The Resurrection
of Christ

Gerd Lüdemann

The Resurrection of Christ
A Historical Inquiry   of Christ

Prometheus Books
59 John Glenn Drive
Amherst, New York 14228–2197

Published 2004 by Prometheus Books

Inquiries should be addressed to
Prometheus Books
59 John Glenn Drive
Amherst, New York 14228-2197
VOICE: 716-691-0133, ext. 207
FAX: 716-564-2711
WWW.PROMETHEUSBOOKS.COM

08 07 06 05 04   5 4 3 2 1

Library of Congress Cataloging-in-Publication Data

Lüdemann, Gerd.
    The resurrection of Christ : a historical inquiry / Gerd Lüdemann.
        p. cm.
    Includes bibliographical references and index.
    ISBN 1-59102-245-2 (hardcover: alk. paper)
    1. Jesus Christ—Resurrection. 2. Bible. N.T.—Criticism, interpretation, etc.
I. Title.

BT481.L83 2004
232'.5—dc22

2004011812

Printed in the United States of America on acid-free paper

Contents

Preface

Crises clear the ground, firstly of a host of institutions from which life has long since departed, and which, given their historical privilege, could not have been swept away in any other fashion. Further, of true pseudo-organisms which ought never to have existed, but which had nevertheless, in the course of time, gained a firm hold upon the fabric of life, and were, indeed, mainly to blame for the preference of mediocrity and the hatred of excellence. Crises also abolish the cumulative dread of "disturbance" and clear the way for strong personalities.[1]

My book *The Resurrection of Jesus: History, Experience, Theology* (Philadelphia: Fortress Press, 1994)[2] has received a great deal of attention not only from the public but also within the theological guild.[3] Indeed, it has succeeded in initiating further discussions.[4] Its aim was to prove the nonhistoricity of the resurrection of Jesus and simultaneously to encourage Christians to change their faith accordingly by basing it entirely on the historical Jesus. Yet in the meantime, objections from fellow theologians along with further work of my own on the subject[5] have convinced me that disproving the historicity of the resurrection of Jesus ultimately annuls the Chris-

7

tian heritage as error. While the 1994 book may still be consulted for secondary literature—especially from the nineteenth century—the present work not only presents a completely revised and less technical analysis of the resurrection texts (including translations), but also spells out in detail why the result of the nonhistoricity of the resurrection of Jesus leaves little if any room for Christianity.

Unless otherwise indicated, translations are my own. I have employed underlines, italics, and bold-faced type to stress key words and ideas, and thus foster a close and discerning reading of the texts.

I take the opportunity to thank the following persons who have helped me with the present work: My friend Dr. John Bowden translated the 1994 book on the resurrection and many other studies of mine that underlie this book. Though everything has been completely rewritten, I will always remain in his debt. The staff of Vanderbilt Divinity School library made every possible effort to get me the books that I needed. Maria Mayo Robbins has helped me with a host of details; my Nashville neighbor, friend, and former colleague Gene TeSelle has offered valuable suggestions; Samuel Robbins has discussed the content of the book with me and helped me with more than technical matters. Yet I am most grateful to my friend Tom Hall, who has seen the project through from the beginning to the end. I owe a great deal to his generous sharing of ideas and to his revisions of difficult passages.

Gerd Lüdemann
Amherst, NY
July 12, 2004

NOTES

1. Jacob Burckhardt, *Reflections on History* (London: George Allen & Unwin, 1943), p. 158.

2. See also the popular version of the 1994 book, *What Really Happened to Jesus: A Historical Approach to the Resurrection* (London: SCM Press and Louisville: Westminster John Knox Press, 1995).

3. Reactions are enumerated in passing by Martin Rese, "Exegetische

Anmerkungen zu G. Lüdemanns Deutung der Auferstehung Jesu," in *Resurrection in the New Testament*, ed. R. Bieringer, V. Koperski, and B. Lataire Festschrift J. Lambrecht (Leuven: University Press, 2002), pp. 55–71.

4. See Hansjürgen Verweyen, ed., *Osterglaube ohne Auferstehung? Diskussion mit Gerd Lüdemann* (Freiburg/Basel/Wien: Herder Verlag, 1995). In this book, which goes back to an interdisciplinary colloquy at the University of Freiburg from June 30 to July 1, 1994, there are contributions by Ingo Broer, Gerd Lüdemann, Lorenz Oberlinner, Karl-Heinz Ohlig, and Hansjürgen Verweyen. See further, Alexander Bommarius, ed., *Fand die Auferstehung wirklich statt? Eine Diskussion mit Gerd Lüdemann*. Mit Beiträgen von Gerd Lüdemann, Klaus Berger, Hugo Staudinger, Michael Murrmann-Kahl und Alexander Bommarius (Düsseldorf und Bonn: Parerga Verlag, 1995); Ulrich Wilckens, *Hoffnung gegen den Tod. Die Wirklichkeit der Auferstehung Jesu* (Neuhausen-Stuttgart: Hänssler Verlag, 1996), pp. 9–27; Peter Carnley, "Response," in *The Resurrection: An Interdisciplinary Symposium on the Resurrection of Jesus*, ed. Stephen T. Davis, Daniel Kendall, and Gerald O'Collins (Oxford and New York: Oxford University Press, 1997), pp. 29–40; Ulrich B. Müller, *Die Entstehung des Glaubens an die Auferstehung Jesu. Historische Aspekte und Bedingungen* (Stuttgart: Verlag Katholisches Bibelwerk GmbH, 1998); Ingolf U. Dalferth, "Volles Grab, leerer Glaube? Zum Streit um die Auferweckung des Gekreuzigten," *Zeitschrift für Theologie und Kirche* 95 (1998): 379–409; A. J. M. Wedderburn, *Beyond Resurrection* (London: SCM Press, 1999); Werner Zager, *Jesus und die frühchristliche Verkündigung. Historische Rückfragen nach den Anfängen* (Neukirchen-Vluyn: Neukirchener Verlag, 1999), pp. 63–87 ("Die Auferstehung Jesu in historisch-kritischer und psychologischer Perspektive"); Bernd Oberdorfer, ",Was sucht ihr den Lebenden bei den Toten?' Überlegungen zur Realität der Auferstehung in Auseinandersetzung mit Gerd Lüdemann," *Kerygma und Dogma* 46 (2000): 225–40; *Jesus' Resurrection: Fact or Figment? A Debate between William Lane Craig and Gerd Lüdemann*, ed. Paul Copan and Ronald K. Tacelli (Downers Grove, IL: InterVarsity Press, 2000). The debate between Craig and Lüdemann took place September 18, 1997, at Boston College and afterward was edited by Copan and Tacelli who invited contributions by other scholars. These are Stephen T. Davis, Michael Goulder, Robert H. Gundry, and Roy W. Hoover. See further, Carsten Peter Thiede [versus] Gerd Lüdemann, *Die Auferstehung Jesu—Fiktion oder Wirklichkeit? Ein Streitgespräch* (Basel and Giessen: Brunnen Verlag, 2001).

5. See my two books *The Great Deception: And What Jesus Really Said and Did* (Amherst, NY: Prometheus Books, 1999), pp. ix–xxii, and *Jesus After*

Two Thousand Years (Amherst: NY: Prometheus Books, 2001), pp. 686–93 ("A Short Life of Jesus"). A revised version of the piece from *The Great Deception* has been published under the title "The Decline of Academic Theology at Göttingen" in *Faith, Truth, and Freedom: The Expulsion of Professor Gerd Lüdemann from the Theology Faculty at the University of Göttingen*, ed. Jacob Neusner (Binghamton, NY, 2002), pp. 1–11. See also *Religion* 32 (2002): 87–94.

1

On the Need for a Fresh Investigation into the Historicity of the Resurrection of Jesus

We who have come out of liberal theology could not have remained theologians had we not been encountered by the seriousness of the radical integrity of liberal theology. We perceived the work of all shades of orthodox theology in the universities as an effort at compromise. G. Krüger is always to be thanked because he saw in that oft-named essay on "unchurchly theology," the danger to the soul in the vocation of the theologian, the entrance into doubt, the shattering of naive credulity. Here—so we perceived—was the atmosphere of truthfulness, in which we were able to breathe.[1]

An examination of the historicity of Jesus' resurrection is called for because according to early Christian testimony it is an event in time and space. Probably the earliest Easter confession runs thus: "God raised Jesus from the dead."[2] Quite apart from the person who utters the confession, this claim includes at the historical level an action of God with respect to the dead Jesus. Therefore "this event has come to us in the form of historicizing reports."[3] The evangelist Luke[4] follows the earliest witnesses, including Paul,[5] who assert that the risen one was not a spirit but Jesus Christ himself.

Indeed, the defenders of the church tradition of the second century have emphasized that claim by introducing the doctrine of the fleshly nature of Jesus' resurrected body.[6] Following the late Marburg theologian Hans Grass, the historical question of "the basis and justification for this testimony . . . remains decisive. Without this basis any theology of resurrection, even the theology of the New Testament, is groundless speculation."[7] At another point Grass emphatically affirms the importance of the "historical investigation into the Easter accounts and the Easter events, something which nowadays is often too quickly pushed to one side or even dismissed altogether."[8]

No other systematic theologian of the present day has assessed the scholarly discussion of Jesus' resurrection from the dead as clearly as Wolfhart Pannenberg from the University of Munich in Germany. It is only consistent with his insights that he considers the resurrection a historical event:

> There is no justification for affirming Jesus' resurrection as an event that really happened if it is not to be affirmed as a historical event as such. Whether or not a particular event happened two thousand years ago is not made certain by faith but only by historical research, to the extent that certainty can be attained at all about questions of this kind.[9]

Regardless of how we may judge Pannenberg's results, it is in any case welcome that on a decisive point of Christian faith he has justified historical enquiry and thus again made it possible for Christianity to come to an understanding with the sciences. Pannenberg is right in noting that "behind the foggy talk of 'Easter faith' many an author shamefully evades the interest of his readers in what he thinks about the reliability of the Easter tradition, which has become the basis for Christian faith."[10]

THEOLOGICAL ARGUMENTS AGAINST RESEARCH INTO THE HISTORICITY OF THE RESURRECTION OF JESUS AND A PRELIMINARY RESPONSE

For theological reasons the relevance of historical research for the resurrection of Jesus is often played down. For example, Hans Conzelmann, one of my New Testament teachers at the University of Göttingen, decrees:

> The question of whether the resurrection of Christ is a "historical event" is theologically inapposite. Of course it is a historical event for Paul, in so far as he cannot know the modern theoretical distinction between historical and supra-historical (in effect: unhistorical). We for our part cannot retreat behind this reflection. But for faith, the particular stage of consciousness reached by thought is quite unimportant. Faith at any stage is—faith. Its object cannot be experienced. Only the cross can be perceived. . . . The question of the historicity of the resurrection must be excluded from theology as being a misleading one.[11]

Presupposing the illegitimacy of any research about the historicity of the resurrection, the most influential New Testament scholar of the last century, Rudolf Bultmann, adds that it is also irrelevant to know how the Easter faith came into existence:

> How the Easter faith arose in individual disciples has been obscured in the tradition by legend and is not of basic importance.[12]

Reference should also be made to the verdict of his pupil Willi Marxsen:

> For my faith in Jesus, it is completely unimportant how Peter arrived at his faith in Jesus after Good Friday. It is equally unimportant how the person found faith who then communicated his faith to me, so that I, in my turn, could believe.[13]

Here two objections must be taken into account. First, the faith of the early Christians is related to God's raising Jesus from the dead as well as to the latter's making himself known as the "Risen One." Second, the opposition between proclamation and history does not do justice to what the early Christians actually believed. History is necessarily part of the proclamation although the notion of "fact" was coined only in modern times.[14] Yet even if "the concept of factuality was unknown to the writers of sacred history . . . [and in] their narrations of events they thus allow heterogeneous elements to flow together which the historian today must fundamentally separate,"[15] from the Early Christian perspective, a lack of factual basis would deprive the proclamation about Jesus of all meaning. In other words, the early Christian preaching had a reference point in history, namely that God did raise Jesus from the dead. The confessional statement includes the idea that the whole Jesus, including his body, came back to life.[16]

Even more directly than members of the Bultmann school, certain systematic theologians reject the merely historical question as irrelevant for the topic of Jesus' resurrection. For example, Jürgen Moltmann writes:

> If we look at Christ's resurrection from the standpoint of this modern paradigm "history," using the categories of the modern historical mind, then—in spite of all the disputes—it makes no great difference whether we see the resurrection as a product of the disciples' imagination, or view it as a historical fact; for as a past event that is becoming ever more past and ever more remote, Christ's resurrection can neither determine the present nor have any relevance for the future. The modern category "history" has already turned the happening into something past and gone; for anything historical is something that comes to pass, and then passes away.[17]

Similarly, the American theologian Richard R. Niebuhr stresses:

> The resurrection of Jesus is neither simply the appearance of Jesus, nor is it the resurrection of an anonymous man, nor is it the rise of faith in his disciples. It is a single and indivisible event, which does not thrust forward one facet or aspect for our consideration to the neglect of the others. It offers no possibility of generalizing and

projecting universal laws; it offers only itself as an analogy of what is to come, and we have no rules by which to determine what is to be negated and what affirmed in this analogy.[18]

To me that is cloudy talk, the more so since—as C. F. Evans rightly responded—"the difficulty is . . . that we have no criteria for judging an event which is strictly without parallel."[19]

Last but not least, the most influential systematic theologian of the last century, Karl Barth, states:

It is sheer superstition to suppose that only things which are open to "historical" verification can have happened in time. There may have been events that happened far more really in time than the kind of things the "historian" can prove. There are good grounds for supposing that the history of the resurrection of Jesus is a pre-eminent instance of such an event.[20]

To this statement Rudolf Bultmann replies:

Barth . . . concedes to me . . . that the resurrection of Jesus is not an historical fact which can be established by the means at the disposal of historical science. But from this he thinks that it does not follow that it did not *happen* . . . My question is, what does Barth understand by "have taken place in history" and "history"? What kind of events are those about which it can be said that "they have really taken place as history in time far more certainly than everything which the 'historian' can establish as such"?[21]

Bultmann's objection to Barth deserves an exclamation mark, the more so since Barth has "exempted himself from any possibilities of assessing the historical truth of his claims."[22] At the same time, though, Bultmann's own approach to the issue of Jesus' resurrection calls for critical comments. Without any scientifically sound reason[23] Bultmann deliberately omits a historical look behind the preaching of the Easter message. Moreover, on the issue of Jesus' resurrection he declares that "Jesus has risen into the proclamation" while simultaneously presupposing the nonhistoricity of Jesus' resurrection.[24] Yet for the reasons given above, the early Christian confession, "God raised Jesus from the dead," cannot possibly be interpreted in Bultmann's way, for once again it witnesses to an act of God concerning a specific historical person.

Paul Hoffmann, a Catholic New Testament scholar from the University of Bamberg, has formulated another fundamental objection to the necessity and even the possibility of raising the historical question concerning the resurrection of Jesus. He argues that "the Easter question points comprehensively to the question of God and can only be solved from that perspective in a systematic theological way."[25] Though the first point is well taken since "God" per se cannot be the object of historical research, the Easter event ought to remain an object of historical study. After all, the early Christians understood it as a statement of historical fact in their dispute both with Jewish contemporaries[26] and later with Gentile critics such as Celsus[27] and Porphyry.[28] Moreover, they insisted on it from the very beginning in discussions with dissenters from their own communities.[29] But Hoffmann goes even further by claiming that the "old questions of the historicity of the empty tomb or the quality of the Easter appearances have been dealt with in numerous publications with long-known arguments without leading to any progress in knowledge. . . . That also applies to the primarily apologetic-systematic question of the factual character of the resurrection."[30] He continues: "*Only the earliest Christian faith in the resurrection can be the object of historical investigation, not the resurrection itself.*"[31]

Why does Hoffmann insist on this last point—as if it were all but self-evident? For apologetic reasons? Is he afraid to be naked in the case of a negative answer? And what do we grasp historically of Easter faith if we do not investigate its historical starting point? Moreover, the first Christians reported not only an empty tomb but also the imperishability of Jesus' body,[32] thus understanding both in a factual sense.

FURTHER THEOLOGICAL ARGUMENTS AGAINST RESEARCH INTO THE HISTORICITY OF THE RESURRECTION OF JESUS AND A FINAL REBUTTAL

Evasive arguments in this connection are legion. Let me give just one example. In an introductory essay to the April issue (1997) of the scholarly journal *Evangelische Theologie* that was dedicated to the "resurrection of Jesus," the Bern New Testament scholar Ulrich Luz wrote:

> The discussion of the resurrection of Jesus is still defined by Gerd Lüdemann's book from 1994. This is really regrettable. Lüdemann's book reduced the quest for the reality of the resurrection to the question of what really happened then. He makes the equation "historical = real." To be sure, such a narrow approach does allow a discussion of the resurrection, but only insufficiently. In order to avoid narrowness in this issue, we have not left the topic of the resurrection solely to New Testament scholars, but have summoned representatives of all other theological disciplines to participate. They are being asked to write about the resurrection of Jesus from the standpoint of their own discipline or of their own theological opinion. With this we have the hope that through various theological disciplines something of the manifold dimensions of the reality of the resurrection may become visible.[33]

I do not think that these statements take us any further. If you want to do justice to the early Christian Easter texts, it is meaningless to write anything about the "reality of the resurrection" if its nonhistoricity is certain. For in that case everything that is said about the reality of the resurrection would be mere fiction without any basis in *real* reality. Therefore the historical reconstruction, far from having a narrowing effect, is decisive—just as a decisive proof for the nonexistence of Jesus would certainly have a negative consequence for the theological quest for Jesus. Thus it is no wonder that critics of my work have accused me of historical positivism[34] or of focusing too narrowly on the empty tomb,[35] or have accused me of a lack of metacritical reflection.[36]

Let me answer these objections with a quotation from the work of the late Heidelberg church historian Hans von Campenhausen. He writes:

> The Easter Narratives have in the past generation, as indeed always, been studied scientifically, and the general progress in the study of primitive Christianity has naturally furthered this work. Yet it seems to me that, with all the various researches into literary history, history of tradition, motif-history and form-history, there has been undue neglect of the inquiry into history pure and simple, that is, the inquiry into the historical core of that to which tradition gives its historical testimony. Interest in these types of approach to the Easter event threatens to smother the event itself. But the philological work that necessarily has the first word in assessing the sources must not lead us to hold as secondary the strictly historical inquiry into what took place, the actual sequence of events and their interconnection, nor to relegate these matters to the fringe as crude and commonplace. Our legitimately critical attitude, justified as it is, towards a naive psychologism and historicism has held us back from a direct exploitation and interpretation of ancient texts. It does not, however, absolve us, on the grounds of a better and more promising method, from the task of posing anew and answering the question the historian is bound to face; that is, of deciding how far and with what degree of probability the actual events and their sequence can still be ascertained.[37]

At the same time, von Campenhausen raises the suspicion that most New Testament scholars regard the Easter history as being without any historical value:

> For them there remains only the somewhat awkward expedient of following the old Christians in their confession of the risen Lord, instead of the Jews in what occasioned this confession.[38]

In this polemic against modern mainstream New Testament research, von Campenhausen obviously equates the Jewish report of the theft of Jesus' body with the tacit acknowledgment of the non-bodily resurrection of Jesus by many a New Testament scholar. For despite their denials, according to von Campenhausen, the latter, along with nonbelieving Jews of Matthew's community, do contradict the core of early Christian belief in the bodily resurrection of Jesus. At the same time, far from seeing any difficulty in accepting the bodily resurrection of Jesus, von Campenhausen considers it theologically natural:

> Here we are dealing with an event unique in every sense, with which the new "aeon" begins and in which therefore, the old world with its laws definitely ends. Consequently, from the nature of the case, such an event is not to be assented to as merely "probable"; it must be seen as necessary and theologically "natural," as it were.[39]

THE NECESSITY OF THE TASK AND ITS FEASIBILITY

While agreeing with von Campenhausen's criticism of modern liberal theology, I would add that if Jesus' resurrection did not take place and consequently Jesus was not revived and changed into a divine being, then neither revival myths nor metaphorical interpretation nor the introduction of a new notion of history nor sermons guised in hermeneutical reflections[40] can help. In that case Christian faith is as dead as Jesus and can be kept alive only by self-deception. Therefore an investigation into the historicity of Jesus' resurrection has as much relevance for the life or death of the church as it has for scholarship.

Every day pastors comfort mourners with the message of the resurrection of the dead. The church derives its right to exist from the authority bestowed on it by the risen Christ, for he—not the historical Jesus—has given her the authority to forgive sins and has sent her into the world. Further, Jesus' resurrection secures the Christian hope of being raised into eternal life. A basic rule applies here: As with Jesus, so with Christians. Yet many modern Christians and even liberal theologians no longer believe in the literal resurrection of Jesus, nor in their own. This disjunction persists despite the fact that the literal understanding of the resurrection and of the whole Christian fabric of salvation has long been the reason why Christian churches play an important role in Western societies, not to mention Christianity's impact on the countries of the third world.

Since I am well aware of the objections to a purely historical discourse on the resurrection of Jesus, I shall here list the most important of them and offer rebuttals.

1. We have no eyewitness accounts of the resurrection of Jesus.

Rebuttal: But we do have the testimony of Paul himself who claims to have seen the "Risen One." Though this is not a description of the occurrence of the resurrection itself, it does shed light on what happened to the other resurrection witnesses—the more so since Paul puts his own encounter with the "Risen One" in parallel to that of other witnesses (1 Cor. 15:8). Moreover, even if the above objection is correct, the question of the manner of the resurrection must be legitimate as long as theology makes a claim to be scientific and to be related to the enlightenment.

2. The resurrection traditions cannot be disentangled, and the historical sources are inadequate.

Rebuttal: This way out seems a bit too easy. Relying exclusively on the biblical witness as the only remaining source serves an apologetic agenda. Again Hans von Campenhausen remarks acutely:

> The covenant thus concluded between an allegedly radical faith and historical skepticism in reality serves only to withdraw it altogether from the particular assault of history and historical reason.[41]

In other words, to say that what really happened at Easter is inexplicable seems formally to become an indispensable requisite for doing theology.

3. The resurrection of Jesus is a miracle that completely evades our grasp—what can historical research achieve here?

Rebuttal: Indeed, the miraculous or revelatory aspect of Jesus cannot be the object of any scientific approach. However, as long as theology is "paired" with historical thought (as it is on the one hand by the character of its central sources and on the other by modern criteria of truth),[42] then it must be interested in a natural explanation of the miracle—or it must admit that even on historical grounds a supernatural explanation is more plausible.

4. It is impossible to talk meaningfully about the resurrection of Jesus outside the experience of faith.

Rebuttal: This amounts to "I believe in order to understand" and a resultant separation of faith from reason based on an immunization strategy. As long as absurdity is not to be made the criterion of the truth of theological statements, academic theologians must be concerned that their remarks are comprehensible. It is their task to interpret past and present testimonies of faith, but also to criticize them if they stand in direct opposition to present knowledge.

5. Event and interpretation are always interlocked so that it is impossible to have access to the event of the resurrection without the interpretation. Thus many Easter texts are unfit for historical investigation.[43]

Rebuttal: The interlocking of event and interpretation applies to all texts with which the historian deals, and thus is in no way a peculiarity of religious or Christian source-texts.[44] Since this fundamental fact compels one to see and respect any given source as an expression of human life, one must not and cannot shrug off the responsibility of investigating the New Testament texts to discover to what extent, given their nature, they can be used as historical material. Perhaps one can compare the work to be done by historical research with psychoanalysis, where similarly in the framework of a "hermeneutic of suspicion" the utterances of the patient have to be read against the grain, i.e., against his or her explicit interpretations. No analyst will dispense with such a method simply because it is in tension with what the patient claims.

It is almost superfluous to say that the following analyses move within the realm of the probable and that the argument is hypothetical; this from the very beginning sets limits to the present investigation. To conceive of the predicates "purely hypothetical" or a "series of hypotheses" as indicating the possibility of refutation rests on a misunderstanding of historical work. Like any form of interpretation, historical reconstruction cannot proceed without hypotheses and assessments of probabilities. Indeed, it is the central task of historical investigation both to work out the most appropriate hypotheses and clearly to weigh probabilities in the process. The value of a reconstruction is decided by whether it is based on the best hypotheses—that is, those that resolve the most (and most important) open questions or existing problems, and provoke the fewest (and weakest) counterarguments.[45] I shall adopt an approach similar to that of Kirsopp Lake's study of nearly a century ago, *The Historical Evidence for the Resurrection of Jesus Christ*:

> The first task of the historical inquirer is to collect the pieces of evidence; the second is to discuss the trustworthiness and meaning of each separate piece; and the third is to reconstruct the events to which the evidence relates.[46]

Lake then turns to law courts, adopting a legal metaphor in order to illustrate the spirit of sober historical study:

> [The critic] has to play in turn the parts of solicitor, barrister, and judge, for he has to draw up the case, to argue its meaning, and to decide on its merits. Such an inquirer is necessarily bound by the limitation of the evidence. The evidence of even the best witnesses can in the end represent nothing more than their belief; and if the witnesses differ, either the point at issue must be left open, or an explanation must be given of their difference. It is, of course, impossible to apply the laws of evidence to historical problems with the same rigour as obtains in a law court, but in principle the judge and the historian are both guided by them, and the qualities which are demanded for the one are equally necessary in the other.[47]

THE PROCEDURE

The plan of the book is as follows:

Chapter 2 surveys the early Christian sources for the resurrection of Jesus. Here I not only compare the content of the individual texts, but also classify them by characteristics of form in order to arrive at a starting point for the history of the resurrection traditions. This task is especially important for the present work, not only since it is about the resurrection of Jesus, but also because it deals with the origins of the resurrection traditions. In other words, should certain of the earliest texts about the resurrection prove to be lacking in historical value, there would be no need to subject them to a detailed historical investigation.

The task of chapter 3 is to offer fresh translations of the most important early Christian texts concerning Jesus' resurrection and to assess their historical value. Because of the large number of sources to be examined it requires much more space than the other chapters. I analyze the texts in three steps—purpose, reworked tradition, and historical elements. Sometimes two steps are carried out in one. Critics have charged this approach with being too mechanical. Yet in working with these and similar texts, this approach has proved fruitful, for it takes into account that since the authors of these and similar texts were not eyewitnesses, the various accounts necessarily reflect the use of imagination and/or earlier tradition.

Among the chief tools for identifying the purpose of the author and the reworked tradition are linguistic and stylistic considerations, and observation of contradictions or tensions in the text. In translating the texts, I have, unless otherwise indicated, set in italics those portions that are likely redactional, and have employed underlines, italics, and bold-faced type to stress key words and ideas in order to foster a close and discerning reading of the text. Only after establishing the purpose of the author and the reworked tradition may one meaningfully evaluate the historical worth of the text and so gain a credible understanding of the events it relates.

Today it is almost universally recognized that the gospel

accounts of the resurrection appearances are secondary narrative expressions of resurrection faith.[48] Therefore my analysis begins with the old kerygmatic formulations and only after that turns to the texts of the Gospels and of other noncanonical early Christian texts. Starting from 1 Cor. 15:3–8, the aim of chapter 3 is to offer a reconstruction of the course of events as well as the circumstances surrounding Jesus' death on the cross, the burial of his body, and his reported resurrection on the third day and subsequent appearances to various disciples. All this prepares the path for chapter 4, where I shall argue that both primary witnesses to Jesus' resurrection, Peter and Paul, became victims of self-deception. For that very reason I shall narrate the early Christian belief in Jesus' resurrection as a history of self-deception. In the fifth and final chapter, I shall ask whether in light of the nonhistoricity of Jesus' resurrection one can legitimately and with good conscience still call oneself a Christian. A brief epilogue addresses the question of whether the negative historical conclusions must result in spiritual despair or moral misconduct. Three appendices present material which, though it would have interrupted the flow of thought in the text, is necessary as a basis for the argument in various chapters of the book.

NOTES

1. Rudolf Bultmann, *Glauben und Verstehen* (Tübingen: J. C. B. Mohr, 1933), 1:2–3. The English translation is from Van A. Harvey, *The Historian and the Believer: The Morality of Historical Knowledge and Christian Belief. With a New Introduction by the Author* (Urbana and Chicago: University of Illinois Press, 1996), pp. 7–8. The article that Bultmann refers to in the quote is Gustav Krüger, "Die unkirchliche Theologie," *Die Christliche Welt* 14 (1900): 804–807.

2. For details see below, pp. 30–32, 153.

3. Hans Grass, *Ostergeschehen und Osterberichte*, 4th ed. (Göttingen: Vandenhoeck & Ruprecht, 1970), p. 13.

4. Here and throughout I use the traditional names Luke, Matthew, Mark, and John for the authors of the New Testament though the actual authors remain unknown to us. At any rate, the question of real authorship has little or no consequence for my analyses.

5. See below, p. 178.

6. See my *Heretics: The Other Side of Early Christianity* (SCM Press: London and Louisville: Westminster John Knox Press, 1996), pp. 143–46, 187–89.

7. Grass, *Ostergeschehen*, p. 14.

8. Ibid., p. 4.

9. Wolfhart Pannenberg, *Jesus—God and Man* (Philadelphia: Westminster Press, 1968), p. 99.

10. Wolfhart Pannenberg, *Grundzüge der Christologie*, 5th ed. (Gütersloh: Gerd Mohn 1976), p. 417.

11. Hans Conzelmann, *An Outline of the Theology of the New Testament* (London: SCM Press and New York and Evanston: Harper & Row, 1969), p. 204. Cf. Lloyd Geering, *Resurrection: A Symbol of Hope* (London/Auckland/Sydney/Toronto: Hodder and Stoughton, 1971), p. 26, who adds, "the truth of Christianity cannot be proved by historical evidence or by any other rational process" (ibid.).

12. Rudolf Bultmann, *Theology of the New Testament* (New York: Charles Scribner's Sons, 1955), 1:45.

13. Willi Marxsen, *The Resurrection of Jesus of Nazareth* (Philadelphia: Fortress Press, 1970), pp. 126–27.

14. Cf. the brilliant essay by Christian Hartlich, "Historical-Critical Method in Its Application to Statements Concerning Events in the Holy Scriptures," *Journal of Higher Criticism* 2, no. 2 (Fall 1995): 122–39.

15. Ibid., p. 134. In a Bultmannian fashion, Hartlich fails to pay enough attention to the importance of the historical basis of the proclamation and typically ignores that Luke/Acts purports itself to be a historical account of early Christianity (see Luke 1:1–4/Acts 1:1) and that Heilsgeschichte does matter not only to Luke but also to Paul. Cf. Oscar Cullmann, *Immortality of the Soul or Resurrection of the Dead? The Witness of the New Testament* (New York: Macmillan, 1958), pp. 16–17: "The whole of early Christian thought is based on *Heilsgeschichte*, and everything that is said about death and eternal life stands or falls with a belief in a real occurrence, in real events which took place in time." See further, Oscar Cullmann, *Christ and Time: The Primitive Christian Conception of Time and History* (Philadelphia: Westminster Press, 1964).

16. Joachim Gnilka, *Die frühen Christen: Ursprünge und Anfänge der Kirche* (Freiburg: Herder Verlag, 1999), p. 216. Earlier Gnilka had written: "Within the context of the monistic anthropology of Judaism the sentence does presuppose the reviving of the whole human being" (p. 197).

17. Jürgen Moltmann, "The Resurrection of Christ: Hope for the World," in *Resurrection Reconsidered*, ed. Gavin D'Costa (Oxford: Oneworld Publications, 1996), p. 77.

18. Richard R. Niebuhr, *Resurrection and Historical Reason: A Study of Theological Method* (New York: Charles Scribner's Sons, 1957), pp. 176–77.

19. C. F. Evans, *Resurrection and the New Testament* (London: SCM Press, 1970), p. 177.

20. Karl Barth, *Church Dogmatics*, vol. 3, pt. 2 (Edinburgh: T. & T. Clark, 1960), p. 446.

21. Rudolf Bultmann, *Essays: Philosophical and Theological* (London: SCM Press, 1955), p. 260.

22. Harvey, *The Historian and the Believer*, p. 157.

23. Bultmann, however, would respond that there is a sound reason to proceed in this and no other way: Faith should not base itself on historical facts, and humans should not boast of works before God. On this see below, pp. 193–95.

24. See my *Paul: The Founder of Christianity* (Amherst, NY: Prometheus Books, 2002), pp. 232–37.

25. Paul Hoffmann, "Einführung," Hoffmann, ed., *Zur neutestamentlichen Überlieferung von der Auferstehung Jesu*, WdF 522 (Darmstadt: Wissenschaftliche Buchgesellschaft, 1988), p. 13.

26. Matt. 28:15. On this text see below, pp. 95–97.

27. Origen *Contra Celsum* 2.59–60.

28. See Joseph R. Hoffmann, *Porphyry's Against the Christians: The Literary Remains*, edited and translated, with an introduction and epilogue (Amherst, NY: Prometheus Books, 1994).

29. Cf. Luke 24:37. On this text see below, pp. 108–12.

30. Hoffmann, "Einführung," p. 2.

31. Ibid. (italics mine).

32. Acts 2:27; Acts 13:35. On these texts see below, pp. 110–12.

33. Ulrich Luz, "Editorial," *Evangelische Theologie* 57 (1997): 177.

34. See Eckart Reinmuth, "Historik und Exegese—zum Streit um die Auferstehung nach der Moderne," in *Exegese und Methodendiskussion*, ed. Stefan Alkier and Ralph Brucker (Tübingen and Basel: A. Francke Verlag, 1998), p. 6; Jacob Kremer, "Die dreifache Wiedergabe des Damaskuserlebnisses Pauli in der Apostelgeschichte. Eine Hilfe für das rechte Verständnis der lukanischen Ostergeschichte," in *The Unity of Luke-Acts*, ed. Joseph Verheyden (Leuven: Leuven University Press, 1999), pp. 354–55.

35. Joachim Ringleben, *Wahrhaft auferstanden: Zur Begründung der The-*

ologie des lebendigen Gottes (Tübingen: J. C. B. Mohr/Paul Siebeck, 1998), p. 3. See my *Die Auferweckung Jesu von den Toten: Ursprung und Geschichte einer Selbsttäuschung* (Lüneburg: zu Klampen, 2002), pp. 218–25, for a rebuttal of this book.

36. Adolf Martin Ritter in Carl Andresen and Adolf Martin Ritter, *Handbuch der Dogmen- und Theologiegeschichte. Band 1: Die Lehrentwicklung im Rahmen der Katholizität*, 2d ed. (Göttingen: Vandenhoeck & Ruprecht, 1999), p. 16.

37. Hans von Campenhausen, "The Events of Easter and the Empty Tomb," in Campenhausen, *Tradition and Life in the Church: Essays and Lectures in Church History* (Philadelphia: Fortress Press, 1968), p. 42.

38. Ibid., p. 87.

39. Ibid., p. 86.

40. Cf. the following example: "The dispute over the empty tomb has approximately the same role for New Testament theology as if I say: 'I love you' and want to prove this by a bouquet of flowers presented years ago. For the 'I love you' was lacking if theology refuses to spell out these words and instead repeats the quarrel of how it was with the past bouquet" (Eckart Reinmuth, "Lüdemann ist das genaue Spiegelbild, das er beschwört," in *Faith, Truth, and Freedom: The Expulsion of Professor Gerd Lüdemann from the Theology Faculty of the University of Göttingen. Symposium and Documents*, ed. Jacob Neusner (Binghamton, NY: Global Publications, 2002), p. 92.

41. Campenhausen, "The Events of Easter and the Empty Tomb," pp. 88–89.

42. Cf. Gerhard Ebeling, *Theology and Proclamation: Dialogue with Bultmann* (Philadelphia: Fortress Press, 1966), pp. 13–21 ("The tension between 'scientific theology' and 'church proclamation'").

43. See the Emmaus story in Luke 24:13–35.

44. On the postmodernist slogan "There are no facts, only interpretations," see Harvey, *The Historian and the Believer*, pp. xxiv–xxvi, esp. pp. xxvi–xxvii: The slogan "shunts aside all those concrete and practical questions with which the historian is naturally concerned. . . .(I)n historical inquiry we wish to establish whether, in fact, it was necessary to drop the atomic bomb on Hiroshima to end the war by asking whether Japan had already initiated proposals for surrender. . . . So, too, it is legitimate to ask, whether, in fact, Jesus was born in Bethlehem, whether he ever claimed to be the Messiah, or whether he was put to death by the Romans under pressure from the Jewish authorities. The postmodernist slogan "There are no

facts, only interpretations" does not help us at all with these sorts of questions in which appeals to evidence are not only unproblematic but essential. To argue that all these questions rest on an outmoded dualism or depend on whether 'gloves' and 'DNA' are theory-laden concepts only demonstrates the irrelevance of a certain type of academic theory of history."

45. On the nature of the historical method and its relationship to theology, cf. my *Opposition to Paul in Jewish Christianity* (Minneapolis: Fortress Press, 1989), p. 220n56 (discussion of B. G. Niebuhr and F. C. Baur; E. Zeller, E. Troeltsch); Ernst Troeltsch, *Writings on Theology and Religion*, trans. and ed. Robert Morgan and Michael Pye (Atlanta: John Knox Press, 1977). The book includes an appendix, "Troeltsch in English Translation," pp. 253–55. See further, Harvey, *The Historian and the Believer*; Hartlich, "Historical-Critical Method in Its Application to Statements Concerning Events in the Holy Scriptures."

46. Kirsopp Lake, *The Historical Evidence for the Resurrection of Jesus Christ* (London: Williams & Norgate and New York: G. P. Putnam's Sons, 1912), p. 6.

47. Ibid.

48. One should not, however, exclude the possibility that some of their elements may be as old as the aforementioned confessions.

2

The Various Early Christian Texts on the Resurrection of Jesus

Survey and Classification

The god hypothesis is no longer of any pragmatic value for the interpretation or comprehension of nature, and indeed often stands in the way of better and truer interpretation. Operationally, God is beginning to resemble not a ruler but the last fading smile of a cosmic Cheshire cat.

It will soon be as impossible for an intelligent, educated man or woman to believe in a god as it is now to believe that the earth is flat, that flies can be spontaneously generated, that disease is a divine punishment, or that death is always due to witchcraft. Gods will doubtless survive, sometimes under the protection of vested interests, or in the shelter of lazy minds, or as puppets used by politicians, or as refuges for unhappy and ignorant souls.[1]

Depending on their form, the statements about the resurrection may be divided into six groups.[2] They occur as follows:

a) As descriptive phrases or clauses: e.g., "God who has raised Jesus from the dead;"

b) As catechetical statements about the resurrection of Jesus and his postresurrection appearances: "he (Jesus) appeared to XYZ" —statements that are already being developed into sequences;

c)   In extended appearance stories;

d)   In stories about the empty tomb;

e)   In resurrection stories that are dated back into the life of
      Jesus;

f)   In various other stories.

Let me now present the various groups of statements about Jesus'
resurrection in a sequence:

On a) "God has raised Jesus from the dead":

The oldest example of this type appears in 1 Thess. 1:10:

> [You] wait for [God's] son from heaven whom he has raised from
> the dead, Jesus who saves us from the coming wrath.

Compare further 2 Cor. 4:14:

> We know that he who raised the Lord Jesus will raise us also with
> Jesus.

Many other passages in Paul's letters contain similar formula-like
statements.[3] All of them are older than the letters in which they
appear and surely originated with or before the time of the earliest
extant letter, 1 Thess. Depending on the dating of this letter—41 or
50 CE—they stem from the thirties or the forties of the first century.[4]

At this point, anticipating the detailed exegesis, reference should
be made to the close parallel between these and other pre-Pauline
formulaic passages: 2 Cor. 1:9, "God who raises the dead," and Rom.
4:17: "God who gives life to the dead and calls into existence things
that do not exist." These two passages have a parallel in the second
of the Jewish Eighteen Benedictions, which differs only slightly in its
various versions and goes back to the first century BCE:

> Thou art mighty, humbling the proud; strong, and judging the vio-
> lent; though livest for ever and raisest the dead; though blowest the
> wind and bringest down the dew; thou providest for the living and

makest the dead alive; in an instant thou causest our salvation to spring forth: Blessed art thou, Lord, who makest the dead alive.[5]

On b) Catechetical statements:

These can be divided into statements about the death and resurrection of Jesus, and statements about his appearances.

1) Statements about the death and resurrection of Jesus (1 Thess. 4:14; 1 Cor. 15:3c–4; Rom. 4:25; Rom. 14:9)

1 Thess. 4:14: "Jesus died and rose."

1 Cor. 15:3c–4: "Christ died for our sins according to the scriptures; he was buried; he has been raised on the third day according to the scriptures."

Rom. 4:25: Jesus "was put to death for our trespasses and raised for our justification."

Rom. 14:9: "To this end Christ died and lived again, that he might be Lord both of the dead and of the living."

2) Statements about Jesus' appearances (1 Cor. 15:5–8; Luke 24:34; Mark 16:9–20)

1 Cor. 15:5–8: (5) Christ appeared to Cephas, then to the Twelve, (6) he appeared to more than 500 brothers at one time, (7) he appeared to James, then to the apostles, (8) he appeared to Paul.

The reports about the christophanies listed here (verses 5–7) are doubtless very old, since they all go back to the time before the appearance of Christ to Paul (verse 8). Yet there needs to be an explanation of how many of the appearances here mentioned Paul had already communicated to the Corinthians during the time of the founding of the community there. If one reads 1 Cor. 15:1–11 straight through, it is not evident which verses report what was related during the foundational preaching and what information

Paul is now adding. In any case, it is clear that the statement about the appearance to Cephas had been communicated to the Corinthians during the first mission shortly after the founding of the community at Thessalonica. That would mean that since the report of the christophany to Cephas was handed down to Paul before he came to Europe, it is chronologically at least as old as the formula listed under a) "God raised Jesus from the dead," which indeed goes back even before the time of the composition of the first letter to the Thessalonians (see 1 Thess. 1:10). One may even hypothesize that Jesus' appearance to Cephas led to the conclusion: "God raised Jesus from the dead" (more on this see below, p. 153).

Luke 24:34: "The Lord was really raised and appeared to Simon."

This is an old "cry of Easter-jubilation."[6] Placing the assertion of Jesus' resurrection ahead of the report of the appearance to Simon reflects the idea that God's raising of Jesus is both the presupposition of and the reason for Jesus' appearance to Simon.

Mark 16:9–20: For the text see below, pp. 88–90.

The longer ending of Mark was composed in the second century recalling 1 Cor. 15:3–8 in its list of the sequences of appearances.[7]

On c) Extended appearance stories

We may follow C. H. Dodd in dividing these stories into two groups.[8]

1. The first group of narratives is to be found in Matt. 28:9–10, 16–20, and John 20:19–21. It consists of five elements: a) Exposition: Jesus' followers are robbed of their Lord. b) Appearance of the Lord (Matt. 28:9, 17; John 20:20). c) Greeting (Matt. 28:9; John 20:19). d) Recognition (Matt. 28:9, 17; John 20:29). e) Commission (Matt. 28:10, 19; John 20:21–23).

2. The second group of narratives consists of Luke 24:13–35 and

John 21:1–14. It differs from the first group of resurrection stories in the fact that the "Risen One"—although he can be seen and heard—is not immediately recognized as such. Since these narratives betray a higher state of reflection, their historical value diminishes accordingly.

Last but not least, Mark 16:14–15 ("The appearance to the Eleven"), Luke 24:36–49 ("The appearance to the Eleven and to those who were there"), John 20:26–29 ("The doubting Thomas") and John 20:11–17 ("Mary Magdalene at the tomb") are mixed types of resurrection stories.

On d) Stories about the empty tomb

The tomb story in Mark 16:1–8 has a special role. Since it does not report an appearance of the Risen Christ himself, but rather proclaims that Jesus was raised from the dead (verse 6), it is perhaps a resurrection story, but one already cast in the form of a reflection.

To the problem of how to understand Mark 16:1–8 must be added the question of the chronological order of the other New Testament stories about the tomb, since the Gospel writers emphasize very different facets of the narrative (especially Matthew and John). Certainly we must assume that Mark 16 is the basis for Matt. 28:1–10 as well as Luke 24:1–10, and that John 20 is later in terms of literary form and tradition. Yet Matthew's and Luke's innovations may not result exclusively from literary revisions of Mark, nor must the peculiarities of John be understood only as a literary reshaping of the Synoptic text. We need always consider the possible role of oral traditions. For the reason just mentioned I shall also examine two noncanonical texts—the *Gospel of Peter* and the *Epistle of the Apostles*—both of which contain narratives of the discovery of the empty tomb.

On e) Resurrection stories dated back into the life of Jesus

Those biographical accounts in the Gospels that may be seen as predated resurrection stories form a further complex. To be sure, in this area it is always difficult to arrive at conclusions with a high

degree of probability. In general, however, the possibility of insert-
ing adapted Easter stories into the life of Jesus can hardly be disputed. Indeed, the words of Jesus the man were worth reporting to
the community only because they were also read and understood as
words of the Jesus who was (now) exalted to God. In the past,
scholars have understood the following passages as originally Easter
narratives: Mark 6:45–52 (Jesus walking on the lake); Matt.
14:28–31 (Peter first goes to meet Jesus walking on the lake and then
loses his nerve);[9] Mark 9:2–8 (the transfiguration); Matt. 16:17–19
(Jesus' promise to Peter); Luke 5:1–11 (Peter's fishing trip).[10] However, only the last two passages will be considered in the subsequent
analysis.

On f) Various other stories

Here I should mention those of the so-called apocryphal Gospels that contain accounts of Jesus' resurrection or of post-resurrection appearances. The *Gospel of the Hebrews* relates Jesus' epiphany to
James (for the text see below, p. 81). The *Gospel of Peter* depicts the
resurrection occurrence in detail and links that up with an introduction to what was apparently an account of Jesus' appearance to Peter
and the other disciples ("we the twelve") in Galilee. The *Epistle of the
Apostles* contains narratives about the "Lord's" appearance to the
women and to the disciples.

PRELIMINARY RESULTS AND CONSEQUENCES

The following preliminary results and consequences arise from the
foregoing classification and comments on the texts dealing with
Jesus' resurrection:

1. A large number of the existing narratives do not come from
eyewitnesses, but passed through the hands of the community and/
or a theological expositor. Only in the relatively numerous passages
in Paul, our primary source, do we have an eyewitness account—not

of the resurrection event itself, of course, but of appearances of the risen Lord. Since Paul explicitly conjoins the appearances of Jesus to himself and others (1 Cor. 15:8), it is above all here that we must expect to find the source of the risen Christ's appearances to the rest of the eyewitnesses. Thus, the analysis of the Pauline texts is of key importance.

Of course it is also clear that in 1 Cor. 15 *ophthe* is an umbrella term for a variety of appearances both to individuals and to groups, and that it derives from the language of the Greek Bible, the Septuagint. Some have even been inclined to conclude that different kinds of events were meant here, and that therefore the above-mentioned assumption that Paul's was the only eyewitness account is an improbable one. Yet, since Paul knew Cephas and the other people in Jerusalem personally,[11] he must have known what he was talking about. In other words, Paul's is in all probability the only eyewitness account.

2. According to the texts, the primary eyewitness besides Paul is Peter. And while we do not have his first-person report, the tradition of an appearance to him remains extremely valuable, all the more so since pre-Easter reports about Peter—i.e., his denial of Jesus[12]—are available and can be related hypothetically to such an experience. Therefore the Peter tradition also has an important role, and here as in the case of Paul we must examine the relationship between the appearance to Peter and his "pre-Easter" period.

3. At this point we can already differentiate between the historical values of the individual pieces of information. Paul's report in 1 Cor. 15:3–8 and the details in the Gospels and Acts which accord with it are of paramount significance. Those reports within the Gospel narratives that stress the bodily nature of the risen Christ are presumably of later origin.[13] Their emphasis on the reality of the resurrected body of Jesus shows signs of secondary apologetic concern in the face of the docetic challenge, according to which Jesus only seemed to have risen. Differently put, while according to the oldest traditions Jesus appears from heaven, in the later reports he is still on this earth meeting his disciples as some sort of bodily presence, and not until his ascension will he assume his heavenly status.

4. The stories about the empty tomb pose a different problem, and closely connected with this we need an answer to whether the tradition of the appearance to the women and/or to Mary Magdalene is historically valid. Hence we must thoroughly analyze Mark 16:1–8 and John 20:1–18 and further ask whether the tradition of an appearance to women may not have been preserved in noncanonical texts. After all, the historicity of a first appearance to women would not necessarily be irreconcilable with Paul's report in 1 Cor. 15, since in view of his misogyny the apostle might deliberately have omitted such a report.[14]

5. As for the place of the resurrection appearances, the Gospels offer a choice between two locales: Galilee and the Jerusalem area. However, since the appearances in Galilee can hardly be explained if we assume the priority of those in Jerusalem, we may reasonably conclude that the first appearances took place in Galilee, and those in Jerusalem came only later. In that case, however, the recently emphasized first appearance to Mary Magdalene would have to be disputed, since this—largely because of its apparent connection to the tomb tradition—is probably conceivable only in Jerusalem. The flight of the disciples after the death of Jesus—or before his crucifixion (Mark 14:50)—would support the priority of the Galilee tradition, since Galilee, being their home and the place of Jesus' ministry, would be their most plausible destination.

6. The time of the resurrection or the appearances of the risen Christ also has to be governed by an answer to the Galilee/Jerusalem controversy. At least it can be said at the outset that the resurrection on the third day—if literally understood—with the appearances immediately following is incompatible with the priority of the Galilee tradition. The disciples could not possibly have journeyed from Jerusalem to Galilee between Friday afternoon and early Sunday morning, even if we neglect the fact that the Sabbath lay in between, and they would hardly have traveled on that day. However, a word of caution is appropriate here: if "on the third day" is not to be understood literally (see below, pp. 71–72), then the argument advanced in this paragraph becomes moot.

NOTES

1. John A. T. Robinson, *Honest to God* (London: SCM Press and Philadelphia: Westminster Press, 1963), pp. 37–38 (quoting and endorsing the view of the English biologist Julian Huxley).

2. N. T. Wright, *The Resurrection of the Son of God* (Minneapolis: Fortress Press, 2003), fails to classify the different strata of resurrection traditions in earliest Christianity and engages in bitter polemic against "a highly developed tradition-history, in which the post-Bultmannian world has gone on adding hypothetical stones to a pile which itself originated in guesswork" (p. 19). I do insist, however, that the discovery of pre-Pauline confessional formulations is one of the great achievements of recent New Testament scholarship. Cf. Ethelbert Stauffer, *New Testament Theology* (New York: Macmillan, 1956), pp. 338–39 (appendix 3: "Twelve Criteria of Creedal Formulations in the New Testament"); Werner Kramer, *Christ, Lord, Son of God* (London: SCM Press, 1966); Hans Conzelmann, *An Outline of the Theology of the New Testament* (London: SCM Press and New York: Harper & Row, 1969), pp. 62–93.

3. See Gal. 1:1; Rom. 4:24b; Rom. 8:11a, etc.

4. On the two possible dates of 1 Thess., see my *Paul: The Founder of Christianity* (Amherst, NY: Prometheus Books, 2002), pp. 22–64.

5. Translation based on Emil Schürer, *The History of the Jewish People in the Age of Jesus Christ (175 B.C.–A.D. 135)*, rev. and ed. Geza Vermes, Fergus Millar, and Matthew Black (Edinburgh: T&T Clark, 1979), 2:460 ("Palestinian Recension").

6. Joachim Jeremias, *Die Sprache des Lukasevangeliums* (Göttingen: Vandenhoeck & Ruprecht, 1980), p. 319.

7. Verse 9: "first to Maria Magdalene"; verse 12: "after that . . . to two of them"; verse 14: "still later . . . to them (the Eleven)".

8. C. H. Dodd, "The Appearances of the Risen Christ: An Essay in Form-Criticism of the Gospels," Dodd, *More New Testament Studies* (Grand Rapids, MI: William B. Eerdmans, 1968), pp. 102–33.

9. In fact, Matt. 14:28–31 was added by the first evangelist to Mark 6:45–52.

10. See further, John E. Alsup, *The Post-Resurrection Appearance Stories of the Gospel-Tradition* (Stuttgart: Calwer Verlag, 1975), pp. 139–44.

11. See Gal. 1:18: Three years after his conversion Paul traveled to Jerusalem in order to get to know Cephas and stayed there fifteen days. On that occasion he also met James, the brother of Jesus. Gal. 2:1: Fourteen

years after that Paul traveled again to Jerusalem and met James, Cephas, John, and many members of the Jerusalem community.

12. Mark 14:54, 66–72.

13. Admittedly, we cannot exclude the possibility that elements in them may be earlier.

14. To be sure, Paul was not an enemy of women though sometimes an ambivalent attitude shines through. See my *Paul: The Founder of Christianity*, pp. 143–46.

3

Translation and Analysis of the Early Christian Texts on the Resurrection of Jesus

Whether or not supernatural beings exist is a question for metaphysics.
. . . But the historian does require a world in which these normal phenomena are not interfered with by arbitrary and *ad hoc* divine interventions to produce abnormal events with special historical consequences. This is not a matter of personal preference, but of professional necessity, for the historian's task . . . is to calculate the most
probable explanation of the preserved evidence. . . . In all of this I am,
of course, contradicting the . . . statement . . . that when writing the
history of religion we are only concerned to determine what ancient
beliefs were, not whether or not they were true. This is false, because a
great many ancient beliefs concerned supposed cases of divine inter-
vention in history, and these are questions of historical fact.[1]

The really decisive and revolutionary thing about the critical historical method came from the fact that the modern historian sees
himself compelled to take the sources of the past and set them,
too, in the light of the new self-evident assumptions. Not that he
foists these new self-evident assumptions on to the witnesses of
the past, as if they had been self-evident assumptions also for
them, but he does examine the factual content of their testimony
on the basis of these self-evident assumptions. Thus he will not
accept the truth, e.g. of the statements which presuppose the Ptole-

maic picture of the world, not even when for the rest the source has a high degree of historical dependability. The modern historian is rightly convinced that he knows certain things better. The fact that for the modern age all that is metaphysical and metahistorical has entered the dimension of the problematical is also a thing the modern historian cannot simply put out of his mind when reading sources which presuppose the self-evident character of the metaphysical and metahistorical.[2]

1 COR. 15:1–11: THE EASTER TRADITIONS IN PAUL'S FIRST LETTER TO THE CORINTHIANS

(1) And now, brothers, I must remind you of the gospel that I preached to you, the gospel that you received, in which you stand, (2) by which you are saved, if you hold fast—unless you believed in vain. (3) For I delivered to you as of first importance what I also received, that **Christ died for our sins** *in accordance with the scriptures*, (4) **and that he was buried,** that he has been raised[3] on the third day *in accordance with the scriptures* (5) **and that he appeared to Cephas, then to the Twelve.**

(6) Thereafter he appeared to more than five hundred brothers *at one time, most of whom are still alive, though some have fallen asleep.* (7) Thereafter he appeared to James, then to all the apostles.

(8) Last of all, as to one untimely born, he appeared also to me. (9) For I am the least of the apostles, unfit to be called an apostle, because I persecuted the church of God. (10) But by the grace of God I am what I am, and his grace toward me was not in vain. On the contrary, I worked harder than any of them, though it was not I, but the grace of God that is with me. (11) Whether then it was I, or they, so we preach and so you believed.

PAUL'S PURPOSE

At the outset Paul reminds the addressees of the content of his preaching during the founding of the community (verses 1, 3a) and stresses that he himself had received it (verse 3b). It attested to Christ's death and resurrection along with his appearance to Cephas, then to the Twelve (1 Cor. 15:3c–5). Paul adds the other appearances of Christ which he asserts had been reported to him: the appearance to more than five hundred brothers at one time and the appearance to James, then to all the apostles. At the end of the list he introduces Christ's appearance to himself.

Paul's way of presenting the material had the primary purpose of providing historical proof of the resurrection. He underlines this by adding verse 6b, implying that those who were still skeptical about what they have heard could ask the witnesses directly, since most of them were still alive. In addition, the expression "at one time" in verse 6a is probably meant to intensify the objectivity, because in Paul's opinion more than five hundred witnesses could hardly all have been deluded. Second, Paul was evidently concerned with placing himself within the tradition he had proclaimed on his founding visit, which already included Jesus' appearance to Cephas. That being the case, it was necessary for him to add appearances of the same kind that chronologically preceded his own. Thus it is clear that in verse 8 Paul is claiming to have received the same vision as all the other people listed in this sequence. In this way the statements in verses 5–7 are used by Paul to support the assertion that Christ also appeared to him.

Why does Paul place his experience within a successive pattern of appearances? Why does he stress the identity of his vision with that of all the people mentioned earlier? One cannot avoid the inference that Paul did this to defend his apostolic authority. Indeed, verses 8–10 clearly have an apologetic ring. This follows both from the reference to his own work (verse 10b) and from the surprising length of his comments about himself. Note that the statement in verse 7 that Christ appeared to James, then to all the apostles, strictly speaking, excludes a further appearance to another apostle. In other words, at least James and the group of apostles living in Jerusalem would strongly object to the claim that Christ appeared to the "apostle" Paul. As if aware of this, Paul points out that the appearance to him happened as to one who was "untimely born."[4]

THE TRADITIONS REWORKED BY PAUL

It is evident that the report in verses 3c–5 printed in boldface is different in structure from the elements of appearance tradition that follow in verses 6–7. (Another sentence construction begins after "then to the Twelve," employing a different conjunction.) Therefore both pieces must be investigated separately.

a) 1 Cor. 15:3c–5:

> (Line 1) Christ died <u>for our sins</u> in accordance with the scriptures and was buried.

> (Line 2) He has been raised <u>on the third day</u> in accordance with the scriptures and appeared to Cephas, then to the Twelve.

Verses 3c–5 offer a twofold proof: first from the scriptures (we know them as the Old Testament), and second from confirmation by facts. The reference to the burial confirms the reality of Jesus' death,[5] while the reference to his appearance to Cephas underscores the reality of the resurrection. In addition, "for our sins" and "on the third day"—underlined in the translation above—parallel each other. (For that reason one may already at this point question the correctness of a literal understanding of "on the third day.")

There are different views about the origin of this piece of tradition. One branch of scholarship derives it from the Greek-speaking communities in and around Antioch to whom Paul had particularly close ties. A primary reason for this contention is the observation that "Christ" here—as in the composite phrase "Jesus Christ"—is already a name and no longer a title,[6] for otherwise one would have expected to find "the Christ." Another contingent of scholars derives it from the Aramaic-speaking community of Jerusalem, in which case we must assume a translation into Greek. On the whole, the dichotomy of "Jerusalem or Antioch" seems to be an exaggeration, for even if—as it is likely—members of the Christian community in Antioch mediated the tradition to Paul, they would have reproduced more or less what they had received from Jerusalem. (Former members of the Jerusalem community—the "Hellenists"—had founded the community of Antioch.)[7]

Within the report of the first appearance of Christ to Cephas in verse 5, the clause "he appeared to Cephas, then to the Twelve" can be detached as an independent unit from the tradition handed down by Paul during his founding visit. This is suggested not only by the parallel to Luke 24:34 ("the Lord was really raised and appeared to Simon"), but by Mark 16:7 ("tell his disciples and Peter").

b) 1 Cor. 15:6–7:

Verse 6 reports an appearance of Christ to more than five hundred brothers at one time, and verse 7 announces one to James and all the apostles. The latter is formulated in the same way as the report of the appearance of Christ to Cephas and the apostles. This parallelism could be explained in two ways: either Paul was modeling his language in verse 7 on verse 5, which employed a tradition about an appearance to James and to all the apostles, or Paul was reproducing two independent traditions. In the latter case either the one formula had already been modeled earlier on the basis of the other or the two formulae have a common origin. In either case, it is clear that verses 5 and 7 both derive from earlier tradition.

HISTORICAL ELEMENTS

In the following, for practical reasons, I shall limit myself to answering the following question: What really happened when Christ "appeared" to various persons, including Paul?[8]

To begin with, the verb "appeared" is the English rendering of the Greek *ophthe*, which is the third person aorist passive of *horan*, to see. The Greek phrase *ophthe Kepha* could be translated either "he appeared to Cephas" or "he was seen by Cephas." Furthermore, it should be observed that in 1 Cor. 15:3–7 Paul lumps together the very different phenomena of individual encounters and mass manifestations under the single term *ophthe*. The appearances exhibit other differences, too: for Cephas the experience denoted by *ophthe* does not depend upon a previous process of communication with the Risen One, nor is it contingent upon the consolidation of a community (and thus other members in a chain of witnesses), but is first of all an immediate event, a primary experience. The latter also applies to Paul (see below, pp. 166–72). But a difference between Peter and Paul lies in the fact that Peter had seen Jesus before, whereas Paul had not; he was "seeing him" him for the first time. In other words, the appearance to Peter and others is at least based on their acquaintance with Jesus during his lifetime, but the vision of the later apostolic witnesses is based on the proclamation of Jesus as the risen Christ by the earlier ones. And the appearance to Paul must be further distinguished from those to "later" figures, because—by reversing Paul's stance from persecutor to advocate—it affects the opponent of a community, and is therefore a primary experience.

Yet by using "he appeared" with reference to himself (verse 8), Paul places his encounter with Christ in parallel with the appearances of Christ to the other witnesses; moreover, he elsewhere uses different verbs to express his own encounter. Therefore one may legitimately employ these passages to clarify the phenomenon mentioned in 1 Cor. 15:3–8.

OTHER SELF-TESTIMONIES OF PAUL ABOUT THE APPEARANCE OF CHRIST

1 Cor. 9:1:

> Am I not free? Am I not an apostle? Have I not seen Jesus? Are you not my own handiwork in the Lord?

Here, in the form of a rhetorical question, Paul claims to have seen Jesus. By using the first person perfect active form of *horan, heoraka*, he expresses the substantive content of 1 Cor. 15:8 as his own active sensory perception, and thus asserts the visual nature of the appearance mentioned in 1 Cor. 15:8. This is not surprising, for as noted above, the phrase "he appeared" could also be translated by "he was seen." 1 Cor. 9:1 is then the active perception of Christ which the "appearance" stated in 1 Cor. 15:8 presupposes.

Most likely, here and in 1 Cor. 15, Paul "visualized the resurrected Christ as a heavenly body, luminous."[9] Otherwise it is hard to understand why Paul would employ the phrase "he appeared" in 1 Cor. 15:4–8 to argue for the certainty of the bodily resurrection. The statements about the future resurrection bodies of the believers (1 Cor. 15:35–49) must also be derived from the resurrection body of Christ, all the more so since Paul's guiding principle is evident: as Christ, so Christians. When conceiving the resurrection as bodily though, Paul "emphasizes change within the continuity of corporeality."[10] In verse 40 he contrasts "celestial bodies" with "terrestrial bodies" and writes, "It is sown in dishonor, it is raised in glory" (verse 43). Later he continues, "As was the man of dust, so are those who are of the dust; and as is the man of heaven, so are those who are of heaven" (verse 48), and he writes in verse 54, "The perishable puts on the imperishable, and the mortal puts on immortality." Similarly, Paul expects a bodily transformation in Phil. 3:21 (the Lord Jesus Christ at his coming "will change our lowly body to be like his glorious body"), again in accordance with the transformation of the heavenly body of Christ.[11]

Gal. 1:15–17a:

> (15) But when he who had set me apart before I was born, and had called me through his grace, (16) was pleased to reveal his Son to me, in order that I might preach him among the Gentiles, I did not confer with flesh and blood, (17a) nor did I go up to Jerusalem to those who were apostles before me.

Since this passage stands in the framework of an account of the pre-Christian and earliest Christian activity of Paul, the "revelation" must refer to a particular event. Here, verse 12 ("I did not receive [the gospel] from man, nor was I taught it, but it came through a revelation of Jesus Christ") combined with verse 16 (cited above) makes it clear that the content of the event was a revelation whose object (objective genitive) or author (subjective genitive) was Christ.

The theme of revelation fits the seeing in 1 Cor. 9:1 which in turn presupposes the appearance in 1 Cor. 15:8.

Let me hasten to note that in Gal. 1:15–17 Paul interprets his own calling in the light of such callings of Old Testament prophets as we find in Isa. 49:5 and Jer. 1:5. This interpretation is clearly the result of his reflection on the Damascus event. It corresponds to the fact that as a rule visionaries pondered their visions, and not infrequently believed that they were granted visions based on earlier visions. Hence they developed a propensity to give new interpretations to earlier visions.

Phil. 3:8a:

> Indeed, I count everything as loss because of the surpassing worth of knowing Christ Jesus my Lord.

In this verse Paul returns to a discussion of the "Damascus event." He is speaking of the knowledge (in Greek: *gnosis*) of Christ, which has led him to see his life hitherto as "loss." The context of verse 8a, verses 2–11, has a polemical character. Paul stresses his blameless life in Judaism (verses 4–6) and distinguishes from it the righteousness that comes from faith revealed to him by the knowledge of Christ (verses 8–10).

In the present section we again find a theological interpretation of the "Damascus event" and no more than an intimation of what actually happened. Hence, those scholars who think that there is no visionary element in Phil. 3 are overlooking the historical context. It is not that the visionary element is lacking here, but that it must be set within the historical framework: 1 Cor. 9:1, Paul's statement that he has seen Jesus, provides the key for a historical understanding of the polemical statements of Phil. 3:4–10.

2 Cor. 4:6:

> For it is the same God who said, "Let light shine out in darkness," who has shone in our hearts to give the light of knowledge of the glory of God in the face of Christ.

This text may also reflect the "Damascus event," in which at his conversion Paul is reported to have seen Christ in the form of light; this would fit his remarks about the heavenly man (1 Cor. 15:49). But more than this, Paul would be putting his vision of Christ in parallel with the dawning of light on the morning of creation to express what had happened to him before Damascus.[12]

THE VISIONARY NATURE OF CHRIST'S APPEARANCE TO PAUL

Specifically, "Christ appeared to Paul," means that Paul saw the risen Christ in his glory. In and of itself, this statement could signify either an inner vision or an outward vision, but clearly it reports an extraordinary event and a revelation. In other words, the visionary received insights into an otherworldly sphere of reality, one which had an esoteric character and therefore represented secret knowledge. The whole event had a character of light and, like the vision of John,[13] happened in the spirit, i.e., in ecstasy.

As it is commonly understood, the word "visions" intends both appearances—persons, things, or happenings—and auditory experiences—voices or other sounds—that do not originate in objective stimuli. Like dreams, they occur entirely within the human person, though visionaries often claim that the images and sounds have external origins. This was the experience of Paul, who never had a moment's doubt that he had seen Christ just outside Damascus. Moreover, the experience had as profound an effect on him—both immediate and long-term—as an objective event would have had. Still, the objectivity that his account assigned to the event in no way impugns the fact that his report details a subjective rather than an objective occurrence. At the same time, the vision is interpreted not to be the object, but the lens *through which* the object is seen, presumably because it is *caused* by the object. A vision is a spiritual experience unlimited by the protocols of the time-space world or subject-object relationships. Its context is a nonrational modality, and must necessarily be understood as such. Given Paul's historical context, the most apt description of what happened to him near

Damascus is that he had a vision of a kind that we find reported in the Old Testament,[14] in other Jewish sources,[15] in numerous parallels from the Hellenistic and Roman environment of the New Testament,[16] and in the New Testament itself.[17]

Let me hasten to add that I intend neither to offer a typology of visions at this point nor to posit a genetic relationship between Paul's Damascus vision and any of the visions enumerated. Rather I adopt a psychological viewpoint in proposing that Paul experienced something that many people from his culture did, as well as have any number of human beings both before and since that time.[18] The phenomenon also surfaces in ghost stories, which were as common in antiquity as they are today.[19] Yet it is also clear that the images that constitute these visions are culturally transmitted. As Eric Robertson Dodds remarks:

> Man shares with a few others of the higher mammals the curious privilege of citizenship in two worlds. He enjoys in daily alternation two distinct kinds of experience . . . each of which has its own logic and its own limitations; and he has no obvious reason for thinking one of them more significant than the other. If the waking world has certain advantages of solidity and continuity, its social opportunities are terribly restricted. In it we meet, as a rule, only the neighbours, whereas the dream world offers the chance of intercourse, however fugitive, with our distant friends, our dead, and our gods.[20]

Lest my all-too-brief statements about human minds as the source of apparitions of heavenly beings remain too general, I shall turn to visions of Mary in order to put flesh on the bones of my suggestions. Indeed, apparitions of Mary seem to entirely consonant with appearances of Jesus.

VISIONS OF MARY—AN ANALOGY FOR VISIONS OF JESUS

Numerous visions of "the virgin" Mary have also been reported. As a matter of fact, the last century witnessed a marked increase in such appearances.[21] Lest the phenomenon spin out of control, ecclesiastical commissions have invested a great deal of time and energy in evaluating their authenticity, for a reasonable number of otherwise unexplained healings must be attributed to the particular site of a reported appearance before the Church can grant recognition. For example, Mary is supposed to have appeared to Bernadette Soubirous in 1858 in the Pyrenees town of Lourdes, France—a place where the Catholic Church has recognized sixty-five instances of miraculous healing. The fourteen-year-old girl reported seeing a "young, wondrously beautiful lady, bathed in light" in a cave in Lourdes, but later admitted that she had been "overcome with confusion" and now thought it was a "deception." The Church, however, issued a different finding. It is easy to see why. After interviewing the girl, the local bishop directed her to ask the "wondrously beautiful lady" her name. After the question was put to her three times, the lady supposedly identified herself as "Immaculate Conception." This utterance nicely corroborated the papal dogma of the same name proclaimed just four years earlier, and enhanced the validity of the Church's institutionalized acceptance of Mary's appearance at Lourdes. Later, when Bernadette repeatedly testified that the lady's appearance confirmed the pope's words, the dogma he had announced gained divine corroboration. The two dogmas, the Immaculate Conception and papal infallibility, illustrate analogous principles: the virgin was free of sin, and the pope was incapable of error.

But even if one ignores the problem of the Church's political agenda in maintaining the historicity of the Lourdes appearances, ecclesiastical sanction can never enter into the critical historian's deliberations. No scholar can help seeing the parallels between the reported appearances of Mary and those of Jesus, nor fail to recognize their subjective nature. Once we understand that visions commonly arise from the frustrations, the hopes, and even yearning for power on the part of both individuals and groups, we are able to examine history as well as human motivation in a more revealing light.

HISTORICAL FACTS BEHIND 1 COR. 15:3–8

The death of Jesus (1 Cor. 15:3)

Jesus' death as a consequence of crucifixion is indisputable.[22]

The burial of Jesus (1 Cor. 15:4a)

Reports of Jesus' burial can be found in the following sources: Matt. 27:57–61; Mark 15:42–47; Luke 23:50–56; John 19:38–42; Gospel of Peter 2:3–5 and 6:21–24; Acts 13:27–29.

With respect to the first three texts, there is agreement that both Matthew and Luke use Mark (or an account that very closely resembles Mark). Therefore any analysis must begin with Mark's account, and should then proceed to examine the other two accounts with due regard to how they have changed Mark's report.

Since the accounts of John and the Gospel of Peter are sometimes regarded as independent of Mark, a separate investigation of each is called for.[23] After analyzing each individual text about the burial of Jesus, I shall try both to sketch the history of the tradition of Jesus' burial and then to answer the question of how or indeed whether Jesus was really buried.

Mark 15:42–47:

(42) And when it was already evening, and because it was the day of preparation, that is, the day before the Sabbath, (43) Joseph of Arimathea, a respected member of the council, who was also living in the expectation of the kingdom of God, took courage and went to Pilate, and asked for the body of Jesus. (44) *And Pilate wondered if he was actually dead; and summoning the centurion, he asked him whether he had already died. (45) And when he learned that from the centurion, he gave Joseph the corpse.* (46) And he bought a linen cloth, took him down, wrapped him in the linen shroud, and laid him in a tomb that had been hewn out of a rock; and he rolled a stone against the door of the tomb.

(47) But Mary, the woman from Magdala, and Mary, the mother of Joses, saw where he was laid.

CONTEXT

This passage serves to connect the crucifixion narrative (15:20b–41) to that of the empty tomb (16:1–8). "In the evening" (verse 42) harks back to both "the third hour" (15:25), the time of the crucifixion, and "the sixth to ninth hour" (15:33), the period of preternatural darkness. In short, Jesus died at 3 o'clock in the afternoon and by early evening his body was entombed. The double reference to the crucifixion scene in verse 44 emphasizes Pilate's surprise at how quickly Jesus died. The unusually short period of suffering makes especially good sense in the context of Mark's sterilized passion narrative.

The interrogation of the centurion (verse 44) links the present scene with that in verse 39 (the centurion under the cross). Note also that 15:46b and 16:3b are nearly verbatim, and that the women who observe the crucifixion from afar also witness the burial and later visit the empty tomb (15:40, 47; 16:1).

MARK'S PURPOSE AND THE TRADITION REWORKED BY HIM

Verse 42: The note of time "and when it was already evening" goes back to Mark, as do 4:35; 6:47; 14:17.

Verse 43: Mark uses the terms "respected" and "member of the council" only here in his gospel. However, we cannot infer from this that the characterization of Joseph stems from tradition. To be sure, the statement about Joseph's being a member of the council derives from tradition, but the idea that he was respected and also that he was waiting for the kingdom of God are likely Mark's inventions. Mark then affirms that Joseph belongs to the council that condemned Jesus to death,[24] but by adding the above qualifications, he mitigates that blemish. Mark's assertion that Joseph was "also living in the expectation of the kingdom of God" suggests that others were doing the same thing. This includes not only the disciples[25] but also the scribe whom Jesus claims to be "not far from the kingdom of God."[26] In other words, while Mark does not depict Joseph as a

Christian, he does single him out from Jesus' enemies in the High Council. In view of the strong positive significance of "kingdom of God" in Mark's gospel,[27] he dissociates him from the opposition of the Sanhedrin to Jesus. Certainly Mark would rather have reported that Jesus was buried by his followers (cf. Mark 6:29, the burial of John the Baptist by his disciples). But no tradition to that effect was available, and since reports of Joseph of Arimathea's role were already widely known, Mark contented himself with these enhancements to Joseph's character.

The information that "he took courage and went to Pilate" is passed over in the parallels. This piece of information, offered only by Mark, makes Joseph a good deal more sympathetic to the reader.

Verses 44–45: These verses certainly derive from Mark and bracket the scene with the context. They provide official authentication of the death of Jesus and have the subsidiary apologetic aim of stressing its reality.[28]

Verse 46: The account of Jesus' burial comes from the tradition. And yet specifying a rock-hewn tomb with a stone to close it prepares for 16:3; and Joseph's purchase of linen—which, it seems, must be new—is curious, since it likely comes from Mark, who is at pains not to allow any hint of dishonor to mar the burial of Jesus. To be sure, the tradition may have included the linen wrapping (but it would have been used material), which is a customary element in Jewish burials, but other circumstances are also anomalous. Jesus was not placed in a family tomb in Nazareth, as would normally have been true of an honorable burial. Furthermore, Mark's earlier report of an anointing of Jesus was described as a preparation for death (14:3–9), but this is hardly the anointing of a corpse that one would find in a burial ritual. One cannot help wondering whether Mark is disinfecting a tradition that contained the account of a dishonorable burial.

RESULT

The tradition underlying Mark 15:42–47 reports a burial of Jesus' body by Joseph of Arimathea, a member of the Supreme Council.

Matt. 27:57–61:

(57) Now when it was evening, there came a *rich* man from Arimathea, named Joseph, *who had also become a disciple of Jesus*. (58) He went to Pilate and asked for the body of Jesus. Then Pilate ordered [it] to be given. (59) And Joseph took the body, and wrapped it in a *clean* linen cloth, (60) and laid it in *his own new tomb*, which he had hewn in the rock; and he rolled a *great* stone to the door of the tomb, and departed.

MATTHEW'S PURPOSE

Matthew is using Mark 15:42–47. On the curious omission of Mark 15:44–45 from both Matthew and Luke, see below on Luke 23:52 (p. 54).

Verse 57: Joseph becomes a disciple of Jesus. The fact that as a councilor he had been a member of the Supreme Council that had condemned Jesus to death is left out.

Verse 58: Joseph's courage to ask for the body (Mark 15:43) is passed over.

Verse 59: Matthew omits the detail that the linen cloth was purchased by Joseph and writes "clean linen cloth" rather than "bought a linen cloth." By affirming both the newness and cleanliness of the linen cloth, Matthew works to convince his audience of Jesus' uniqueness. Further, Matthew wants to show that Jesus' body will be the exception; according to Jewish belief, corpses are unclean[29] but Jesus will be miraculously raised, so he must be buried appropriately.

Verse 60: This description of Jesus' tomb is especially significant. Because it belongs to Joseph, who was a rich man, it stands to reason that the tomb is new. In other words, it has not yet been made unclean by another corpse. This was something one would not expect since tombs for individuals were rare. In this way Matthew reinforces the idea in verse 59.

Luke 23:50–56:

(50) *And look,* there was a man *named* Joseph, a member of the Council, *who was a good and righteous man;* (51) *he had not consented to their council and action.* He was from Arimathea, *a town of the Jews,* and lived in expectation of the kingdom of God. (52) This [man] approached Pilate and asked for the body of Jesus, (53) and he took it down, wrapped it in a linen cloth, and laid it in a rock cut tomb, *in which no one had yet been laid.*

(54) And it was the day of preparation, and the Sabbath was dawning. (55) *And the women who had come with him from Galilee followed, and saw the tomb, and how his body was laid in it.* (56) *They returned and prepared fragrant oils and ointments. And on the Sabbath they rested according to the law.*

LUKE'S PURPOSE

Verses 50–51: These verses draw an even more positive picture of Joseph than Mark 15:43.

Verse 52: Neither Luke nor Matthew include Mark 15:44–45 in their account. Either it did not appear in their copies of Mark, or they left it out as unnecessary.

Verse 53: Luke also describes Jesus' burial more positively than Mark 15:46. As in Matthew, no one had yet lain in the tomb. However, Luke does not explicitly state that it was new, nor does he say that it was Joseph's tomb which he had hewn in the rock.

Verse 54: Luke introduces a note of time here based on Mark 15:42.

Verses 55–56: These verses improve on Mark 16:1 and show the women readying the spices ahead of time. Resting on the Sabbath corresponds to the faithfulness that Luke's main characters show to the Jewish law.[30]

John 19:38–42:

(38a) And *after this* Joseph of Arimathea, who was a **disciple of Jesus** *but secretly, for fear of the Jews,* asked Pilate that he might take away <u>the body of Jesus,</u> (38b) and Pilate allowed it. (38c) So <u>he came</u> and took away his body. (39a) And *Nicodemus also came, who had at first come to him by night,* (39b) bringing a mixture of myrrh and aloes, about a hundred pounds' weight. (40) They took the body of Jesus, and wrapped **it** in linen cloths with the **spices**, *as is the burial custom of the Jews.* (41a) Now in the place where he was crucified there was a garden, (41b) and in the garden a **new tomb** where no one had ever been laid. (42) There now—because of the Jews' day of preparation, *as the tomb was near—they* <u>buried Jesus.</u>

JOHN'S PURPOSE

The section demonstrates knowledge of all three synoptic accounts of Jesus' burial (Mark 15:42–47; Matt 27:57–61; Luke 23:50–56). Verbatim or almost verbatim agreements with Mark are underlined, additional agreements with Matthew and/or Luke are set in bold-face, and features that derive from John are italicized.

Verse 38a: Cf. Mark 15:43; Matt. 27:57–58a; Luke 23:50–52. As in Matt., Joseph of Arimathea has become a disciple of Jesus. Yet, for fear of the Jews, he keeps it hidden.[31]

Verse 38b: Cf. Mark 15:45; Matt. 27:58.

Verse 38c: Jesus' body is removed from the cross. The Synoptics also assumed this action but did not mention it.[32]

Verse 39a: Here, John has Nicodemus join Joseph to prepare the body for burial, making mention of the nocturnal scene in John 3:1–21.

Verse 39b: Cf. the amount of costly ointment used by Mary in 12:3.

Verse 40: Cf. Matt. 27:59; Luke 23:53a (Mark 15:46a); "spices" as in Luke 23:56.

Verse 41a: Moving the tomb into the garden[33] recasts the interment as an almost idyllic scene.

Verse 41b: Cf. Matt. 27:60 ("his new tomb"); Luke 23:53 ("in which no one had yet been laid").

Verse 42: Cf. Mark 15:46; Matt. 27:60; Luke 23:53.

RESULT

John's account is in every respect a further development of the synoptic accounts of the burial of Jesus.

Gospel of Peter 2:3–5 and 6:23–24

INTRODUCTORY INFORMATION ABOUT THE GOSPEL OF PETER

At this point some basic information about the Gospel of Peter must be given since as an apocryphal writing it is known to few but specialists.[34]

Until 1886/87, when a lengthy fragment of it was discovered in the tomb of a Christian monk in Upper Egypt, the existence of a Gospel of Peter was known only from general remarks of the church fathers Origen and Eusebius. Though neither quoted any passages from it, one historical detail about it was available. Eusebius[35]—relying on Bishop Serapion of Antioch's book "Concerning what is known as the Gospel of Peter"—reported that Serapion (c. 200) first allowed the Gospel of Peter to be read during worship in the community of Rhossos but after a closer examination banned it, explaining that while "the most part indeed was in accordance with the true teaching of the Savior . . . some things were added."[36] Indeed, since the attribution to Peter was false, we must reject it "as men of experience, knowing that such were not handed down to us."[37]

Some have divided the text of the fragment into fourteen chapters and others into sixty verses. Following established custom, I note both numberings in the table of contents and in the translation given below.

Written entirely in the first person with Peter as the speaker (7:26; 14:60), the text begins with the scene in which Pilate washes his hands. Then the account continues with the request of Joseph of Arimathea for the body of Jesus—who in the Gospel of Peter is called only "the Lord" (2:3–5)—, then the mockery (3:6–9), the crucifixion (4:10), the inscription on the cross (4:11), dividing of the garments (4:12), rebuke of the crucifiers (the Jews) by one of the two malefactors crucified with the Lord (4:13–14), darkness (5:15), drinking gall and vinegar (5:16), the last cry and death of the Lord (5:19), rending of the veil of the temple (5:20), deposition from the cross (6:21), earthquake (6:21), end of the darkness (6:22), burial (6:23–24), repentance of the Jews (7:25), behavior of Peter and the disciples (7:26–27), setting of guards over the tomb (8:28–33), mass visit of the inhabitants of Jerusalem to the tomb (9:34), resurrection (9:35–10:42), report of Pilate and command to the soldiers to keep silent (11:43–49), the women at the empty tomb (12:50–13:47), and the return home of the disciples (14:58–59), where Peter, Andrew, and Levi go back to fishing (14:60). Here the fragment breaks off, but on the basis of the parallels in the canonical Gospels one can justifiably assume that there followed an appearance of "the Lord" by Lake Tiberias.

Gospel of Peter 2:3–5:

> (2:3) Now there stood Joseph the friend of Pilate and of *the Lord*, and knowing that they were about to crucify him, he came to Pilate and <u>requested</u> the body of *the Lord* for burial. (4) And Pilate sending unto Herod, <u>requested</u> his body. (5) And Herod said: "Brother Pilate, even if no one had <u>requested</u> him, we should bury him, since the Sabbath is drawing on. For it is written in the law: The sun should not set on one that has been put to death." And he delivered him to the people on the day before the unleavened bread.

[3:6–6:22—see above table of contents]

> (6:23) And the Jews rejoiced, and gave his body to Joseph to bury it, because he had beheld all the good that he [Jesus] had done (24) And he took *the Lord*, washed him and wrapped him in linen and brought him unto his own tomb, called Joseph's Garden.

PURPOSE AND TRADITIONS REWORKED

In general it is striking that Jesus is never named, but called "the Lord" (here three times, set in italics).

2:3: The designation of Joseph as a "friend of the Lord" reflects a later tendency of the tradition that continues the positive picture drawn by the Synoptics and John. The great distance from the earliest tradition becomes especially evident when the text calls Joseph a friend of Pilate, since this entails making Pilate a Christian. Thus Joseph no longer needs courage—as he does in Mark 15:43—to request Jesus' body. Placing the request for Jesus' body at this point of the narrative—before the report of the execution—points to later origin. This literary device ensures at the outset that Jesus will receive an honorable burial.

2:4: The detail that Pilate must request Jesus' body from Herod —whom the author regards as supreme ruler and judge—illustrates his "ignorance of political realities of 1st-cent. Judea."[38]

2:5: Cf. Luke 23:54; see further John 19:31; Mark 15:15 par.; Mark 14:12 par. Herod's remark to "brother Pilate" that Jesus would have been buried anyway according to Jewish law[39] gives the strong impression of a secondary reflection.

6:23: Their joy at Jesus' death makes the Jews appear especially guilty, while Joseph—who recognizes all the good that Jesus has done—will be more than exonerated.

6:24: The report of washing Jesus' body cannot be found in the synoptic Gospels. It goes back to the narrator, who adds this customary step of the burial practice (cf. Acts 9:37). The notice that it is Joseph's tomb is based on Matt. 27:60. Its location in the garden corresponds to John 19:41.

RESULT

The details of Jesus' burial by Joseph of Arimathea in the Gospel of Peter are totally dependent on the Synoptics and John. Everything that goes beyond it is due to the purpose of the narrator. Thus the

Gospel of Peter does not contribute anything to the historical question of Jesus' burial.

Acts 13:(27–)29

([27] For those who live in Jerusalem and their leaders, because they did not recognize him [Jesus] nor understand the utterances of the prophets which are read every Sabbath, fulfilled these by condemning him. [28] Though they found no charge against him worthy of death, they demanded of Pilate to have him [Jesus] killed.) (29) When they thus brought about all that was written of him, they took him down from the tree, and laid him in a tomb.

LUKE'S PURPOSE AND THE TRADITION REWORKED BY HIM

The passage is part of the report of a sermon delivered by Paul at Antioch in Pisidia. It is often asserted that this text is exclusively governed by Luke's language and theology, but that is questionable. While it is true that in the mission speeches of Acts Luke lays the blame for the death of Jesus on the Jews,[40] in this case Jews see to taking the body away and burying it—an action that cannot be linked with the motif of attaching blame. So this might well be an independent tradition,[41] and a reminiscence of it may have been preserved in the *Epistle of James to Philip* from Nag Hammadi where we read about a shameful burial of Jesus.[42]

Two Different Traditions of Jesus' Burial

The tradition of a burial of Jesus occurs in two different narratives: a) Joseph of Arimathea asks Pilate for the corpse of Jesus and buries it; b) Jews ask Pilate for the corpse of Jesus and bury it. The latter tradition is doubtless earlier; the former, with its positive portrayal of Joseph's character, is clearly a Christian interpretation.

ON THE LITERARY DEVELOPMENT OF JOSEPH'S CHARACTER

The parallel reports, Matthew and Luke along with John, have christianized the figure of Joseph, drawing it even more positively than Mark had before them. Matthew differed from his Markan model by making Joseph a rich man and a disciple of Jesus (Matt. 27:57). Luke describes him as a good and just man (Luke 23:50) who did not take part in the hearing of the Supreme Council against Jesus (Luke 23:51); and according to the Gospel of Peter 6:23 Joseph not only "beheld all the good that he [Jesus] had done," but he was even "a friend of the Lord" (2:3).

In John, too, Joseph of Arimathea is described as a disciple of Jesus (19:38), but he keeps his discipleship hidden for fear of the Jews (12:42; 9:22). The story contains the further detail that Nicodemus, "who had at first[43] come to him [Jesus] by night" (19:39a), came to help Joseph prepare the body of Jesus for the burial (19:39b). Adding Nicodemus to Joseph commended itself because like Joseph, he was both a councilor and a secret disciple.

The direction taken by the early Christian narrative tradition of the burial of Jesus by Joseph of Arimathea has become sufficiently clear. The councilor has become a disciple of Jesus—one could almost say the enemy has become a friend—and finally yet another friend assists in the burial.

ON THE LITERARY DEVELOPMENT OF THE BURIAL

But the burial, too, is painted in increasingly positive colors. Whereas Mark says merely that it was a rock tomb, the parallels further identify it as Joseph's own tomb,[44] and John 20:15 and Gospel of Peter 6:24 give it the distinction of a garden location.[45] Finally, Matt. 27:60, Luke 23:53, and John 19:41 describe the tomb as new, thus both ascribing honor to Jesus and excluding the possibility that Jesus was put, for example, in a grave for criminals.

Let me reiterate at this point that only Mark's account—or the report reworked there—and Acts 13:29 are sources relevant to the locating of the historical kernel of the tradition.

It must be noted, of course, that if the post-Markan tendency is to transform a member of the hostile Sanhedrin into a Christian, then Mark's narrative may have initiated this trend in its portrayal of Joseph as someone who expects the kingdom of God. But in that case a similar conclusion recommends itself for the story of Jesus' burial: if the story of the burial increasingly bestows honor on Jesus, did it perhaps serve to displace knowledge of a dishonorable burial? In other words, Mark's way of telling the story of Jesus' burial may have been a cover-up.

WAS JESUS REALLY BURIED?

Roman legal practice quite often provided for someone who died on the cross to serve as a warning to the living, and thus to rot there or to be devoured by vultures, jackals, or other animals. "It was a stereotyped picture that the crucified victim served as food for wild beasts and birds of prey."[46] This may not have applied in the case of Jesus, for the traditions relating to him agree in reporting that his corpse was taken down from the cross, and 1 Cor. 15:4 also assumes this. The report of Jesus' burial could reflect one of those cases in which the Roman authorities released the body. Note, for example, the witness of the apostle Paul's older contemporary from Alexandria, the Jewish philosopher Philo in *Against Flaccus* 83:

> I know of instances before now of persons who had been impaled, when a holiday of this kind was at hand, being taken down and given up to their relatives in order to receive the honor of sepulture and to enjoy the customary rites. For it was proper that even corpses should enjoy some good on the emperor's birthday and at the same time that the sanctity of the festival should be observed.[47]

However, we cannot completely rule out the possibility that both in Mark's account and in 1 Cor. 15:4 the burial of Jesus was only postulated—in 1 Cor. 15:4 because in this way Jesus' death would be confirmed, and in Mark 15:42–47 in order to avert the rumor of a dishonorable burial which perhaps included the devouring of the corpse by vultures and jackals. A passage from the prophet Isaiah could have been a catalyst for the formation of the tradition, the more so since the book of Isaiah served in many other cases as a storehouse of proof text for the earliest Christians.[48]

Isa. 53:9:

> And he was given the tomb with the godless and the transgressors (or "with the rich") when he had died, although he had done no injustice to anyone and no deceit was in his mouth.

In that case there would have been no burial for Jesus. Yet apparently Jesus' body was taken down from the cross, and the most likely reason is that Pilate ordered it done. According to Jewish law, a dead person ought not to hang on the cross overnight,[49] and especially since it was soon to be Passover, one of the most important Jewish festivals of the year, such a gesture would reduce the possibility of serious unrest among the throng of celebrants at the festival. It is not beyond imagining that the second or third century BCE tale of Tobit, whose title character buried executed Jews at the risk of his own life, might have encouraged a devout Jew to do the same and to attend to the burial of Jesus.[50]

The two pieces of tradition reconstructed above to be the earliest independent strata of information—Mark 15 and Acts 13—seem to agree in knowing Joseph of Arimathea. While someone of that name may have taken upon himself or been charged with the burial of Jesus, it is improbable that he was a disciple or friend of Jesus. The conclusion that he was one of Jesus' enemies is equally dubious, since Jesus' condemnation by the Supreme Council is historically improbable.[51] The simple fact is that we can no longer say where Joseph (or Jews unknown to us) put the body.

Yet anticipating the results of the analysis of the stories of the empty tomb and of the appearances of the "Risen One," let me hasten to add that Jesus' corpse decayed. This statement is based not on the discovery of Jesus' bones, but on the nature of the available sources and on the natural law that human corpses decompose.[52]

The Resurrection on the third day (1 Cor. 15:4b)

Resurrection in Greek and Roman Religion

The notion of resurrection, let alone bodily resurrection as a means to overcome death permanently, was in general alien to Greek and Roman religion. While it is true that since Homer there had existed the idea that the dead drink[53] and are able in the underworld to hold swords in their hands,[54] the explicit idea of bodily resurrection is not present.[55] Some five hundred years before the rise of Christianity, the tragedian Aeschylus had enunciated the Greek view of the matter. In the course of dramatizing the mythic origin of the Aereopagitican court under the aegis of the city's eponymous goddess Athene, he put these words on the lips of the divine Apollo: "When the dust has soaked up a man's blood, once he is dead, there is no resurrection."[56] It is worth noting that his word for resurrection, *anastasis*, is the same as Paul's in Acts 17:31f.

A Roman critic of the notion of resurrection is Fronto (d. before 175 CE), the teacher of the emperor Marcus Aurelius. Part of his speech against the Christians has been preserved in the work of the Christian apologist Minucius Felix who composed his work "Octavius" around 200 CE. We have a unique opportunity of listening to Fronto's objections:

> (7) Yet I should be glad to be informed whether or no you rise again with bodies; and if so, with what bodies—whether with the same or with renewed bodies? Without a body? Then, as far as I know, there will neither be mind, nor soul, nor life. With the same body? But this has already been previously destroyed. With another body? Then it is a new person who is born, not the former one restored; (8) and yet so long a time has passed away, innumerable ages have flowed by, and what single individual has returned from the dead either by the fate of Protesilaus[57] with permission to sojourn even for a few hours, or that we might believe it for an example? (9) All such figments [are] of an unhealthy belief, and vain sources of comfort.[58]

It is true that neither Aeschylus nor Fronto was a contemporary of Jesus and the first disciples. But they most likely said what many Greeks and Romans thought about the Christian preaching of the resurrection. It is important to note that while several, influenced by Plato, maintained some idea of the soul's immortality,[59] many altogether denied any real existence to the deceased, as we see from a well-known text of an often-used epitaph: "I wasn't, I was, I am not, I don't care."[60]

Resurrection in Judaism

Greek-speaking Jews living outside Palestine such as Philo of Alexandria[61]—an older contemporary of the apostle Paul—to a more or lesser extent adopted the concept of the immortality of the soul,[62] and most likely shared the disdain of the Greeks and the Romans for the doctrine of resurrection whose origin is much debated.[63] Indeed, the hope for resurrection as a means to overcome death permanently is quite alien to the Old Testament and occurs only at its fringes.[64]

Ezek. 37:1–14, the report about the vision of the reviving of the bones of the dead, is an image of the future restitution of Israel that was at the time (sixth century BCE) captive in Babylon.[65] Even verse 12 ("Therefore prophesy, and say to them, 'Thus says the Lord God: Behold, I will open your graves and raise you from your graves, O my people; and I will bring you home into the land of Israel'") does not intend the resurrection of the individual believer.

Isa. 24–27, the so-called little apocalypse of Isaiah, contains in its Greek translation (second century BCE) an indisputable reference to the bodily resurrection of the dead.

Isa. 26:19a:

The dead shall rise, and they that are in the tombs shall be raised, and they that are in the earth shall rejoice.

The Book of Daniel reworks many texts from Isaiah, especially Is. 26:19a. We read, for example,

Dan. 12:2–3:

(2) And many of those who sleep in the land of the dust shall awake, some to everlasting life, and some to shame and everlasting contempt. (3) And those who are wise shall shine like the brightness of the firmament; and those who turn many to righteousness, like the stars forever and ever.

The "land of the dust" designates the underworld. However, it remains unclear whether only the shades of the dead or, less likely, the bones of the dead rest in it.[66] "Sleeping" is a euphemism for "being dead."[67] The claim that some of the resurrected will shine "like the brightness of the firmament" fails to specify whether they will be reunited with their previous bodies. More probable is the notion that by receiving heavenly bodies they will participate in astral immortality.[68]

The Book of Jubilees from the middle of the second century BCE shows a similar notion of the relationship between the old earthly body and the new heavenly one. Its description of the time of salvation runs thus:

Jubilees 23:30–31:

(30) And then the Lord will heal his servants, and they will rise up and see great peace. And they will drive out their enemies, and the righteous ones will see and give praise, and rejoice forever and ever with joy; and they will see all of their judgments and all of their curses among their enemies. (31) *And their bones will rest in the earth, and their spirits will increase joy;* and they will know that the Lord is an executor of judgment; but he will show mercy to hundreds and thousands, to all who love him.[69]

This text—especially verse 31a—suggests that decay of a body and "resurrection" could stand side by side in Palestinian Judaism. For the spirits of the dead remain conscious and are "aware of postmortem events while their bones rest in peace."[70]

However, it must be noted that many texts from second temple Judaism presuppose a notion of bodily resurrection that undoubt-

edly included the corpse, meaning that the old body was transformed into the new.[71] There is no reason to go into detail at this
point. The important thing to remember is that the notions of resurrection were quite variegated in Judaism, and that occasionally the
decay of the body was admitted even while the resurrection of the
body was affirmed.

Resurrection in the New Testament

The same must be said with respect to the New Testament, which is
also an important source for understanding Jewish belief about resurrection. In it resurrection is understood in the following manner:

a) Resuscitation to Life

In the stories of resuscitation like John 11:1-44 ("The Raising of
Lazarus"), resurrection means the revival of the corpse with the
result that death will occur again.[72] A similar case can be found
when Herod Antipas regards Jesus as the resuscitated John the Baptist whom he had decapitated earlier. See Mark 6:16b: "The one
whom I beheaded, John, was raised."

Elsewhere in the New Testament, however, resuscitation is part
of a final overcoming of death or belongs to the description of the
final judgment:

1) Matt. 27:52b-53 reports that at the moment of Jesus' death,
tombs opened up in Jerusalem, "and many bodies of the deceased
saints were raised and left the tombs after his resurrection and
entered the holy city and appeared to many." While "after the resurrection" is an addition by Matthew in order to harmonize this passage with the raising of Jesus on the third day, the original idea
behind the present text is that death and resurrection on the same
day constitute the beginning of the general resurrection.[73] Paul, in
two places, uses the same concept. In Rom 1:4 he writes that Jesus
was adopted as Son of God since the (general) resurrection, and 1
Cor. 15:20, when writing about the first fruit of those who have
fallen asleep, says the same thing.

2) In John 5:28–29 Jesus gives instructions about the hour, "when all who are in the tombs will hear his [the Son of God's] voice (29) and come forth, those who have done good to resurrection and life, and those who have done evil to the resurrection of judgment."

3) In 1 Thess. 4:16–17 those Thessalonians who have prematurely died are restored to their earlier bodies and together with the surviving Christians will be lifted up to meet the Lord in the air. Paul presumes that the dead will receive their former bodies again so that the surviving Christians will be able to recognize them. Their resurrection makes up for the earlier disadvantage of having died prematurely. They will not die again and will be, along with the survivors, united with Jesus forever.

b) Transformation

The hope set forth in 1 Thess. 4:16–17 reappears in expanded form in 1 Cor. 15:51–52:

> (51) We will not **all** sleep, but will **all** be transformed (53) suddenly—in the twinkling of an eye—on that last day, for when the trumpet sounds, the dead will be raised to immortality, and we will be transformed.

Note that two groups will be transformed: not only those who have already died, but also those who are still alive at the parousia. This expansion of 1 Thess. 4:13–17 demonstrates Paul effectively equating resuscitation and transformation, exchanging one concept for the other.

c) Being like the angels

The account of Jesus being challenged by the Sadducees is also pertinent, since it clearly reflects a Jewish notion of the resurrection that specifies transformation at one point: the ceasing of sexuality. A discussion of Mark's text will suffice, for Matt. 22:23–33 and Luke 20:27–40 depend on Mark and contribute nothing additional to the matter at hand.

Mark 12:18–27:

(18) Then some Sadducees, *who say there is no resurrection,* posed him this question: (19) "Teacher, Moses wrote that 'If a man's brother dies and leaves a wife but no children, then his brother must marry her and father children for his brother.' (20) Now once there were seven brothers. The first took a wife, but died leaving no children. (21) The second married her and also died without begetting offspring, and the third likewise. (22) And so all seven, leaving no child; and finally the woman herself died. (23) Now at the resurrection—inasmuch as *all seven had married her*—whose wife will she be? (24) Jesus said to them, "Do you know why you are wrong? It's because you understand neither scripture nor God's power. (25) For when people rise from death, they neither marry nor are given in marriage; rather they are like the angels in heaven.

(26) But as for the raising of the dead, haven't you read Moses' account of how God spoke to him from a burning bush, saying, 'I am the God of Abraham and the God of Isaac and the God of Jacob'? (27) He is God not of the dead, but of the living. You are badly mistaken."

MARK'S PURPOSE

Aside from the explanation offered in verse 18 (cf. the analogous explanation of Jewish legal practice in Mark 7:3–4) and the clarification in verse 23b—both are italicized—no Markan modifications of the traditions he received are evident. Mark has inserted tradition at this point because of its content. *First,* the Sadducees are here rebuffed just as the Pharisees vainly challenged Jesus in the previous section (Mark 12:13–17). *Second,* the present text may well be intended as a preparation for the resurrection message to the women—and the reader—announced by the young man in the tomb (Mark 16:5–7).

THE TRADITION REWORKED BY MARK

While no doubt the underlying tradition reflected a controversy, we must differentiate verses 18–25 (the original controversy) from verses 26–27 (a later addition). The purpose of this elaboration was to argue the general resurrection as the consequence of Jesus' resurrection on the basis of the purported dialogue with the Sadducees, who repudiated the very idea of resurrection. All in all, however, it amounts to little more than a legalistic quibble, since in Jesus' day the institution of levirate marriage no longer existed.

Still, the addition of verses 26–27 further supports the resurrection claim. For while the Old Testament God is the God of the living, Old Testament conservatives conclude that in death they are excluded from any relationship with God (cf. Psalm 6:6, "For in death no one remembers you; who will thank you among the dead?"). Thus verses 26–27 offer an interpretation founded, like that of verses 19–25, on faith in Jesus' resurrection. In both cases the exegesis clearly reflects community formation.

Paul and the empty tomb

Already at this point the question arises how Paul imagined the relationship of the dead body of Jesus to the raised one. Did he think that the tomb was empty? Two questions must be distinguished here: a) Did Paul know about reports of the empty tomb? b) If someone had asked him about it, would he have presumed that the tomb was empty?

Before addressing these questions let me introduce a presupposition that John Dominic Crossan posits in an analysis of Mark's account of the empty tomb (Mark 16:1–8). I am convinced that it equally applies to the present work. Crossan writes, "a *presumption* is not the same as a *tradition*. It is possible that those who believed Jesus was with God might have presumed there was, therefore and somewhere, an empty grave. But this not yet a tradition of where it is, how it was found, when, by whom, etc."[74] He continues, "No doubt Mk presumed Jesus had an infancy but there is no tradition of an infancy in Mk as there is in Matthew and Luke. Presumption of fact is not tradition of event."[75]

On a) Paul does not seem to be acquainted with any source about the empty tomb, for in 1 Cor. 15:4—apart from Rom. 6:3-4 the only text in his letters in which he speaks of Jesus' burial in the immediate context of his resurrection—the reference to the burial confirms only Jesus' death and not his resurrection. Therefore one must assume that the formula used by Paul in 1 Cor. 15:3c-5 does not contain the notion of an empty tomb.

On b) Paul thinks of the resurrection in bodily terms. This requires the idea of Jesus' body leaving the tomb if the apostle joins in with the very Jewish tradition that presupposes that the identity of the corpse is the same as that of the raised body. At any rate, he uses this notion in 1 Thess. 4:16-17 with respect to the deceased Christians from Thessalonica. Furthermore, in 1 Cor. 15:5-8 he thoroughly catalogues the attestations of Jesus' resurrection, and after that in verses 16-19 emphasizes the necessity of believing in the future bodily resurrection—which has its basis in the bodily resurrection of Christ. Therefore, it is reasonable to assume that Paul considered Jesus' tomb to have been empty.

This hypothesis becomes even more plausible after examining the following counter thesis: *According to Paul Jesus' tomb was full and his corpse decayed in it. At the same time Paul assumed a bodily resurrection of Christ, just as he expected the bodily resurrection of those Christians who would die before Jesus' return from heaven.*

Rebuttal: Such a thesis is unconvincing because it overlooks Paul's conviction that Jesus was without sin (2 Cor. 5:21), and therefore has no part in flesh and blood that will not inherit the kingdom of God (1 Cor. 15:50). In Paul's way of thinking, "flesh and blood" means that although Christians are God's creatures, they live under the yoke of sin and the shadow of mortality. Since this does not apply to Jesus, however, to argue from the bodily resurrection of humans—which includes their bodily decay—to that of Jesus is not valid. As Jesus' body was not subject to sin, he was not subject to decay. Using Paul's logic one might say that through his death Jesus paid for the sins of all the people, but his body did not decay. After doing the job on earth that he was sent to do, Jesus was exalted from the cross directly to God.

At the same time one must take into account that the various notions of resurrection were quite fluid. Indeed, Paul did not even try to harmonize contradictions if he ever saw any. Remember that he was able to read the empty tomb into a text that did not contain such an idea.

"On the third day"

We should first recall that "on the third day" in the second line of 1 Cor. 15:3c–5 has a function analogous to "for our sins" in line 1 (see above, p. 42) and thus in all likelihood is an interpretation, not part of a historical report.

To derive the phrase "on the third day" from the Bible is surely indicated because "according to the scriptures" follows. Here Hos. 6:2 in its Greek translation comes to mind: The Lord "will make us healthy after two days, on the third day we will rise and live before him." In Judaism this passage was used to point to the final resurrection.[76] If such an understanding underlies 1 Cor. 15:4, Jesus' resurrection would have been understood as the fulfillment of an Old Testament prophecy.

Various commentators have objected that Hos. 6:2 is never quoted in the New Testament and that it occurs only in rabbinic texts from a later time. However, the date of the attestation of such an exegesis of Hos. 6:2 need not coincide with its origin. 1 Cor. 15:4 might very well reflect a common Jewish understanding of Hos. 6:2 in the context of an eschatological hope. Against such a view Martin Hengel writes:

> The third day . . . as the day of [God's] raising Jesus from the grave has certainly not been deduced from Hos. 6:2 or similar texts. For such an action the statements of the report are too basic. All of them derive from the beginning of the primitive community. Indeed, they are documents of its foundation and belong to the original proclamation of the resurrection. This statement of time is connected with the date of the discovery of the empty tomb.[77]

Hengel combines God's raising Jesus from the dead on the third day with the discovery of the empty tomb by women on the third day. Yet the two events must be distinguished from one another, all the more so since the narrative about the discovery of the empty tomb on the third day—something that Hengel considers historical—is a conclusion derived from an appearance of Jesus to the disciples and Peter (Mark 16:7). In other words, the report of an appearance of the risen Jesus to his disciples and Peter must be earlier than the report of the discovery of the empty tomb on the third day and therefore cannot be harmonized with it. Rather Mark 16:7 has a genetic connection with 1 Cor. 15:5, neither of which in its original setting presupposes an empty tomb or the discovery of an empty tomb on the third day.[78]

The appearance to Cephas and the appearance to the Twelve (1 Cor. 15:5)

THE APPEARANCE TO CEPHAS

The relationship of the appearance to Peter to the appearance to the Twelve can be defined in two ways: First, the two appearances might originally have been one. Paul could have replaced a *kai* with an *eita* and thereby altered "Cephas and the Twelve" to "Cephas, then to the Twelve," simply because of the other appearances which he intended to cite in sequence. However, such a view is improbable (see below). Second, the appearance to Cephas and the appearance to the Twelve derive from two different events. This thesis is probably correct. Indeed, it is supported by the very formulation in 1 Cor. 15:5 and moreover on historical grounds.

Peter was the leader of the earliest community in Jerusalem. This must be concluded from Gal. 1:18, according to which Paul went to Jerusalem three years after his conversion, to make acquaintance with Cephas in order to introduce himself to the most important leader of the Jerusalem community of that time. As reflected in 1 Cor. 15:5 and Luke 24:34, Peter most likely was appointed to this position of prominence as a result of witnessing an appearance of the risen Jesus.

THE APPEARANCE TO THE TWELVE

We have no explicit account of the appearance to the Twelve in the New Testament unless one connects parts of Matt. 28:16–20, Luke 24:36–43, and John 20:19–23. Furthermore, the previously reported defection and death of Judas renders at least the number problematic, if not the story itself.

From the "Proclamation of Peter" (Kerygma Petri),[79] an apologetic writing from the beginning of the second century of which only fragments are preserved, the church father Clement of Alexandria took the following report of what the Lord said to his disciples after the resurrection:

> I have chosen you twelve because I judged you worthy to be my disciples. . . . And I sent them, of whom I was persuaded that they would be true apostles, into the world to proclaim to men in all the world the joyous message that they may know that there is [only] one God, and to reveal what future happenings there would be through faith in me, to the end that those who hear and believe may be saved; and that those who believe not may testify that they have heard it and not be able to excuse themselves saying, "We have not heard."[80]

The text certainly has no genetic relationship to the appearance to the Twelve and is wholly indebted to the theology of the unknown author, which is centered on the preaching of the one God and the mission of the twelve apostles to the whole earth. We may further assume that the existing fragment is part of a conversation between Jesus and his disciples after the resurrection, and this similarly points to a later period.[81]

The appearance to more than five hundred brothers at one time (1 Cor. 15:6)

It is to be supposed that this appearance is a kind of foundation legend of the Christian community and can be derived from the event that underlies Acts 2.[82]

We may start by reflecting that it is improbable that such an event witnessed by more than five hundred people should otherwise have left no trace. Moreover, Paul emphasizes that those concerned can still be asked questions about it since only a few of them have died. This assumes that their witness corresponds to his own, a notion surely significant for the Christians in Corinth, and one that tells in favor of the significance of this event in primitive Christianity.

Acts 2:1–13:

(1) *And* when the day of Pentecost was fulfilled, they were all together in one place. (2) *And* suddenly there came from heaven a sound like a mighty rushing wind, *and* it filled the entire house where they were sitting. (3) *And* divided tongues as of fire appeared to them *and* rested on each one of them. (4) *And* they were all filled with the Holy Spirit *and* began to speak in other tongues as the Spirit gave them utterance.

(5) But there were dwelling in Jerusalem Jews, devout men from every nation under heaven. (6) But at this noise the multitude came together, and they were bewildered, because each one was hearing them speak in his own language. (7) But they were amazed and astonished, saying, "Are not all these who are speaking Galileans? (8) And how is it that we hear, each of us in his own native language? (9) Parthians and Medes and Elamites and residents of Mesopotamia, Judea and Cappadocia, Pontus and Asia, (10) Phrygia and Pamphylia, Egypt and the parts of Libya belonging to Cyrene, and visitors from Rome, (11) both Jews and proselytes, Cretans and Arabians—we hear them telling in our own tongues the mighty works of God." (12) But all were amazed and perplexed, saying to one another, 'What does this mean?' (13) But others mocking said, "They are filled with new wine."

LUKE'S PURPOSE

The text can be divided into two parts: verses 1–4 describe speaking in tongues, verses 5–13 a linguistic miracle.

Verses 1–4: This section reflects numerous elements typical of Luke's language and style. Note, for example, the use of "and," seven times in a row (marked by italics). The manner of expression in verses 2–3 is reminiscent of descriptions of the Sinai theophany.[83] Note Philo, *Decalogue 46* (on Exod. 19:16 ff.):

> Then from the midst of the fire that streamed from heaven there uttered a voice . . . for the flame became articulate speech in the language familiar to the audience, and so clearly and distinctly were the words formed by it that they seemed to see rather than hear them.

In Philo's presentation the stress on the interconnection of fire, voice, and language is particularly striking. This matches Luke's account of Pentecost in Acts 2:1–4. And finally Luke's indication of time, "Pentecost" (verse 1), fits the Sinai complex of motifs to which I have referred, if in his time Pentecost was indeed understood as "a festival celebrating the making of the covenant."[84]

The unit of text culminates in the sentence of verse 4b: "And they began to speak in other tongues (*heterais glossais*) as the Spirit gave them utterance." The context indicates that the phrase "other tongues" refers to the fact that those present could understand the Spirit-filled disciples; verse 11: "We hear them telling in our tongues (*tais hemeterais glossais*) the mighty works of God."[85] Thus verse 4 is the expression of a language miracle and its context is developed in the narrative in the following verses.

Another observation shows that Luke shaped the text under review:

Verses 2 and 3 have an almost completely parallel construction:

A: And suddenly there came from heaven a sound
A1: And divided tongues appeared to them
B: like a mighty rushing wind
B1: as of fire
C: and it filled the entire house where they were sitting
C1: and it rested on each one of them.

Verses 5–13: This section also contains elements of Luke's language and style. The frequent use of "and" (*kai*) in verses 1–4 is replaced by the use of "but" (*de*) marked by underlining. Furthermore, it is skillfully connected to the previous unit. Verse 6 points back to verse 2: "noise" recalls "sound." Verses 6, 8, 11 take up verse 4 and show that the event is a language miracle. A list of the various peoples is framed within the unit of verses 5–13 by "we hear" in verses 8, 11. The way in which the reaction of the hearers is described twice in verses 12 and 13 is in accordance with Luke's narrative style.[86]

THE FUNCTION OF VERSES 1–13 IN THE CONTEXT

With the account of the receiving of the Spirit, the promise Jesus made in 1:8 is fulfilled.[87] It is no coincidence that the ensuing speech of Peter (verses 14–40) begins with this theme (verses 17–18). From now on the receiving of the Spirit is constitutive for being a Christian.[88] However, its specific effects have still to be defined in each case.

It may be that as well as describing the receiving of the Spirit, Luke's purpose is to depict the Pentecost event as a miracle of language. The fact that on the very day on which the Christian religion is founded the Holy Spirit equips the members of this new movement with the languages of all other peoples undoubtedly expresses Luke's conviction of the universal nature of Christianity. However, the universalism of preaching of the gospel is not yet expressed in this passage in terms of the Gentile mission, since the section describes the audience as Diaspora Jews, who only with some difficulty can be considered representatives of the nations of the world.[89]

THE TRADITION REWORKED BY LUKE

The last two sections make it clear that the present text is a self-contained unit. The following analysis will first demonstrate the discontinuities in the passage, and then attempt to identify the elements of tradition that they reveal.

1. The event depicted in verses 1–4 takes place in a house (verse 2), but the sequel (verses 5–13) evidently occurs in the open air.

2. Verses 9–11 interrupt the argument and likely go back to a source. That the list of peoples nevertheless fits very well in verses 5–13 may well be an indication of Luke's editorial work.

The disparity between verses 1–4 and 5–13 to which I have drawn attention can be intensified at one point. Verse 4 says that the disciples spoke in "other tongues." If we regard "other" (*heterais*) as an edit, then a language miracle would become speaking in tongues, i.e., glossolalia, which we know from 1 Cor. 14. In that case the tradition contained in verses 1–4 (and verse 13?) reports an ecstatic experience in a house of a group of disciples, and it was Luke who first interpreted this tradition as a language miracle in order to prepare the reader for the idea of the worldwide mission. The evidence that Luke probably no longer knew of the original glossolalia supports this suggestion. In Acts 19:6 he identifies it with prophecy (cf. 10:46). This makes "the synthesis with the language miracle easier."[90] So a distinction needs to be made between glossolalia (verses 1–4) and language miracle (verses 5–13) in the framework of the analysis of the tradition.

Glossolalia is generally an incomprehensible ecstatic speech. Of the Corinthian glossolalia in particular it can be said with certainty that it was not speaking in foreign languages. It had to be translated (1 Cor. 14:5) not because it was a foreign language but because it was incomprehensible (cf. 1 Cor. 14:19, 23). In Paul's worldview, it was the language of the angels (1 Cor. 13:1, cf. 2 Cor. 12:4).

In analyzing the tradition of the language miracle (verses 5–13) attention should be paid above all to a later rabbinic legend about a language miracle at Sinai, in which the voice of God divided itself into seventy world languages and the law was made known to all nations (cf. Gen. 10:1–31). "This means that there are striking points of contact between Sinai and a miracle in foreign tongues—something that was certainly useful for Luke's purposes."[91]

SUMMARY OF THE ANALYSIS OF THE TRADITION

The two traditions that can be extracted are the story of the ecstasy of the disciples in a Jerusalem house (perhaps verse 13 also belongs to this), and the list of peoples. The language miracle is not an independent tradition, but a composition of Luke on the basis of knowledge of the Sinai tradition; his interest in the language miracle is evident from his adoption of the list of peoples.

The possibility that the language miracle is the bedrock of the tradition[92] is remote. In that case one would have to assume that the report of the glossolalia had already become attached at the level of tradition. Yet as was demonstrated above, Luke no longer has any idea of it. Therefore the proposal would be based on a second-degree hypothesis.

HISTORICAL ELEMENTS

At various times it has been suggested that Pentecost should be identified with the "appearance to more than five hundred brothers." Hans Conzelmann has objected to this:

> The development from a christophany (sc. like 1 Cor. 15:5) to this theophany (sc. like Acts 2) is really not conceivable, because in the older version of the Easter christophany the Spirit is not mentioned.[93]

Yet, in all likelihood, Luke introduced the features of a theophany into the story of Acts 2 where the theme of the glossolalia constitutes the kernel of the tradition. I therefore regard it as at least possible that the report of an appearance of Christ to more than 500 brothers has a genetic connection with the tradition behind Acts 2:1–4. As for Conzelmann's reference to the older version of Easter christophany not mentioning the Spirit, one has to keep in mind that for Paul, our earliest witness, Christ and the Spirit were at least partly identical from the start.

Since this statement about the close relationship of Christ and the Spirit needs some substantiation, let us look at a central Pauline text, Rom. 8:9–11:

(9) But you are not in the flesh, you are in the Spirit, if the Spirit of God really dwells in you. If someone does not possess the Spirit of Christ, he does not belong to him. (10) But if Christ [dwells] in you, then although the body is a dead thing because of sin, yet the Spirit is life itself because of righteousness. (11) If the Spirit of him who raised Jesus from the dead dwells in you, he who raised Jesus from the dead will give life to your mortal bodies also through his Spirit which dwells in you.

In verse 9 the Spirit of God and the Spirit of Christ are used interchangeably to describe what dwells within Christians. Indeed, Christ abides in Christians (verse 10) and the Spirit of the one who raised Jesus from the dead dwells in them (verse 11). However, in binding the Spirit to God—just as he bound ecstasy to God in 2 Cor. 12—Paul precludes the autonomy of those who bear the Spirit, and thus understands the gift of the Spirit as sheer grace. That does not alter the fact that Spirit (of God) and Christ stand in parallel and are ultimately identical. In much the same way, the formulae "in Christ" (Gal. 3:28, etc.) and "in the Spirit" (Gal. 5:25, etc.) correspond.

This coalescing of the Spirit and Christ in Paul's thought confirms what has been said about the Damascus event, in which Paul saw Jesus as a spiritual heavenly being. Against this claim it might be argued that despite 2 Cor. 3:17–18 Paul never designates "the Risen One" who appeared to him and to the other apostles explicitly as Spirit, or attributes the vision to the working of the Spirit. But 1 Cor. 15 with its reference to the spiritual body of 'the Risen One' (verse 45) is an answer to the question of what figure of "the Risen Lord" Paul saw before Damascus.

Precisely how are we to imagine and to understand that kind of appearance to "more than five hundred brothers at one time"? We have no explanations or even helpful indications of the historical context similar to those that we have in the cases of Peter and Paul. But perhaps conclusions from research into mass psychology may help us here.

Some 90 years ago Gustave Le Bon studied the phenomenon that people differ from one another most in intelligence, morality, and ideas, and least in animal instinct and emotions. Thus, according to Le Bon, the power of the mass is the greater the more its members resemble one another, since the things in which they differ are for the moment put aside. They then possess a collective mind in which the aptitudes for understanding and in consequence the individualities are weakened. Thus the "unconscious qualities obtain the upper hand."[94] Le Bon observes further:

> Crowds are to some extent in the position of a sleeper whose reason, suspended for the time being, allows the arousing in his mind of images of extreme intensity which would quickly be dissipated could they be submitted to the action of reflection. Crowds, being incapable both of reflection and of reasoning, are devoid of the notion of improbability; and it is to be noted that in a general way it is the most improbable things that are the most striking.[95]

Everything that stimulates the imagination of the masses appears in the form of a moving, clear image, which needs no interpretation. Indeed, the members of masses are often subject to contagious suggestion. Le Bon cites the following instructive example:

> Before St. George appeared on the walls of Jerusalem to all the Crusaders he was certainly perceived in the first instance by one of those present. By dint of suggestion and contagion the miracle signalised by a single person was immediately perceived by all.[96]

Le Bon explains:

> Such is always the mechanism of the collective hallucination so frequent in history—hallucinations which seem to have all the recognised characteristics of authenticity, since they are phenomena observed by thousands of persons.[97]

Paul Wilhelm Schmiedel[98] no doubt correctly sees the mass visions of Thomas Becket and Savonarola after their deaths as analogies to Christ's appearance to more than five hundred at one time. Suffice it to say that in all the cases mentioned we are dealing not with historical facts, but psychological phenomena.

RESULT

One must understand the "appearance to the more than five hundred brothers at one time" as the report of a mass ecstasy that took place in the early period of the community. One or more individuals provided the stimulus for it. Such an explanation fits in well with what has been worked out so far, namely, that the first appearance to Peter was the impulse to further appearances among the disciples.

The appearance to James (1 Cor. 15:7)

In a fragment of the *Gospel of the Hebrews,* as transmitted by the church father Jerome (347–c 420 CE), we have a description of an appearance to James:

> And when the Lord had given the linen cloth to the servant of the priest, he went to James and appeared to him. For James had sworn that he would not eat bread from that hour in which he had drunk the cup of the Lord until he should see him risen from among them that sleep. And shortly thereafter the Lord said: Bring a table and bread! And immediately it is added: he took the bread, blessed it and broke it and gave it to James the Just and said to him: My brother, eat thy bread, for the Son of Man is raised from among them that sleep.[99]

The text has the following peculiarities:

a) James is the first witness to the resurrection. b) Already before Easter James belonged to the community. c) The focal point of the text is the release of James from a vow. It may well be modeled on Peter's promise to go with the Lord to death (Mark 14:31), and if James has fulfilled the vow while Peter was known to have broken it, the first testimony would understandably be attributed to James.

d) Yet little can be traced of any direct rivalry with other apostles or Peter. Indeed, neither Peter nor the other disciples are mentioned at all. e) Here as in the New Testament gospels we have an anti-docetic motive. The legend of the guard over the tomb from Matt. 27:62–66 is presupposed. (The Lord gave the linen cloth in which his own body has been wrapped to the servant of the high priest.)

Thus the text is already a long way from historical reality. As Wilhelm Pratscher of the University of Vienna observes:

> James no longer needs to fight for his position; his victory is complete. He has been recognized as the first and supreme witness of the Risen Christ, the most important bearer of the tradition, also and particularly over against Peter and the Twelve.[100]

James (and not Jesus) stands at the center, and the fact that he was not one of Jesus' disciples during Jesus' lifetime is forgotten. Furthermore, the attestation to the report is late. Its basis is a New Testament tradition of the Eucharist transformed into a personal legend to glorify James. However intriguing the report that Jesus appeared to James, the rest of the text gives us no reliable information of any kind.

Only vague conjectures are possible about the historical background of this individual vision, which represents a kind of conversion of James. Note that during Jesus' life James did not follow his brother but considered him to be "out of his mind."[101] Because of 1 Cor. 15:7 it seems all but certain that James saw his brother after the latter's death. This might have happened during the appearance to more than five hundred brothers at one time, which may have been followed by an individual vision. The conditions and circumstances of James's vision were therefore different from Peter's, the more so since James must have known of Peter's vision before he in turn "saw" his brother exalted in heaven. That James later became the leader of the earliest community in Jerusalem has more to do with the fact that he was a member of Jesus' biological family. In antiquity family politics predominated—note especially the significance of the family in the Hasmonaean dynasty and the examples in 1 and 2 Maccabees. Scholars have rightly envisaged a kind of caliphate in early Christianity.[102]

The account in the Gospel of the Hebrews was subsequently developed into a narrative on the basis of the already existing traditions of appearances, and certainly does not derive from a report by James or his immediate followers.

The appearance to all the apostles (1 Cor. 15:7)

Although this vision cannot be historically tracked down or further amplified, it will be taken into account in the final reconstruction of the history of the Easter visions of the earliest Christians.

The appearance to Paul (1 Cor. 15:8)

Since the appearances to Paul and Peter played a decisive role in the rise and expansion of the faith in Jesus' resurrection, and since Paul's vision has already been examined as a key to the appearances mentioned in 1 Cor. 15:5–7, I shall later turn my attention to it once more (see below, pp. 166–72).

THE EASTER NARRATIVE IN THE GOSPEL OF MARK

Mark 16:1–8: The Proclamation of the "Risen One" in the Empty Tomb

(1) And when the Sabbath was past, Mary Magdalene, and Mary the mother of James, and Salome bought fragrant oils, so that they might go and anoint him. (2) *And very early on the first day of the week they went to the tomb as the sun was rising.* (3) *And they said to one another, "Who will **roll away** the stone from the door of the tomb for us?"* (4) *And looking up, they see that the stone has been **rolled away**, for it was very large.* (5a) *And entering the tomb, they saw a young man sitting on the right side, clothed with a long white garment;* (5b) *and they were* <u>terrified</u>. (6) *And he says to them, "Do not be <u>terrified</u>; you seek* Jesus of Nazareth, the crucified one. He was raised, *he is not here; see the place where they laid him.* (7) *But go,* tell his disciples and Peter, 'He is going before you to Galilee; there you will see him, as he told you.'" (8) *And they went out and fled from the tomb; for trembling and numbness seized them; and they said nothing to any one, for they were afraid.*

MARK'S PURPOSE AND THE TRADITION REWORKED BY HIM

This passage raises several difficulties. *The first problem* relates to its position at the end of the Gospel: How can a Gospel have ended with the phrase *ephobounto gar,* "for they were afraid"?[103]

Scholars who doubted that Mark's gospel really reached its conclusion in verse 8 have attempted to reconstruct the original ending. They pointed out that various concluding verses were added to it from the second century on (see below, pp. 88–90) and that the parallels in Matthew and Luke add to the copy of Mark they worked from. Hence, they suggested that the original conclusion to Mark disappeared quite early, whether by intentional or accidental excision. If accurate, this argument would neatly resolve the problem posed here. Yet, for methodological reasons we ought first endeavor to appreciate the Gospel of Mark in its given canonical form.

The *second problem* lies in the content of Mark's report. If as verse 8 says, the women did not obey the command of the young man, how did the disciples and Peter learn of the resurrection? To be sure, Christians who believed in the resurrection of Jesus read the Gospel of Mark. Thus, even if this passage is skewed historical data, the message intended by the author would have been transparent to Gospel's audience. Put otherwise, the seeming historical contradiction in verse 8 must be interpreted from within the context of the Gospel as a whole.

Verse 1: As in 15:42 a note of time introduces the story. The dating indicated here is certainly part of the tradition, though we cannot exclude the possibility that it was intended to justify the church's festival of Easter.[104] Underlying the planned anointing the tradition could well have included the motif of funeral lament by the women.[105] The names of the women in the tradition echo those in 15:40 and 15:47, in all three cases headed by Mary Magdalene, who Mark evidently thought was their leader. Since there had been no prior mention of these women disciples in the Gospel, he adds in verse 41 that they had already followed Jesus in Galilee and served him.[106] Furthermore, he points out that additional women went with Jesus to Jerusalem. From this follows a kind of hope for the reader that their faithfulness will be stronger than that of the disciples. The intended anointing recalls 14:3–9, the story of the anointing of Jesus which was performed "for burial" (verse 8), by the anonymous woman in Bethany. By reintroducing here the theme of anointing in connection with women, Mark frames the account of the passion with narratives containing similar motifs.[107]

Verse 2: The time indicators "very early" and "as the sun was rising" are not in tension with each other as is sometimes argued.[108] The clear implausibility of purchasing unguents before sunrise does not concern the narrator. The crucial event is for the women to get to the tomb.

Verse 3: "Stone" and "door of the tomb" employ the same language from 15:46. The women's seemingly belated concern about who will move the stone for them is answered by the following verse.

Verse 4: The mention that the stone was massive heightens the amazing nature of the act of the man in the following verse.

Verse 5a: A young man in white sits in the tomb. He suggests a parallel to the fleeing young man in Mark 14:51–52 and may well represent the same person.

Mark 14:51–52:

(51) And a young man *followed along with him* (Jesus), with nothing but a linen cloth about his body; and they seized him. (52) But he left the linen cloth and fled naked.

These verses contradict the previous verse, which describes the flight of all figures present. There has been a good deal of debate about the man who follows along with Jesus. In Mark 5:37 the verb "to follow along with" refers to the inner circle of disciples. To be sure, the young man remains at Jesus' side longer than the other disciples.[109]

Like the young man in the narrative of the empty tomb, the young man in the incident of the fleeing disciples puzzles the reader by his sudden and unexplained appearance. Furthermore, the clothing of the two receives a special emphasis: a white garment replaces the linen cloth lost during the flight. Mark, speaking here as a preacher of the cross and resurrection of Jesus, seems to imply that nakedness has been clothed by the white garment that symbolizes baptism.

For parallels to the figure of the young man, see the account in the second Book of Maccabees[110] and the report in the Gospel of Peter (9:36) concerning the two young men who descend from heaven in a great radiance of light (see below, pp. 93–94). For "white" cf. Mark 9:3f; Rev. 7:13. Matt. 28:2 identifies the young man as an angel. He may indeed denote a heavenly figure, just as in the book of Tobit the angel Raphael is addressed repeatedly as "young man."[111] The entire scene suggests the appearance of a divine being. The description "sitting on the right" emphasizes the message of the young man and confirms it, since "right" indicates the correct or fortuitous side[112] while "sit" evidently expresses the authority with which the young man speaks.[113] Yet, this symbolic choreography does not exclude the possibility that the young man is the mundane figure from 14:51, where he apparently represents the author of the Gospel himself. Indeed, as a preacher Mark would have been understood by sympathetic audiences as a heavenly messenger. (Should the identification of the "young man" in verse 5 with the author of Mark's gospel be incorrect, the consequences for the historical results of the analysis of Mark 16:1–8 would be negligible.)[114]

Verse 5b: The frightened reaction of the women has the coloring of Mark's language, for the word "terrified" occurs in the New Testament only in Mark 9:15; 14:33; 16:5, 6; cf. further 1:27; 10:24, 32.

Verse 6: "Terrified" harks back to verse 5. "Jesus of Nazareth, the crucified one" recalls the passion narrative (chapters 14–15) and the predictions of the passion,[115] while "of Nazareth"[116] makes identification with the earthly Jesus certain. The report of the young messenger that Jesus has been raised complements Jesus' predictions made in 8:31; 9:31; 10:34. The explicit description ("he is not here") insists on the facticity of Jesus' bodily resurrection. By giving priority to the statement "Jesus was raised," the text aims to silence those skeptics who might aver that one cannot infer a resurrection on the basis of an empty tomb. The text plainly emphasizes the miraculous nature of the event over against rival interpretations.

Verse 7: Here the women are instructed to inform the disciples and Peter that Jesus will precede them to Galilee. The phrase "the disciples and Peter" echoes 1 Cor. 15:5 and can be read as a continuation of the primal tradition of an appearance to Cephas and the twelve. The young man continues, "There you will see him, as he has told you." This phrase makes explicit reference to Mark 14:28 ("But after my resurrection I will go before you into Galilee"). As in Mark 10:32 Jesus' "going before" refers to the "Christian way" which the disciple who obeys Jesus must follow. Here Mark's representation of the primitive Christian tradition as "the way" suggests technical expression of Christian faith.[117]

Verse 8: The flight of the women parallels the disciples' flight in 14:50. The present verse describes their paralyzing fear twice.[118] Their silence represents disobedience to the express command of the young man. This delinquency recalls the failures of the disciples throughout the Gospel of Mark, and thus 16:1–8 is the final instance of faithlessness displayed by those who were with Jesus, only this time it is the women.

RESULT

As a unit, the conclusion of Mark's gospel consolidates the points he considered most crucial to his account: a) Jesus' death and resurrection, b) the ineptitude of the disciples, men and women alike, c) the continuing preaching of the gospel, d) the significance of Galilee as the origin of the gospel. In addition, he has further asserted his own authority as an eyewitness.

It is unlikely that a comprehensive story about the empty tomb existed prior to Mark, as the text abounds with traces of his redactions. But the names of the women, the indirect mention of the third day ("when the Sabbath was past"), and the identification of Peter and the disciples as those to whom the risen Christ will appear are clearly elements of the earliest tradition.[119] By intimating that the women fail to relay the message of the resurrection, Mark implicitly identifies himself as the first to proclaim the story of the empty tomb.[120]

HISTORICAL ELEMENTS

It follows from the analysis of the tradition that its historical merit is insignificant. The story only gives us the claim that the crucified Christ was raised and the further claim that this explains the empty tomb. Further, Mary Magdalene's visit with the other two women to the tomb of Jesus the day after the Sabbath cannot plausibly be termed historical. Third, the tradition that Peter and the disciples will see Jesus is backed by the report in 1 Cor. 15:5. This means that the historical kernel of Mark 16:1–8 is an appearance of the "Risen One" to Peter and the other disciples.

Mark 16:9–20: Various appearances of the "Risen One"

(9) Now, having risen early on the first day of the week, he [Jesus] appeared **first** to Mary Magdalene, from whom he had cast out seven demons. (10) She went and told those who had been with him and were [now] mourning and weeping. (11) But when they heard that he was alive and had been seen by her, they did not believe it.

(12) **After that** he appeared in another form to two of them on the way when they were going through the country. (13) And they went back and proclaimed it to the rest, but they did not believe them.

(14) **Still later,** when the Eleven were reclining at table, he revealed himself to them and rebuked their unbelief and the hardness of heart, that they had not believed those who had seen him after he had risen. (15) And he said to them, "Go into the entire world and preach the gospel to the whole creation. (16) *He who believes* and is baptized will be saved; but he who does not believe will be condemned. (17) And the signs which will follow *those who believe* are these: in my name they will cast out evil spirits, speak in new tongues, (18) pick up snakes, and if they drink anything deadly it will not harm them; they will lay their hands on the sick, and they will recover."

(19) **After** the Lord Jesus had spoken to them, he was taken up into heaven, and sat at the right hand of God, (20) and they went out and preached everywhere. And the Lord worked with them and confirmed the message by the signs that followed.

PURPOSE AND TRADITIONS REWORKED

Verses 9–20 are not part of the original Gospel of Mark. They were added in the second century for the sake of supplying the Gospel with an ending in harmony with those of the other three canonical gospels. The awkward way this addition is attached to Mark 16:1–8 can be seen in the opening verse; for while "early on the first day of the week" obliquely recalls Mark 16:1 ("When the Sabbath was over . . ."), Mary Magdalene's introduction is hardly appropriate for someone who was a leading character in the preceding action. Equally puzzling is the lack of a clear antecedent for "he." Clearly Jesus is intended, but the "he" who is the active subject in verses 1–8 is the young man in white.

The text divides into four sections, each beginning with an adverb of time (set in boldface in the text); and it is worth noting that while it reports that Jesus first appeared to Mary Magdalene, the significance of this appearance is overshadowed by the subsequent list of witnesses. Clearly the emphasis falls on the later appearance to the eleven disciples who receive Jesus' detailed instructions (verses 15–18).

Although the theme of disbelief is noticeable throughout (see the underlined verses 11, 13, 14, and 16), the importance of *correct* belief is emphasized (see italics in verses 16 and 17). It seems evident that the text is a defense of resurrection faith combined with an affidavit of the power of the church (verse 18).

Far from being intended as a conclusion for Mark's gospel, this passage had an independent origin around the beginning of the second century. Likely an Easter catechism for community instruction, it testifies to the author's knowledge of Luke and John, as well as Acts, but it shows no evidence of Mark's or Matthew's influence.[121]

HISTORICAL ELEMENTS

This passage's historical value for the aims of our investigation is negligible.

The short ending of Mark

> But everything that was commanded them [the women] they
> reported concisely to those around Peter. After that Jesus himself
> also issued through them from East to West the holy and imperish-
> able preaching of eternal salvation.

This text, written in Egypt in the fourth century, was intended to
supply the Gospel of Mark with a conclusion complementing the
young man's charge to the women (16:7) and the church's Easter
legend of the disciples' preaching the gospel in the whole world. It
was later conjoined with the long ending (16:9–20), but its author
clearly was unfamiliar with the latter text. Historically it is of even
less account than the long ending, but it does suggest that the early
Christians, like Matthew and Luke before them, were dissatisfied
with the anticlimactic report of terrified women that constituted the
original conclusion of Mark's Gospel.

THE EASTER NARRATIVE IN THE GOSPEL OF MATTHEW

Matthew's resurrection narrative is based on Mark's account of the
empty tomb, but the author supplements this with stories of two
appearances of the "Risen One": Matt. 28:8–9 tells the story of Jesus'
appearance to the women at the tomb, and Matt. 28:16–20 relates
how the risen Jesus sends out his disciples to preach the Gospel in
the whole world. He adds these narratives because the ending of
Mark's Gospel was as unsatisfactory for him as it was for Luke and
later readers of Mark. Moreover, Matthew contributes a story about
the guards at the tomb by way of providing a framework for the story
of the women's journey to the tomb, reported in Mark 16:1–8.

Matthew 27:62–66: The Guard at the Tomb

> (62) *Next day, that is, after the day of Preparation, the chief priests and
> the Pharisees gathered before Pilate* (63) and said, "Lord, we
> remember how this *deceiver* said, while he was still alive, 'After

three days I will be raised.' (64a) Therefore order the tomb to be made secure until the third day, lest his disciples go and steal him away, and tell the people, 'He was raised from the dead,' (64b) and the last *deceit* will be worse than the first."

(65) Pilate said to them, "Take a guard [of soldiers]! Go, make it as secure as you can.' (66) So they went and made the tomb secure by sealing the stone and setting a guard.

MATTHEW'S PURPOSE AND THE TRADITION REWORKED BY HIM

Verse 62: The verse begins the narrative with Matthew's language.[122] The setting in time—"next day"—follows logically from the "evening" of verse 57. The "Pharisees" appear only here in the passion story; historically, they became adversaries of Christian communities only in the time of Matthew.[123] They have been inserted here because they were the chief opponents of Matthew's church and surely skeptical about any claims of Jesus' resurrection. This incident is clearly polemical rather than historical. Incredibly, Matthew pictures these strict followers of Jewish law meeting with Pilate on the Sabbath (Saturday). The historical validity is nil, but the narrative requires it. The death of Jesus on Friday, and the resurrection or discovery of the empty tomb two days later, on the day after the Sabbath, were established by Mark 16:1.

Verse 63: Addressing Pilate as "Lord" is a bit of Matthew's irony. He also has the chief priests and Pharisees "recall" a saying of Jesus: "This deceiver said, while he was still alive, 'After three days I will be raised.'" The reference is to Matt. 12:40: "For as Jonah was three days and three nights in the belly of the whale, so will the Son of man be three days and three nights in the heart of the earth." The Evangelist is at least consistent, for Pharisees were present in that scene (cf. Matt. 12:38), just as here in verse 62. The phrase "after three days" is a formula intended to recall the earlier passage.

Verse 64a: The Jewish authorities advise Pilate to station a guard at the tomb.

Verse 64b: "Deceit" echoes "deceiver" in verse 63. The sentence, "and that last deceit will be worse than the first," recalls 12:45c, "And the last state of this man is worse than the first." If the disciples are able to proclaim the resurrection, matters will be even worse than when Jesus was preaching justice and forgiveness.

Verses 65–66: Pilate agrees to the suggestion of the Jewish authorities. "Guard" as later in 28:14 means Roman soldiers and not the Jewish Temple guard. Verse 65b seems to indicate that Pilate was not convinced that the sealing of the tomb would be a success (cf. 27:24).

The following section, 28:1–10, tells about the empty tomb and the appearance of Jesus to two women disciples; thereafter, Matthew resumes this account with the suborning of the guard at the tomb (28:11–15).

HISTORICAL ELEMENTS

See the remarks on the section 28:11–15.

Matthew 28:1–10: The empty tomb and the appearance of Jesus to two disciples

(1) Now after the Sabbath, toward the dawn of the first day of the week, Mary Magdalene and the other Mary went to see the sepulcher.

(2) *And look,* there was a great earthquake; for an angel of the Lord descended from heaven and came and rolled back the stone, and sat upon it. (3) His appearance was like lightning, and his raiment white as snow. (4) And for fear of him the guards trembled and became like dead men.

(5) But the angel said to the women, "**Do not be afraid**; for I know that you seek Jesus who was crucified. (6) He is not here; he was raised, as he said. Come, see the place where he lay. (7) Then go quickly and tell his disciples that he was raised from the dead. *And look,* he is going before you to Galilee; there you will see him. Look, I have told you." (8) So they departed quickly from the tomb with fear and great joy, and ran to proclaim [it] to his disciples.

(9) *And look, Jesus met them and said, "Hail!" And they came up and took hold of his feet and knelt before him.* (10) *Then Jesus said to*

them, "Do not be afraid! Go and proclaim to my brothers to go to Galilee, and there they will see me."

MATTHEW'S PURPOSE AND THE TRADITION REWORKED BY HIM

Verse 1: This verse must be explained solely on the basis of Mark. The reason why only two women come to the tomb,[124] whereas there were three in Mark, is that Matthew probably felt a tension between Mark 15:47 and Mark 16:1 and glossed over it. The women's aim in Mark's report—to anoint the corpse in the tomb—is lacking in Matthew. The phrase "to see the tomb" is attributable to the influence of Mark 15:47.[125]

Verses 2–4: Tension is evident between verses 2–4 and 5–8, where again Mark's version is the source, for the momentous events related in verses 2–4 have no relation to the expression of the message in verses 5–8. Such powerful events were hardly necessary to do away with these guards and enable the women to view the empty tomb. Verses 2–4 describe the opening of the tomb by a heavenly angel, confronted with whom the guards become powerless. Evidently the tradition used by Matthew had the angel open the tomb so that the revived Jesus could come out. The corroboration for this can be found in an early Christian tradition about the ascent of Jesus from the tomb, a narrative that all but certainly forms the background of Matt. 28:2–4. The Gospel of Peter tells the following story about Jesus' resurrection:

> (9:35) But in the night in which the Lord's day dawned, when the soldiers were safeguarding it two by two in every watch, there was a loud voice in heaven; (9:36) and they saw that the heavens were opened and that two males who had much radiance had come down from there and come near the sepulcher. (9:37) But that stone which had been thrust against the door, having rolled by itself, went a distance off the side; and the sepulcher opened, and both the young men entered. (9:38) And having seen this, the soldiers awakened the centurion and the elders (for they too were

present, keeping watch). (10:39) And while they were relating what they had seen, again they see three males who have come out from the sepulcher, with the two supporting the other one, and a cross following them, (10:40) and the head of the two reaching unto heaven, but that of the one whom they led out by the hand reaching beyond and into the heavens. (10:41) And they heard a voice from the heavens saying, "Have you made proclamation to those who sleep?" (10:42) And an answer was heard from the cross, "Yes." (11:43) Then those people began discussing how to go and make these things clear to Pilate (11:44), but while they were still thinking it through, the heavens appeared to open again, and a man descended and entered into the tomb.

Verse 5: This verse parallels Mark 16:6a.

Verse 6: Cf. Mark 16:6b. However, the announcement of the resurrection derives from Jesus' foretelling (see 26:32). The latter detail is lacking in Mark.

Verse 7: This corresponds to Mark 16:7.

Verse 8: Whereas in Mark 16:8 the women are simply silent out of fear, Matthew adds to that their great joy at being able to pass on the angel's message. That is not surprising, since they have been made at a remove witnesses to the event of the resurrection (verses 2–4), but their joy prepares for verses 9–10 where Jesus will appear to them *in person*.

Verses 9–10: Lacking any parallel in Mark, these verses may be entirely Matthew's creation. They report an encounter between Jesus and the two women who were mentioned in verse 1, who take hold of his feet[126]—and kneel before him (cf. later verse 17).

Note that Matthew has the women "kneel" (cf. 8:2; 9:18; 14:33; 15:25; 20:20), a detail absent from Mark, which is his source. This suggests the sameness of the earthly Jesus and the "Risen One." (Matthew's omission of the sarcastic "worship" reported in Mark 15:19 is consistent with this.) Apart from greeting the women, the risen Jesus does not add anything to what the angel at the tomb said. Compare:

Verses 5–7: "Do not be afraid . . . Go quickly and tell his disciples that he . . . is going before you to Galilee; there you will see him."

Verse 10:"Do not be afraid! Go and tell my brothers to go to Galilee, and there they will see me."

For Jesus' use of "brothers" cf. Matt. 18:15f and 23:8, which also allude to the fellowship of the disciples. It should be noted that here, instead of the "disciples" of verses 7–8, we have "brothers," and despite the mutual brotherhood of the disciples they still have a pupil-teacher status vis-à-vis Jesus (Matt. 23:8, 10).

Matt. 28:11–15: The Bribing of the Guards

(11) *As they started on their way,* some of the guard went to the city and reported to the chief priests what had occurred. (12) The latter, after conferring with the elders, *decided* to give a large sum of money to the soldiers (13) and told them, "Say that his disciples came at night and stole the body while you were asleep." (14) If by chance the governor hears anything, we will cover for you.' (15a) So they took the money and did as they were told. (15b) This story is widely known among Jews to this day.

MATTHEW'S PURPOSE AND THE TRADITION REWORKED BY HIM

Verse 11: Verse 11a ties the previous scene to the present one. The women leave for Galilee, and the guards report the events surrounding Jesus' resurrection to the Jewish leaders.[127] So the chief priests and elders learn what Jesus himself had told them: that he would rise after three days.[128]

Verse 12: The subornation of the guards naturally reminds us of the payoff given to Judas (26:15).

Verse 13: This verse is a follow-up to 27:64. The soldiers are to spread what they know to be the false rumor that while they were asleep, the disciples carried off the body. This, of course, is the very fear that the Jewish authorities had expressed to Pilate (27:64). Now, with Jesus actually risen, they feel obliged, ironically, to bribe the soldiers to spread this false report.

Verse 14: This provides the soldiers with a cover story. Should someone tell the governor that the guards whose posting he had agreed to fell asleep on duty,[129] then the Jewish authorities will somehow make it right with Pilate.

Verse 15a: The story ends with the Roman soldiers doing as the Jewish authorities bid them.

Verse 15b: This is clearly a contemporary comment by Matthew; it attests to widespread knowledge among Jews of his time of the tale that Jesus' disciples had stolen his body. Whether this is the source of Matthew's account is very questionable, not only because the Jewish leaders appear in an extremely negative light, but because they seem to accept Jesus' resurrection as a fact. Besides, they would hardly have put themselves in such a vulnerable position. We may reasonably infer that Matthew himself composed the counter-story for apologetic purposes.

In the middle of the second century, the Christian teacher and philosopher Justin shows his awareness of this story. Without mentioning the guards, Justin addresses the Jew Tryphon thus:

Dial. 108:2:

> After you heard of his resurrection from the dead you failed to convert, but rather selected . . . people and sent them throughout the world with the message that a godless and wicked sect had been instituted by a Galilean named Jesus. After we crucified him, his disciples came by night and stole his body from the tomb where he had been laid after being removed from the cross, and they claimed that he had been raised from the dead and taken up into heaven.[130]

On the basis of the textual evidence, the following history of the tradition is likely: a) From their visions of Christ, the earliest Christians concluded that a bodily resurrection of Jesus had occurred. b) Mark (or his predecessor) composed the story of the empty tomb. c) Jews claimed that the disciples had stolen the corpse of Jesus. d) Matthew reacts to this news with his story of the bribery of the guards at the tomb.

It has often been proposed that the Jewish report of the stolen body authenticates the empty tomb: the Jewish polemic never disputed that the tomb was empty, but simply tried to explain it away. But how could the (unbelieving) Jews have come to think that the tomb was empty except as a result of this particular Christian tradition?

HISTORICAL ELEMENTS

From the above we can derive three historical judgments:

a) While the story of the theft of Jesus' corpse is certainly historical, the theft itself is not. For one thing, the disciples did not know where or even whether Jesus had been buried; and for another, their grief, fear, and disappointment would have rendered them unable to perpetrate such a hoax.

b) The business of bribing the guards—who, in Joseph McCabe's phrase, are nothing but "chocolate soldiers"—cannot be taken seriously, because it is too obviously partisan, and because the guards would have been risking their necks by confessing to sleeping on watch. "No priest could save a Roman soldier from sentence for *that*."[131]

c) The Jewish authorities did not know anything about an actual resurrection of Jesus from a neutral witness. Claiming that they did is a figment rooted in Matthew's anti-Jewish attitude.

Matt. 28:16–20: The appearance of Jesus on a mount in Galilee and his apostolic charge

(16) Now the eleven disciples went to the mountain in Galilee where Jesus had bid them go. (17) And when they saw him they knelt before him, although some were doubtful. (18) And Jesus *came close and said to them,* "I was given full authority in heaven and on earth. (19) *Go, then, and make disciples of* all peoples, and baptize them in the name of the Father and of the Son and of the Holy Spirit, (20) and teach them to *fulfill all* that I have *commanded;* and *remember* that I am with you always, *until the end of the world.*"

MATTHEW'S PURPOSE AND THE TRADITION REWORKED BY HIM

This is Matthew's appearance story. The brevity of the account is striking. It is introduced by a terse "when they saw him" (verse 17a); and the reaction of the eleven disciples in verse 17 ("they knelt") is the same as that of the women in verse 9. The story focuses not on the appearance itself, but on Jesus' speech in verses 18b–20, which can be divided into three parts: a) claim of authority (verse 18b); b) mission command (verses 19–20a); c) assurance (verse 20b).

Verse 16: Here the disciples fulfill Jesus' command given to the women in verse 10 and obviously transmitted to the disciples. It is a characteristic motif of Matthew's redaction that he underscores the disciples' obedience. He eschews Mark's dismal portrait of the Twelve, consistently offering a more encouraging scenario. For example, he omits the disciples' obtuseness reported in Mark 6:52, and Jesus' chastisement is considerably milder in Matthew 16:5–12 than it was in Mark 8:14–21. Matthew also drops from the second passion prediction (Matt. 17:22–23) Mark's indication of their dull-wittedness (9:30–32). To be sure, in the passion narrative Matthew follows Mark's doleful assessment—the Gethsemane scene, the headlong flight of the disciples, Peter's denial—but then he mitigates the Markan gloom by transforming Mark's sympathetic stranger, Joseph of Arimathea, into a disciple. "Mountain" is Matthew's way of suggesting an epiphany.[132]

Verse 17: "They knelt" repeats the verb from verse 9. "Were doubtful" (to doubt) appears elsewhere in the New Testament only in Matt. 14:31[133] and originates with Matthew. The motif of doubt, evident in the Easter stories,[134] reflects the problem of second and third generation Christians, who have no direct tie to the original Easter experience. Here they see their own situation and can more readily accept the risen Jesus' relevance to their lives.

Verse 18: The verb "to come" is typically Matthean.[135] Verse 18b describes Jesus' new status; his exaltation and the power given to him[136] are traditional theological and liturgical elements. Except in Matt. 9:6 (which derives from Mark 2:10), the phrase "in heaven as on earth" appears in part or as a whole only in texts unique to Matthew.[137]

Verse 19: With its call to apostleship, verse 19 deliberately echoes 10:5–6, but here the mission is clearly directed to Gentiles, for "peoples" (*ethnon*) must be understood in the same way as in 10:5–6, where the term clearly designates Gentiles. Matthew has apparently replaced "preach the gospel," the command found in his source, by the exhortation to "make disciples;"[138] the former seems to have been preserved in Mark 16:15. The baptismal formula "in the name of the Father and of the Son and of the Holy Spirit" is notable for its triadic structure, since the earliest baptisms were simply "into Christ"[139] or "in the name of Jesus."[140] This formula's liturgical character probably has a parallel in Didache 7:1: "Baptize in the name of the Father and of the Son and of the Holy Spirit."[141]

Verse 20: As indicated by the italicized words, this verse is replete with favorite terms of Matthew.[142] The present and exclusive authority of Jesus' words remains (see verse 18), but instead of the appearance of the risen Christ that is no longer credible to Matthew's community, we have the word of the exalted Christ who is identical with the earthly Jesus. His teaching resides in Matthew's gospel, which presents Jesus even during his lifetime as Lord and Son of God. Now he has become the ruler of the universe. "The one who speaks thus is not a ghost, but the cosmocrator."[143]

HISTORICAL ELEMENTS

Verses 16–20: Historicity is in very short supply. No doubt Jesus "appeared" to Peter and the Twelve, though like some textual variants of 1 Cor. 15:5 Matthew refers to eleven disciples—a later critical emendation to remove the figure of Judas from the Twelve. Originally the tradition reported an appearance to the Twelve (1 Cor. 15:5), whose leader was Cephas. The historical underpinning was Peter's reestablishment of the Twelve, a group thereafter having both symbolic and eschatological meaning, for like the original Twelve they represented both God's chosen people and his coming kingdom. Based on their vision of the risen Jesus, they founded a Jerusalem community that proclaimed among their Jewish contemporaries his resurrection and exaltation as the Messiah and/or the Son of Man. That is the historical nucleus of Matthew's report. Whether, as the text indicates, such a visionary experience occurred in Galilee cannot be authenticated by the present passage, since "Galilee" was derived from Mark 16:7. Other considerations, however, suggest Galilee as the likely location of this first vision (see further below, p. 139).

Furthermore, in this closing passage Matthew and/or his tradition has included such later theological elements as the "mission to the Gentiles;" but clearly such a formulation does not reflect the Twelve, for spreading the good news among Gentiles goes back to Paul and the Hellenistic Christians from whom he first heard the good news.

THE EASTER NARRATIVE IN THE GOSPEL OF LUKE

Luke 24:1–12: The proclamation of the "Risen One" in the empty tomb

(1) But at dawn on the first day of the week they went to the tomb, bringing with them fragrant oils they had prepared. (2) They found the stone rolled away from the tomb, (3) but when they went in *they did not find the body of the Lord Jesus.* (4) *While they were puzzling over this, suddenly two men* in shining garments stood beside them. (5) The women were frightened *and bowed their faces to the ground,* but the men said to them, *'Why do you seek the living among the dead?* (6) He is not here, but he was raised. *Remember that when he was still in Galilee he told you* (7) *that the Son of man must be handed over to sinful men, and be crucified, and on the third day rise.'* (8) *Then they remembered his words,* (9) and they returned from the tomb *and told all this to the eleven and to all the rest.* (10) Now it was Mary Magdalene and Joanna and Mary the mother of James and the women with them who reported this to the apostles; (11) *but since these words seemed to them a foolish story, they did not believe them.* (12) But Peter *rose* and ran to the tomb, where he stooped and saw only the linen cloths; then he went home, *amazed at what had happened.*

PRELIMINARY TEXTUAL-CRITICAL NOTE

Verse 12 is not found in some ancient manuscripts. Even so, it likely derives from the original text, for its language is distinctively Lukan.

LUKE'S PURPOSE AND THE TRADITION REWORKED BY HIM

Verses 1–11: By comparing this passage with Mark's report, we can see both Luke's sense of the importance of the passage and its basis in tradition. The texts differ significantly on the following points:

1. The women saw both the tomb where Jesus was buried and how his body was placed in it (Luke 23:55). Then, having prepared spices and oil for anointing, they observed the Sabbath by resting the following day (Luke 23:56). In Mark the women saw only where the tomb was located (15.47), and they did not buy spices to anoint the body until *after* the Sabbath (Mark 16:1). Luke 24:1 does not explicitly mention the intention to anoint the body, and assumes the women were able to purchase fragrant oils that early in the morning.

2. Luke mentions the names of the women almost as an afterthought near the end of the passage (verse 10); Mark identifies them at the very beginning (verse 1). Both Luke and Mark mention Mary Magdalene and Mary the mother of James, but Salome (Mark 16:1) does not appear in Luke. Joanna does, however; she had been identified in Luke 8:3 as the wife of Chuza, and is probably a redactional addition here. Luke also alludes to other women who followed Jesus, and again he is probably thinking of Luke 8:2–3.

3. Luke's women are strangely unconcerned about who will move the stone for them (Mark 16:3 differs), but like Mark's (who did not act on their concern!) they find the stone rolled away from the tomb and enter it (Mark 16:4–5/Luke 24:2–3a).

4. The remark about not finding Jesus' body (Luke 24:3b) does not appear in Mark, because the "young man" announces the raising of Jesus and points to the empty tomb. This shift of emphasis, along with the explicit mention in verse 3b of the *body* of Jesus (see also

Luke 23:55), shows how Luke underscores the empty tomb and the bodily resurrection.

5. While in Mark 16:5 a young man in a white robe met the women, in Luke 24:4 we have two men in shining garments who remind us of the "two men in white garments" in the ascension scene in Acts 1:10 (cf. 9:30, 32). The angelic appearances in 24:4–6 and Acts 1:10–12, corresponding as they do in mode of expression and order, derive from Luke.

6. In Mark 16:6 the young man said,

"You seek Jesus of Nazareth, the crucified one. He was raised, he is not here; see the place where they laid him."

In Luke 24:5b–6a this becomes,

"Why do you seek the living among the dead?[144] He is not here, but he was raised."[145]

7. Luke 24:6b–8 differs considerably from Mark 16:7. In Mark (and similarly Matt. 28:7) the women are directed to tell the disciples that Jesus is going to Galilee, and they will see him there. In Luke 24:7, however, the women are reminded of an earlier statement—*made in Galilee*—that the Son of Man had to suffer and be killed and rise again on the third day: Luke 9:22; cf. 9:44; 18:32–33.[146] It should be noted that only 9:22 and 44 were spoken in Galilee, and no indication is given that the women were present at either time. Luke deliberately excludes accounts of apparitions of Jesus in places other than Jerusalem (cf. below on verse 34). For the necessity of Jesus' suffering see below on verse 26).

8. In Mark 16:8 the women fail to relay the message they are charged with; in Luke they show no fear or doubt, and voluntarily pass on the message of the resurrection (verse 9), but are met with unbelief (verse 11).

Verse 12: The report of Peter's inspection of the tomb is indeed striking. Does it come from a tradition earlier than Mark? Almost certainly not, since we can easily imagine a more likely reconstruction: Luke or his tradition knows of both Jesus' appearance to Peter (cf. Luke 24:34) and the women's visit to the tomb. The "logic" of this combination runs as follows: if the tomb was empty **and** Jesus appeared to Cephas, then the latter must have inspected it before he could accept the reality of the appearance. Either Luke or (more likely) the tradition he used must be the source of this combination.[147] In any case, the piece of information behind verse 12 stems from the account in Mark 16:1–8 and the tradition of a first appearance to Peter. Thus the narrative detail reflected in Luke 24:12 is secondary and accordingly lacks historical bearing on the issue at hand.

HISTORICAL ELEMENTS

See on Mark 16:1–8.

Luke 24:13–35: Jesus' appearance to two disciples on the Emmaus road

(13) *And look, that same day* two *of them* were going to a village named Emmaus, about seven miles from Jerusalem, (14) and talking with each other about all these things that had happened. (15) And while they were discussing these events, Jesus himself drew near and walked with them. (16) But their eyes were kept from recognizing him.

(17) And he said to them, "What is this you are talking about as you walk?" And they stood still, looking sad. (18) Then one of them, named Cleopas, replied, "Are you the only visitor to Jerusalem who does not know about what has happened there in recent days?" (19) *And he said to them, "What things?"* And they said to him, *"Concerning Jesus of Nazareth, who was a prophet powerful in deed and word in the eyes of God and the people,* (20) *and how our chief priests and rulers delivered him up to be condemned and crucified,* (21) *though we had hoped that he was the one who would free Israel. Furthermore, it is now the third day since this happened,* (22) *and some women of our group amazed us. They were at the tomb early in the morning* (23) *and did not find his body, but they returned saying that they had had a vision of angels, who told them he was alive.* (24) *Some of our people then went to the tomb, and found it just as the women had said, but they did not see him."* (25) *And he said to them, "How dull you are, how slow of*

heart to believe what the prophets have proclaimed! (26) *Was it not necessary for the Messiah to suffer these things before entering into his glory?"* (27) *Then beginning with Moses and all the prophets, he explained to them everything in the scriptures that referred to him.*

(28) When they approached the village to which they were going, he made it seem that he was going further, (29) but they urged him not to, saying, "Stay with us, for it is nearly evening and the day almost over." So he went in to stay with them, (30) and when they had sat down at the table, he took the bread, blessed and broke it, and gave it to them. (31) And all at once their eyes were opened and they recognized him; *but he vanished from their sight.* (32) They said to each other, "Did not our hearts seem to be on fire while he talked to us on the road and made the scriptures so clear to us?"

(33) *They immediately rose from the table and returned to Jerusalem, where they found assembled the eleven and the rest of their group,* (34) *who said, "The Lord was really raised, and he appeared to Simon!"* (35) *Then they told all about their journey, and how they had recognized him as he broke the bread.*

LUKE'S PURPOSE AND THE TRADITION REWORKED BY HIM

This story about the disciples on the Emmaus road was written with special care; its outline is as follows:

Verses 13–16: Exposition: two disciples meet Jesus on the way from Jerusalem to Emmaus.

Verses 17–27: Conversation on the way.

Verses 28–32: Arrival in the village and meal scene.

Verses 33–35: Return from Emmaus to Jerusalem.

Verse 13: "And look" (*kai idou*) is a Lukan introduction (cf. 23:50); "of them" links this episode with what has gone before; "that same day": according to Luke all the resurrection appearances take place in a single day.

Verse 14: Here we have the same "all these things" as in verse 9: the report of the women which the disciples did not believe (verse 11). Nevertheless, Peter inspected the tomb (verse 12).

Verse 15: Nor can the two disciples disregard what has happened and what the women have reported. Their discussion[148] sets the stage for Jesus to join them on their journey.

Verse 16: That they were kept from recognizing him marks the end of the introduction; the "resolution" will consist in their eyes being opened (verse 31). But before that can occur, both they and the reader must undergo a recognition process. This begins with the conversation in verses 17–27.

Verses 17–19: In typically Lukan fashion, Jesus opens the dialogue with a question about what the disciples have been discussing. Their sorrow is dramatized by the pause in the external scene (they stand still) which heightens the anticipation. In the tension-building exchange of questions and counter-questions from Jesus in verses 17–19, and the first brief item of information in verse 19, it finally becomes clear that they are talking about Jesus himself, who is termed 'a prophet powerful in deed and word in the eyes of God and the people'. Verse 19 is completely shaped by Luke.[149] Jesus is called "prophet" in Luke 7:16; 9:8, 19 and indirectly in 7:39. For the phrase "powerful in deed and word" see Acts 7:22. If one wonders why the two disciples here give Jesus a title ("prophet") that is hardly central to Luke's thought, the answer is that Luke attributes to the uncomprehending disciples an understanding that will be corrected later (verse 26). Thus verse 19, like the previous verse, produces a tension that demands resolution.

Verse 20: This verse offers Luke's characterization of Jesus' death: the Jews crucified Jesus.[150]

Verse 21: This alludes to the disciples' original but disappointed hope that Jesus would free his people.[151] For Luke it has evidently been surpassed by the creation of the Gentile church.[152] "The third day" harks back to the chronology of the Easter stories.

Verse 22–24: This passage paraphrases what has been reported so far. Verse 22 retells the story of the visit of the women to the tomb, while verse 23 connects with verses 3–5, and verse 24 with verse 12. The word "some" generalizes Peter's visit.

Verse 25: This introduces a summary of the disciples' growth in faith—first of all through a rebuke from Jesus similar to the angels' reproach to the women in verses 5–8.

Verse 26: This characterization of Christ's suffering as necessary and in accordance with the scriptures is part of Luke's notion of salvation history, all elements of which he thinks of as necessary. Here he lays particular stress on the paradox that one destined for glory must suffer.

Verse 27: Luke's Christ bespeaks the author's conviction that the books of Moses and the Prophets have foretold his coming;[153] he neglects, however, to produce a single corroborating passage.

Verse 28: Now that the travelers have almost arrived at their destination, Jesus' purpose to continue on raises the dramatic tension; with the climax in sight—i.e., the recognition of Jesus by the two disciples—we cannot have Jesus simply walk on and disappear.

Verse 29: Thus it happens that the two disciples urge Jesus to stay with them.[154]

Verse 30: When Jesus breaks bread with his disciples, blesses it, and gives it to them, the many parallels to the Last Supper (Luke 22:19) indicate that here Luke is, as it were, presenting a second Eucharist.

Verse 31: When their eyes are opened in recognition, their "blindness" (verse 16) is removed. Luke's aim has been to illustrate that communion with Jesus is experienced in the Eucharist. Once that has been established, Jesus can vanish.[155]

Verse 32: In retrospect the disciples recognize the heart-warming effect of Jesus' self-revelation in his elucidation of the scriptures.

Verse 33: Now the two disciples must hurry to report to the rest of their group—just as the women did in verse 9.

Verse 34: Before the two disciples can pass on their news to the eleven, they are told that the Lord had indeed been raised and had appeared to Peter. This spoils their story. Here, as in such passages as Acts 8:14ff and 11:1, 22, Luke underscores the Jerusalem perspective. He also corrects his received tradition by reporting that the first appearance was to Peter (Cephas in Aramaic), thus comporting with the tradition in 1 Cor. 15:5.[156] The second half of the sentence in verse 34 is puzzling: since Simon is one of the eleven, how could such a statement be 'neutral'—and thus historical? Therefore we must wonder what Luke intends with this verse. His point, surely, is that the experience of the two disciples is like that of the members of Luke's community at the eucharistic meal: Jesus' presence is confirmed by the primitive Christian confession that Jesus was raised and appeared to Simon. In other words, all subsequent Easter experiences grow out of the primitive creed. In Acts, Luke further depicts Peter as the leader of the Jerusalem church[157] to which Luke's community is a successor.

Verse 35: This recapitulates Luke's understanding: what happened to the two disciples was that the scriptures were revealed to them, and in the breaking of bread they recognized Jesus.

Although Luke surely worked with existing material, reconstructing the tradition he used is extremely difficult. It is instructive to remove all the contextual references to see that the result displays the basic features of a tradition. In it Christ appears as an unknown traveler in simple human garb to wander among mankind. From time to time he reveals his divine nature, but whenever he is recognized, he immediately disappears. "This story outline resembles *the earliest narratives about the appearance of the deity*; with only minor adaptation it could become part of Genesis."[158]

It should be further noted that similar stories are known not only in the Old Testament,[159] but also in Greco-Roman literature.[160]

If we assume such a legend belongs to the earliest stratum, we could separate it from the Eucharist tradition in verses 28–31; but while the latter may have been added at a later stage of development, it could already have been part of the earliest tradition.

HISTORICAL ELEMENTS

Verse 34: The appearance to Simon (Peter) is a visionary event, and may to that degree be termed historical.

Elements of the passage are certainly old: behind Cleopas in verse 18 may be a cousin of Jesus whose son Symeon followed James as leader of the Jerusalem community.[161] If so, this story would recall an appearance of Jesus to one of his relatives, and thus might be very early indeed. It is worth noting that John 19:25 identifies one of the women at the cross as "Mary (the wife) of Cleopas."

"Emmaus" can no longer be located, but the name might represent historical recollection.

It has been suggested that the Emmaus story reflects the disciples' experience of Jesus' presence while reading and meditating on scripture. But this proposal does not pay enough attention to three important considerations: (a) Jesus and his immediate disciples were probably illiterate. (b) Their attempts to establish a viable movement failed. (c) It required new vision and leadership to reinvigorate the Jesus movement by transforming it into a Christ cult.

Luke 24:36–43: Jesus' appearance to the (eleven) disciples

(36) *As they were discussing these events,* Jesus himself suddenly stood *in their midst* and said to them, "Peace (be) with you!" (37) *They were startled and terrified,* thinking that he was a ghost. (38) But he said to them, "Why are you troubled, and why are your hearts filled with doubt? (39) Look at my hands and my feet, it is I myself; touch me, and be sure; for ghosts do not have flesh and bones as you can see I have." (40) *And having said that, he showed them his hands and feet.* (41) And while out of sheer joy they were still doubtful and bewildered, Jesus said to them, "Do you have anything here to eat?" (42) They gave him a piece of broiled fish, (43) which he took and ate in their presence.

LUKE'S PURPOSE AND THE TRADITION REWORKED BY HIM

Verses 36–43 comprise a narrative with a recognition scene.

Verse 36: "As they were discussing these events" is an authorial transition from the previous scene to what follows.
Verses 37–38: Cf. Acts 12:8–9.
Verse 39: Jesus' invitation to the disciples to look at his hands

and feet in order to recognize him constitutes a *first* demonstration of his resurrection;[162] the invitation to touch him is the *second*. The risen Jesus is no ghost or spirit, but consists of flesh and blood. Such blunt realism must be seen as an attack on docetism, a challenge to those who disavow the bodily reality of Jesus both as a human being and as the "Risen One."

In the same vein, we find at the beginning of the second century Bishop Ignatius of Antioch in *To the Smyrneans* 3:1–3:

> (1) For I know and believe that he (Jesus) was in the flesh even after the resurrection. (2) And when he came to those about Peter, he said to them, "Take, handle me, and see that I am not a bodiless demon." And immediately they touched him and believed, being intermingled with his flesh and spirit. (3) And after the resurrection he ate and drank with them as a being of flesh, although spiritually united with the Father.[163]

Ignatius—who at this point is dependent on neither Luke nor John—begins by stating a theological thesis (1), which he afterwards backs by a quote of unknown origin (2). He then repeats "after the resurrection" and reaffirms the theological thesis by specifying Jesus' mode of existence on this earth—he ate and drank with the disciples—and by affirming Jesus' spiritual union with his heavenly Father (3). The latter claim is a theological emphasis of Ignatius.[164]

Verse 40: This verse is a contextual variant that simply repeats verse 39 for emphasis, and as such derives entirely from Luke.

Verse 41: Now half convinced, the disciples receive a third demonstration to remove any doubt: Jesus asks for something to eat.

Verse 42: They give him a piece of baked fish.

Verse 43: That he consumes it before their eyes proves him neither a spirit nor an angel. Angels may sometimes seem to eat;[165] only human beings do.

The story has more than one intention. (a) From an *external* perspective, Luke inserted this narrative in order to avoid a possible magical-demonic interpretation of Jesus' putative resurrection. For him the expedient is that the person who appears is the *risen* Jesus with his body of flesh and bones. Luke's "crude materialism" in this story is no mere derivation from naive popular belief but has the explicit aim of repressing any possible magical or demonological interpretation.[166] Luke considers this last demonstration so persuasive that he does not even bother to note that the disciples are convinced. Acts 1:4 and 10:41 also report that the risen Jesus ate with his disciples.

(b) From an *internal* perspective, Luke stresses the physical reality of the risen Jesus in order to strengthen his audience's conviction of *Heilsgeschichte*—note his statement of purpose addressed to Theophilus (Luke 1:3–4). Thus he has woven into verses 36–43 a traditional appearance story whose essential point is the physical reality of Jesus after his resurrection.

The story clearly presupposes disagreement about the corporeality of the risen Christ similar to what we find in the Johannine communities[167] and even earlier among Paul's Corinthians.[168] Rooted in controversy and reflection, it documents the bodily nature of the "Risen One."

A close parallel appears in Acts 2:27 as part of Peter's sermon, in which "David" as the putative author of Psalm 16:10 (LXX 15:10) asserts the necessity of the incorruptible nature of Jesus' body.

Psalm 16:10 (LXX 15:10):

> For you will not abandon my soul to Hades, nor let your Holy One suffer decay.

Luke's reason for citing this verse is that David was speaking about the Messiah—whom Luke equates with Jesus and whom God had allegedly promised that neither will his soul remain in Hades nor his body decay. By having Paul use the same text in a sermon at Pisidian Antioch (Acts 13:35), he underscores the special character of Jesus' incorruptible body. Luke clarifies the difference between David and Jesus by making Paul continue: "For David, after he had served the counsel of God in his own generation fell asleep, and was laid with his fathers and saw decay. But he whom God raised up saw no decay" (verses 36–37).

Here the commentary by David Friedrich Strauss is worth recalling for its clarity:

> The author of the sixteenth Psalm, whether David or another, had, as may be imagined, not dreamt of speaking in the name of the Messiah, but merely given vent to his own joyful trust in God; and if he expressed this by saying that God would not leave his soul in hell, nor suffer his holy one to see corruption, he only meant that with God's help he would emerge happily from every trial and danger. "But David," argued a disciple of Jesus, seeking to prop his vacillating faith, "David is dead and moldered to dust; consequently he cannot in this passage have spoken of himself, but rather he spoke prophetically of his great scion, the Messiah—and this of course was Jesus—who, accordingly, cannot have remained in the grave, cannot have succumbed to the nether powers." In Acts St. Peter certainly only recites this model interpretation on the day of Pentecost, after the resurrection of Jesus; but we see here, on the contrary, one of the processes of thought by which the disciples gradually wrought themselves up to the production of the idea of the resuscitation of their martyred Lord.[169]

HISTORICAL ELEMENTS

The historical yield is nil, both with regard to the historical event and concerning visions as the real catalysts for the rise of Christianity. This is so because verses 36–43 are figments of the imagination of the second Christian generation, arising from discussions within the community on the bodily nature of the "Risen One."

Luke 24:44–49: Jesus' final commission

(44) *Then he said to them, "Now you see fulfilled what I told you while I was still with you: that everything written about me in the Law of Moses and the prophets and the psalms must come true." (45) Then he opened their minds so they could understand the scriptures, (46) and*

reminded them, "It was foretold that the Christ would suffer and on the third day rise from the dead, (47) and that the change of heart that leads to forgiveness of sin would be proclaimed in his name to all peoples, commencing in Jerusalem. (48) And since you are my witnesses to all this, (49) I now bestow on you the gift my Father promised; but stay in the city, until you are fortified with power from above."

LUKE'S PURPOSE AND THE TRADITION REWORKED BY HIM

The section is a discourse of Jesus containing instruction for the disciples. It totally derives from Luke.

Verse 44: Jesus reiterates an earlier statement to the disciples, the content of which appears in the second part of this verse. Jesus argued from the scriptures during his lifetime and now does so after his resurrection.

Verse 45: Luke again introduces an interpretation of scripture as he did in the Emmaus story.[170] The content of his teaching is made specific in the following two verses, but only in the form of a citation from scripture.

Verses 46–47: Verse 46 corresponds to Luke 9:22, the report of Jesus' prediction that he would suffer and rise again on the third day. Verse 47 points to the future task of the disciples. Implicit in the proof from scripture is that "repentance and forgiveness of sins" should be preached in Jesus' name "among all people, beginning in Jerusalem."[171]

Verse 48: Jesus directly addresses the disciples as witnesses to "all this," i.e., the passion and resurrection.[172]

Verse 49: This corresponds to Acts 1:4; Acts 2 records the fulfillment of the prophecies about receiving the Spirit.

HISTORICAL ELEMENTS

Jesus' words in this section are inauthentic because they derive from Luke's pen and can be explained by his theological purpose.

Luke 24:50–53: Jesus' Ascension

(50) *Then he led them out as far as Bethany, and raising his hands he blessed them;* (51) *and even as he did so, he left them and was carried upward into heaven.* (52) *And worshipping him, they returned to Jerusalem with great joy,* (53) *and spent their days in the temple praising God.*

LUKE'S PURPOSE AND THE TRADITION REWORKED BY HIM

The present section is a narrative and contains a farewell. Luke's resurrection narratives culminate in the present scene which has a parallel in Acts 1:9–11. The date of it is still Easter Sunday.[173]

Verses 50: Here the ascension occurs from Bethany on Easter Sunday, whereas according to Acts 1:12 the scene is set on the Mount of Olives and occurs forty days after the resurrection. That does not mean that the two scenes represent rival traditions. Since Luke knows from Mark 11:1 that the "Mount of Olives" and "Bethany" are geographically very close and may even overlap, his use of Bethany here may be a variation. "Forty days" likely derives from Luke who introduced it as a round number with many parallels in the Old Testament[174] in order to fill the gap between Passover and Pentecost (Acts 2).[175] For the blessing, compare the word-for-word parallels in Lev. 9:22 and Sir. 50:20.

Verse 51: For Jesus' disappearance see my comments on verse 31 above, p. 107.

Verse 52: "Great joy" repeats the same motif from verse 41.

Verse 53: The habitual gathering of the community in the temple comports with Luke's theology: as the twelve-year-old Jesus remained in the temple,[176] so does the early Christian community.[177] Considered in terms of form, verse 53 is a short summary statement that has numerous parallels in Luke-Acts.[178] At any rate, the last sentence is surely the work of the evangelist, since we must expect to find the author's intention epitomized in his final words.

HISTORICAL ELEMENTS

The section is a composition of Luke. As a rule in such a case we did not ask the historical question. In this particular case let me hasten to add that any historical element behind this scene and/or behind Acts 1:9–11 must be ruled out because there is no such heaven to which Jesus may have been carried. So in this particular case the rule applies that Morton Smith once formulated (see above, p. 39) and that modern historians apply in similar cases.

THE EASTER NARRATIVE IN THE GOSPEL OF JOHN

John 20:1–23: Easter Day

JOHN'S PURPOSE AND THE TRADITION REWORKED BY HIM

As will be shown below, underlying this section is a tradition dependent on Luke 24 but also influenced by Mark 16 and Matt. 28. Verbatim or almost verbatim agreements with Luke are indicated by dotted underlines and agreements with Mark/Matt. by a normal underline. Verses 2–10 have been set in boldface because, as the analysis will show, they are later revisions of the completed work of the evangelist, whose edits are indicated by italics.

> (1a) Early in the morning of the first day of the week, while it is still dark, Mary Magdalene comes to the tomb (b) and sees the stone has been moved away from the tomb.
> (2) Then she runs to Simon Peter and the other disciple, the one whom Jesus loved, and says to them, 'They have taken the Lord out of his tomb, and we do not know where they have put him.' (3) So Peter and the other disciple set out for the tomb (4) running side by side, but the other disciple outran Peter and got to the tomb first. (5) He stoops and sees the linen cloths lying there, but did not enter. (6) Then Simon Peter arrived close behind and went into the tomb, where he saw the linen cloths

lying there, (7) and the napkin that had been on his head not with the linen cloths, but rolled up in a special place by itself. (8) Then the disciple who had reached the tomb first also went in, and he saw and believed. (9) For until then they had not understood the scripture saying that he must rise from the dead. (10) Then the disciples went home again.

(11a) **But Mary stood weeping outside the tomb,** (b) and as she wept she bent [to look] into the tomb (12) and there she saw two angels in white garments, one sitting at the head and one at the feet of where the body of Jesus had lain. (13a) They said to her, "Woman, why are you weeping?" (b) She says to them, "They have taken away my Lord, and I do not know where they have laid him." (14a) *As she had said this,* she turned around (b) and saw Jesus standing there, but she did not recognize him. (15a) *Jesus says to her, "Women, why are you weeping? Whom do you seek?"* (b) *Thinking he must be the gardener, she says to him, "Sir, if you have removed him, tell me where you have laid him, and I will take him away."* (16) Jesus said to her, "Mary." She turned to him and said, "Rabboni!" *which means Teacher* in Hebrew. (17a) Jesus says to her, "Do not cling to me! (b) *For I have not yet ascended to the Father.* (c) But go to my brothers and tell them that (d) *I am ascending to my Father and your Father, to my God and your God."* (18) So Mary Magdalene goes and tells the disciples, "I have seen the Lord"; *and she gives them his message.*

[[(3*) Then Peter and [the other disciples] set out, and (4*) ran to the tomb (5) And [they bend down] and see the linen cloths lying there, (7) and the napkin that had been on his head not with the linen cloths, but rolled up in a (separate) place. [And they were puzzled.] (9) For they had not yet understood the scripture, that he must rise from the dead. (10) Thereupon the disciples returned home.]]

(19a) Late in the evening of that first day of the week, when the disciples had gathered behind closed doors *for fear of the Jews,* (b) Jesus came and stood in their midst and said, "Peace be with you." (20a) Then he showed them his hands *and his side,* (b) and when the disciples saw the Lord, they rejoiced. (21a) *Then he repeated, "Peace be with you. (b) Just as the Father has sent me, I send you."* (22) *And having said this,* he breathed on them, and said, "Receive Holy Spirit. (23) Whoever's sins you forgive, they are forgiven; those you do not forgive will remain unforgiven."

LATER REVISIONS

The text displays numerous inconsistencies, some of which are so serious as to force us to conclude that the section has undergone drastic revision. *First*, the link between verses 1 and 2 is suspicious: for Mary Magdalene to see only that the *stone* has been rolled away from the tomb (verse 1) and to infer that *Jesus* is no longer in his original place (verse 2) is surely a dubious leap. *Second*, we have no report of Mary's return to the tomb after notifying the two disciples (verse 2); yet in verse 11 she is standing at the tomb and behaving as if the events reported in verses 2–10 had never happened. *Third*, one wonders how it is that Mary sees two angels sitting in the tomb (verse 12), when before it contained nothing but a napkin and some linen cloths (verses 5–7). *Fourth*, the message Mary is to take to the disciples (verse 17) has little point if one of them has already come to believe in the resurrection (verse 8).

These tensions are further heightened by the fact that verse 11b could smoothly follow verse 1. One thus suspects that the race between the two disciples and their visit to the tomb is a narrative inserted by later revisers. By verse 2, no doubt derived from verse 13b, they worked this episode into the context; and with verse 11 they returned to the scene in verse 1 by means of a simple but natural elaboration.

The substantiation of this argument requires anticipating the subsequent analysis of verses 1–18 and 19–23. There we shall see that the evangelist has created these two Easter stories from a tradition dependent on Luke 24—which, significantly, also reports an inspection of the tomb. In Luke's account, though, this occurs only after the women have relayed the angels' Easter message to the disciples, and is performed only by Peter (cf. Luke 24:12: "But Peter rose and ran to the tomb, where he stooped and saw only the linen cloths; then he went home, amazed at what had happened"). When we add these data to the problematic location and integrity of verses 2–11a, and note also that the beloved disciple is explicitly or implicitly a later insertion into the sections John 1:35–51; 13:21–30; 19:16b–30; 19:31–37, we are impelled to the following conclusion:

redactors are responsible for the insertion of verses 2–11a between verses 1 and 11b, and they derived their basic material from the evangelist's text at a place corresponding to Luke 24:12, i.e., after verse 18. They both added the beloved disciple and shifted the account to its present place.

Two further questions need to be asked. *First*, what was the intent of these significant interventions? *Second*, what was contained in the evangelist's original text of verses 3–10*?[179]

The answer to the *first* question is clear. Having the beloved disciple win a race with Peter is a simple assertion of his priority over Peter. Transposing the section enabled the beloved disciple rather than Mary Magdalene to be the first to believe in Jesus' resurrection.

The *second* question is far more difficult, and any answer is necessarily hypothetical. Above all it is uncertain whether the evangelist originally had Peter go to the tomb alone or with another disciple or disciples. The plural in verse 9, however, renders the second possibility the likelier. That would also fit in well with 20:18, 19, 20, 25, which make general mention of "the disciples" (cf. also Luke 24:24a which, despite the single observer of Luke 24:12, has the two Emmaus disciples report, "And *some* of us went to the tomb and found it as the women had said"). Moreover, in the process of revising verses 3–10*, a mention of the disciples' failure to grasp the significance of the empty tomb (cf. Luke 24:12) must have been removed from before verse 9. It goes without saying, of course, that the reconstruction of verses 3–10* (enclosed in doubled square brackets between verses 18 and 19 of the text) represents only one of any number of ways in which the original text could have run (variations from the present text have been placed in single brackets).

MARY MAGDALENE AND THE TWO ANGELS (VERSES 1, 11B–13)

Verse 1: Almost every word has an equivalent in Mark 16:1, 2, 4a or Luke 24:1, 2. Here, in contrast to Mark 16:1 and Luke 24:1, Mary does not bring any spices to the tomb because according to 19:40*

Jesus' body has been properly buried already. Note another important difference from the Synoptics: in 19:25 Mary goes to the tomb alone (Mark 16:1: three women; Matt. 28:1: two; Luke 24:1, 10: more than three). The analysis of verses 14–18 will offer a probable explanation for this.

Verses 11b–13: This piece derives largely from tradition. Note the following parallels, listed in the order of their appearance in John: Mark 16:5 ("into the tomb"); Luke 24:4 ('two'); Matt. 28:2 ("angel"); Matt. 28:3/Mark 16:5 ("white"); Matt. 28:6 ("where . . . had lain"); Luke 24:3 ("the body of the Lord Jesus"); Luke 24:5 ("why . . . ?"); Mark 16:6 ("where they have laid him"). Of course, the possibility also exists that the evangelist has intervened redactionally; for example, in 11:35 the motif of weeping has been inserted, and the address "woman" (see 2:4, 4:21, and 19:26) shows the evangelist at work.

THE APPEARANCE OF JESUS TO MARY MAGDALENE (VERSES 14–18)

The scene with the angels ends abruptly; they neither proclaim the resurrection of Jesus,[180] nor charge Mary to pass the resurrection news on to the disciples.[181] Rather, in verses 14–17 we find a competing report about a meeting between Mary Magdalene and Jesus. To be sure, Matthew also added to Mark's story of the tomb a report (apparently his own) about an appearance of Jesus to Mary Magdalene and another Mary.[182] Here the charge, "Go, proclaim to my brothers" (Matt. 28:10), which corresponds to John 20:17c, is particularly striking. The likely explanation is that John's tradition has appropriated Matthew's report about Jesus meeting with the two women and then transformed it into a recognition scene. Two essential differences from the Synoptic tomb stories should be noted. First, the proclamation of the resurrection by one or more angels was dropped, since the encounter with the "Risen One" himself rendered this episode superfluous. Second, the removal of Matthew's "other Mary" focuses the recognition scene entirely on Jesus and

Mary Magdalene. And if this supposition is correct, then John's tradition also accounts for the reduction of the several women listed by the Synoptics to the one we find in verses 1 and 11b–13. The tradition behind verses 14–18 can be only partly reconstructed, however, for the evangelist clearly reworked it considerably.

Verse 14a: "After she had said this" is a transition typical of John's Gospel.[183]

Verse 14b: Cf. Matt. 28:9a ("And look, Jesus met them"). The nonrecognition motif was probably already part of the tradition: it appears also in Luke 24:16 (the Emmaus story) and in John 21:4b. The evangelist has simply added the motif of misunderstanding to the traditional recognition scene (verse 15b).

Verse 15a: "Woman, why are you weeping?" is the same question the two angels ask Mary Magdalene in verse 13. The question "Whom do you seek?" recalls 1:38 and 18:4, 7; cf. also Luke 24:5: "Why do you seek the living among the dead?"

Verse 15b: For the motif of misunderstanding see 2:20; 3:4; 4:11, 15, 33; 6:34, 42; 7:35; 8:22, 52, 57; 11:12, 24.

Verse 16: Mary's turning around clashes with verse 14a, where she has already done so. The translation of "Rabboni" and its identification as a Hebrew word suggest that this exchange derives from tradition. In being addressed by Jesus, Mary recognizes him.

Verse 17: The "do not cling to me" (verse 17a) probably comes from the tradition, for it seems to reflect a customary practice similar to that described in Matt. 28:9b: "And they came up and took hold of his feet." That the commission in verse 17c also comes from the tradition is suggested not only by the parallel in Matt. 28:10 (see above) but also by the term "brothers," a designation not found elsewhere in John. But the prohibition against touching (verse 17b) and the content of the message (verse 17d) are the work of the evangelist, whose point is that once Jesus has returned to heavenly glory, his Father will also become Father to his followers. What originally stood in place of verses 17b and 17d is now beyond discovery.

Verse 18: The report 'I have seen the Lord' does not comport well with Jesus' command in verse 17d, and thus further confirms that the original commission has been modified or replaced by the evangelist. He camouflages his reformulation of verse 17 with the evasive clause, "and [she] gives them his message."

THE INSPECTION OF THE TOMB (VERSES 3–10*)

Verses 3–10*: These verses—hypothetically recreated above—correspond to Luke 24:12. As in Luke, the mention of the linen cloths serves apologetically to identify the tomb as Jesus'. The carefully folded napkin, not found in Luke's description, is probably intended to exclude any suspicion of a tomb robbery.[184] In short, the empty tomb becomes by itself nearly unimpeachable testimony to Jesus' resurrection. Luke 24:7 ("that [he] . . . must . . . rise") and Luke 24:44b–46 seem to have been used in verse 9.

THE APPEARANCE OF JESUS TO THE DISCIPLES (VERSES 19–23)

Verse 19a: The chronological note refers to verse 1. That this verse follows smoothly from verse 10 is further evidence that in the evangelist's work verses 3–10* stood between verses 18 and 19. Parallels in 7:13 and 19:38 (cf. 9:22) show 'for fear of the Jews' to be redactional. This addition also softens the point in the tradition that the Risen Christ can pass through closed doors, since in Luke the fear is a reaction to his appearance (Luke 24:37).

Verses 19b–20a: Note the near-perfect agreement with Luke 24:36, 40. The only notable variation is that the fourth evangelist mentions Jesus' *side* instead of his feet; here he picks up 19:34 while also preparing for the following scene (see 20:25b, 27). (Though since 19:34 reflects tradition, it may be that the wound in the side is an element antedating the evangelist.)

Still, this redactional context raises the issue of Jesus' mention of his ascent in verse 17, particularly in view of his transformed appearance, for the latter would suggest that he has already ascended to his Father and returned to earth. But this is unlikely to be the intent of the evangelist, in whose view Jesus appears to the disciples as the "Ascended One."

Verse 20b: Cf. Luke 24:41 ("the joy of the disciples").

Verse 21: The clause "then he repeated" (cf. 8:12, 21) and the repetition of the greeting that previously appeared in verse 19b indicate the evangelist's insertion of this verse (cf. 4:38).

Verse 22: Except that the clause "having said this" is dependent on the inserted verse 21, we would see this verse as a traditional element, for the archaic idea of the transfer of the Spirit[185] clashes with the Paraclete's assurances found in both the evangelist and later revisers.[186] Similarly, "Holy Spirit" without the article does not appear elsewhere in the Gospel of John. Furthermore, it is noteworthy that in the tradition used by John—in contrast to Luke's[187]— Easter and Pentecost fall on the same day.

Verse 23: The concluding gift of authority also comes from tradition and may represent a combining of Luke 24:47 with Matt. 16:19 and 18:18. Such expressions as "forgiving sins" and "sins remaining unforgiven" do not appear elsewhere in John's Gospel.

HISTORICAL ELEMENTS

Verses 1, 11b–13: These verses presuppose all the Synoptic reports of the tomb. Therefore, regarding their historical significance, reference should be made to the remarks on Mark 16:1–8 (above, pp. 83–88).

Verses 14–18*: These verses depend on the fictional composition found in Matt. 28:9–10 and therefore have no historical value.

Verses 3–10*: For the account of Peter's examination of the tomb, see the commentary above on Luke 24:12 (p. 103).

Verses 19–23*: See the observations on Luke 24:36–43, 44–49 (pp. 94–98). For verse 23 see also the remarks on Matt. 16:19 and 18:18 (pp. 157–59).

John 20:24–29: The appearance of the "Risen One" to Thomas

(24) *One of the twelve, Thomas, called the Twin, was not with them when Jesus came,* (25a) *and so the other disciples told him, 'We have*

seen the Lord.' (b) *He said, 'Unless I see the marks where the nails were in his hands, and put my finger where the nails were, and my hand in his side, I will not believe.'* (26a) *Eight days later, the disciples were in the house once again, and Thomas was with them.* (b) *Even though the doors were shut, Jesus entered and stood in their midst, saying, "Peace be with you."* (27) *Then he says to Thomas, "Put out your finger, here are my hands; and reach out with your hand, and place it in my side; be doubtful no longer, but believe."* (28) *Thomas replied to him, "My Lord and my God!"* (29a) *Jesus said, "Is it because you have seen me that you now believe?* (b) *Blessed are those who have never seen me and (yet) believe."*

JOHN'S PURPOSE AND HISTORICAL ELEMENTS

This story has no parallel in the Synoptics. It conflicts with the preceding section, verses 19–23, which gave no indication that any of the disciples were absent when Jesus appeared.

Verse 24: This verse, with its explicit reference to verse 19, explains why Jesus had not yet appeared to Thomas. Thomas and his nickname "Twin" (in Greek, *Didymos*) were previously mentioned in 11:16, and here he also plays the role of skeptic.

Verse 25a: 'We have seen the Lord' echoes "when they saw the Lord" (20:20b) and thus naturally comports with Mary Magdalene's speech in 20:18.

Verse 25b: The conditions stipulated by Thomas hark back to 20:20a.

Verse 26a: The note of time, "eight days later," places this new gathering, like the first one (verse 19), on a Sunday.

Verse 26b: This verse is a nearly verbatim rehearsal of 20:19b; the closed doors are taken from 20:19a.

Verse 27: Jesus' invitation reiterates Thomas' wish in verse 25b. The evangelist considers the earthly Jesus to have been omniscient[188] and the "Risen One" even more so. (For touching as evidence of Jesus' identity and the reality of his body, see Luke 24:39–43.)

Verse 28: Rather than accept Jesus' invitation, Thomas offers the appropriate confession to the "Risen One,"[189] recognizing God as present in Jesus. Furthermore, "My Lord and my God" amounts to a reformulation of the identification expressed in 1:1 and 18.[190]

Verse 29a: The form of Jesus' question recalls 1:50; in its note of reproach it resembles 3:10; 6:61; and 14:9a.

Verse 29b: This beatitude, restating a theme also found in 4:48, is the final speech that the evangelist attributed to the risen Jesus. Exploring the relationship between seeing and believing is typical of the evangelist.[191]

Ultimately then, since the evangelist has created this narrative to dramatize the same motif of doubt we find in other resurrection stories,[192] its historical value is nil. We may justifiably follow the late Anton Dauer in concluding that the evangelist "has attached to the figure of Thomas the theme of the disciples' unbelief, its overthrow by an encounter with the Risen Lord, and an examination of the problematical value of such faith."[193] Apparently he relocated the motif of doubt from John 20:19–23 to this later narrative.

The question remains of why the fourth evangelist has chosen Thomas to spell out his own belief in the carnal resurrection of Jesus. Here Gregory Riley suggests that the composition of the above unit is a deliberate attempt to refute the symbolic interpretation of Jesus' resurrection by Thomas Christians.[194] However, the text itself says nothing of that sort. In order to defend his thesis, Riley must postulate the existence of Thomas communities in the first century with a symbolic interpretation of the resurrection for which textual evidence is lacking.[195]

INTRODUCTORY COMMENT TO JOHN 21

Several factors make it evident that later editors of the Gospel of John created the whole of chapter 21. First, 20:30–31 is clearly the intended conclusion to the book. Second, according to 21:3 the disciples are all fishermen by trade—a situation totally out of keeping with the commission that Jesus assigned to them in 20:21–23. Third, the evangelist can hardly follow Jesus' appearance in 20:26–29 with any further episodes, since from now on, "Blessed are those who do not see and [yet] believe!" (20:29). Fourth, Peter's appointment to be leader of the church (21:15–17) does not square with the transfer of authority to the disciples as a group (20:21–23). Fifth, in 21:24 a "we" group distinct from the putative author of the book announces its presence. Last but hardly least, chapter 21 differs considerably from chapters 1–20 in language and style.

In what follows, the use of *italics* and the attribution of redaction or purpose indicate the activity not of the evangelist, but of later editors. These will be hereafter referred to as "the authors."

John 21:1–14: Jesus' appearance by the Sea of Tiberias

(1) *Some time later Jesus again showed himself to the disciples* by the Sea of Tiberias, and this is how it happened.

(2) Gathered there were Simon Peter *and Thomas, the Twin and Nathanael from Cana in Galilee* and the [sons] of Zebedee, *and two other of his disciples.* (3) Simon Peter says to them, 'I am going fishing,' and they reply, 'We will come with you.' They got into the boat and set out, but all night they caught nothing. (4a) Just as day was breaking, Jesus was standing there on the shore, (b) but the disciples did not recognize him. (5) *Jesus calls to them, "Friends, have you caught anything to eat" "No," they answered him.* (6) *Then* he said to them, "Cast your net to starboard, and you will get a good catch." So they cast (the net), and soon it contained so many fish that they could not pull it in. (7) *Then the disciple Jesus loved said to Peter, "It is the Lord!" When Simon Peter heard that, he pulled on his shirt—for he had been naked—and jumped into the water.*

(8) The *other* disciples, since they were only about a hundred yards from shore, followed in the boat, *dragging the fishing net.* (9) When they came ashore, they saw a charcoal fire with fish cooking on it, and bread. (10) *Jesus says to them, "Bring some of the fish that you have caught."* (11) So Simon Peter got back into the boat and drew ashore the net filled with a hundred and fifty-three large fish. And in spite of there being so many, the net did not tear. (12a) Jesus says to them, "Come and have breakfast." (b) None of the disciples dared to ask him who he was, (c) *for they knew it was the Lord.* (13) Jesus steps up and takes the bread and hands it to them, along with the fried fish.

(14) *This was now three times that Jesus appeared to the disciples after being raised from (the) dead.*

PURPOSE AND TRADITION REWORKED

This section is marked by numerous inconsistencies, but it will suffice to note two of the more striking ones. First, because the disciples have caught nothing to eat (verses 5–6), Jesus directs them to cast the net on the right side of the boat and promises a good catch; but according to verse 9, fish is already cooking there before the miraculous catch is landed. Second, according to verse 7 Peter jumps into the sea, evidently because he wants to get to Jesus as quickly as possible; but then in verse 11, having gotten back into the boat, he single-handedly pulls ashore (!) a net so full that the other six together could not draw it in (verse 6). These and other inconsistencies no doubt indicate that in verses 1–14 the authors of chapter 21 have interwoven and redactionally bonded together two different traditions: the story of a miraculous catch of fish and an Easter recognition legend. Underlined in the above text is a variant of the tradition behind Luke 5:1–11 which has probably been preserved in its entirety (see below, p. 157). The dotted underline indicates the recognition legend, only fragments of which have been preserved.

Verse 1: This and verse 14, which together frame the story, are the creation of the authors of chapter 21. ("After this" and "again" refer to the preceding Easter stories.)

Verse 2: The sons of Zebedeee (who appear only here in the Fourth Gospel) and Peter originally belong to the miraculous catch story (cf. Luke 5:3, 10). Thomas[196] and Nathanael,[197] by contrast, have been included by the authors, as have the two unnamed disciples ("of his disciples" points back to verse 1). Thus seven disciples are present, a number possibly intended to symbolize the future church.[198]

Verse 3: The failure to catch any fish[199] is the dramatic precondition for the miracle.

Verse 4a: After a long night of failure, the miracle-worker arrives on the shore at the dawn of the new day.

Verse 4b: The disciples' inability to recognize Jesus[200] is a motif that makes sense in an Easter narrative, but not in a miracle story; therefore this must be part of a recognition legend. But its beginning has been lost in linking it to the tradition of the catch. Probably the missing portion merely noted that Jesus arrived on the shore and somehow gained the attention of the disciples in the boat. It may have been this exposition (Jesus standing on the shore, the disciples fishing) that prompted the combining of the recognition legend and the miraculous catch narrative.

Verse 5: It is because this verse serves to connect the two traditions that the phrase "anything to eat" has been employed, for this eases somewhat the tension with verse 9, where fish is already "cooking" on the charcoal fire. Since the familiar form of address, "friends" (literally "children"), appears in the New Testament only here and in 1 John 2:14 and 18, it thus provides additional evidence for the derivative nature of this verse.

Verse 6: This verse originally followed verse 4a. It tersely reports the preparation for and execution of the miracle.[201]

Verse 7: This verse stems entirely from the pen of authors of chapter 21. Once again (cf. 20:8) we are told of the priority of the beloved disciple: he is quicker than Peter to recognize Jesus.[202]

Verses 8–9: These verses extend the recognition legend begun in verse 4b. At the invitation of the unknown man the disciples steer their boat ashore, where they find a meal completely prepared. The reference to "the other disciples" (instead of "the disciples") results from the insertion of verse 7. The middle part of verse 8 ("dragging the fishing net") might also be redactional since it serves to link the two traditions.

Verse 10: Jesus adds a couple of fish from the miraculous catch to those already prepared. This helps overcome any impression that the miraculous catch was an unrelated element and serves as a strong link between the two stories.

Verse 11: Though addressed to all, the invitation to bring the fish (verse 10) is accepted only by Peter—and far from adequately; for instead of immediately rushing to the fire with the catch, Peter merely counts the fish while the author assures us that the net was not damaged. This marks the conclusion of the tradition: Peter comes ashore, pulls in the overloaded net (verse 6), and confirms the miracle.

Verse 12a: In the Easter legend the invitation to breakfast followed verse 9.

Verse 12b: Their hesitance to ask who the mysterious host is indicates that the disciples have not yet recognized Jesus (cf. verse 4b). Note that this stands in contrast to the author's awkward redaction in verse 7.

Verse 12c: This stands in tension with verse 12b because now the disciples know their host is Jesus; hence no reason exists for wondering about his identity, much less for hesitating to ask this question.

Verse 13: In Luke 24:30–31 the two disciples on the Emmaus road recognize Jesus when he breaks bread before them. This recognition story probably ended the same way, but here the authors have replaced the original conclusion ("Then the disciples know that it is the Lord") with verse 12c. Rewording this element and placing it before verse 13 was necessitated by the authors' decision to allow the beloved disciple to establish Jesus' identity in verse 7.

Verse 14: This closing frame of the story derives entirely from the authors (cf. verse 1). Describing Jesus' appearance in verses 2–13 as the third means that 20:19–23 was the first and 20:26–29 the second. One assumes that the appearance to Mary Magdalene (20:14–18) did not count because the author did not recognize her as Jesus' disciple.

HISTORICAL ELEMENTS

The Easter meal scene and the miracle of the fish lack historical credibility.

John 21:15–19: The "Risen One" and Simon Peter

(15) *After breakfast Jesus says to Simon Peter, "Simon, [son] of John, do you love me more than these?" He says to him, "Yes, Lord; you know that I love you." He says to him, "Feed my lambs."*

(16) *He says to him a second time, "Simon, [son] of John, do you love me?" He says to him, "Yes, Lord; you know that I love you." He said to him, "Tend my sheep."*
(17) *He says to him the third time, "Simon, [son] of John, do you love me?" Peter was deeply hurt at being asked a third time, "Do you love me?" And he says to him, "Lord, you know everything; you know that I love you." Jesus said to him, "Feed my sheep.* (18) *And know this for sure: when you were young, you used to dress and travel as you pleased; but when you are old, you will stretch out your hands, and someone else will gird you and take you where you do not wish to go."* (19a) *He said this to indicate the manner of death by which Peter would glorify God.* (b) *Then he added, "Follow me."*

PURPOSE AND TRADITION REWORKED

The second section of this added chapter is rather tenuously attached to the first by the chronological note "after breakfast," which in turn refers to 21:12–13. The purpose of this episode is the rehabilitation of Peter, whose standing had been seriously compromised by his denial of Jesus.

Verses 15–17: These verses form a carefully constructed unit. Three times Jesus asks Simon Peter, the son of John,[203] whether he loves him, and three times Peter assures him that he does. Each time his answer elicits Jesus' appointment of him to be shepherd of the sheep,[204] i.e., the leader of the church. This triple affirmation corresponds, of course, to his threefold denial in the high priest's courtyard,[205] and the thrice-repeated commission exonerates Peter.

Verse 18: In this continuation of the conversation, Jesus predicts Peter's martyrdom.

Verse 19a: This interpretation, based on 12:33 and/or 18:32, indicates that the manner of his death—apparently crucifixion—is decisive for Peter.

Verse 19b: Jesus extends Peter's commission to lead and protect the community by a call to personal discipleship. Because of verses 18–19a this is also to be understood as involving eventual martyrdom (cf. 13:36).

In sum, express and implicit references to 1:42; 10:1–18; 13:36–38 and 18:17, 25–27 show that this scene is entirely the product of the authors of this chapter. Its aim is to show that Peter's primacy in the church—despite his earlier denial of his Lord[206]—is to be ascribed to the "Risen One."

HISTORICAL ELEMENTS

The scene is unhistorical.

John 21:20–25: Peter and the Beloved Disciple

(20) *Then Peter turns around and sees following them the disciple Jesus loved—the one who had also reclined close to Jesus at the supper and asked, "Lord, who is it who is going to hand you over?"* (21) *Seeing him, Peter says to Jesus, "Lord, what will become of him?"* (22) *Jesus says to him, "If I desire that he should remain until I come, what* [does that matter] *to you? Just be sure that you yourself follow me."* (23a) *This was taken to mean, according to the catch-phrase known among the brothers, "That disciple will not die."* (b) *But Jesus had not said he would not die, but only, "If I desire that he remain until I come, what* [does that matter] *to you?"*

(24) *It is this same disciple who hereby bears witness to these things, and who here has written them down; and we know that his testimony is true.*

PURPOSE AND TRADITION REWORKED

This passage concludes the supplementary chapter. Picking up the theme found in 20:3–10 and 21:7, verses 20–23 once again examine the relationship between the beloved disciple and Peter. Verse 24 contains the second conclusion to the book. Verse 25 has been omitted, since it is a notably inferior flourish added subsequently to the drafting of verses 1–24.

Verse 20: Following the dialogue with Jesus in 21:15–19, Peter turns and finds behind them the beloved disciple, whose company at the last supper was particularly noted (cf. 13:23–26a).

Verse 21: If Peter has been made leader of the church, of what significance is the beloved disciple?

Verse 22: Jesus dismisses Peter's query. It must not be Peter's concern whether the beloved disciple lives to see Jesus' return (at the parousia). Since Peter has already been told all that matters to him, Jesus need only repeat the call to discipleship in verse 19b. Clearly, the beloved disciple has a close relationship to Jesus regardless of Peter's authority over the church.

Verse 23a: The authors cite a report circulating in the community that Jesus has assured the beloved disciple that he will live to witness the parousia.

Verse 23b: But that report was erroneous: Jesus has not foretold the beloved disciple's survival, but merely indicated its possibility. This description fits with the report in verse 22.

Verse 24: This verse reveals at long last the secret of the beloved disciple: he is the author of the book. Despite his death (implied in verse 23) he is thus the guarantor of the future of the Johannine community. Further, the Gospel of John affords the community the written testimony of a specially recognized eyewitness and reliable informant. Whereas Peter must die a martyr, in this book the beloved disciple remains alive.

RESULT

The entire section is the creation of the authors of chapter 21. Doubtless the purpose of verses 20–23 is to refute the saying quoted in verse 23a. Evidently the actual sequence of the saying in verse 22 and the misunderstanding in verse 23a was precisely the opposite. First the saying "That disciple will not die" (verse 23a) arose in the community—probably on the basis of the advanced age of the author depicting the beloved disciple—and was soon attributed to Jesus. When the disciple died nonetheless, the saying had to be revised, and accordingly the explanation was made that Jesus had merely suggested that the disciple might survive until his return (verses 22, 23b). Thus the historical value of this section is negligible.

THE EASTER NARRATIVE IN THE GOSPEL OF PETER[207]

Gospel of Peter 12:50–13:57: The women in the tomb

(12:50) Now at dawn on the **Lord**'s Day Mary Magdalene, a female disciple of the **Lord** (though for fear of the *Jews* who were inflamed with anger, she had not done at the tomb of the **Lord** what women were accustomed to do for loved ones who had died), (51) together with her women friends came to the tomb where he had been placed. (52) And they <u>feared</u> lest the *Jews* should <u>see them</u> and were saying, "Although on the day he was crucified we could not <u>weep</u> <u>and beat our breasts</u>, yet now at his tomb we may do these things. (53) But who will roll away for us the stone placed against the door of the tomb so that we may enter and sit beside him and do the expected things?" (54) (Remember, the stone was large.) "We <u>fear</u> that someone will <u>see us</u>. And if we cannot [roll it away], let us at least lay against the door the memorial we have brought for him, and <u>weep and beat our breasts</u> until we return to our homes."

(13:55) So they went, and they found the sepulcher open. They went up to it and <u>bent down and saw</u> sitting there in he middle of the sepulcher a handsome young man clothed in a splendid robe. He said to them, (56) "Why have you come? Whom do you seek? Surely not the one who was crucified? *He rose and went away.* If you do not believe it, <u>bend down and see</u> the place where he lay, because he is not here. Indeed, *he rose and went away* to the place he was sent from." (57) Then the women fled in fear.

PURPOSE AND TRADITION REWORKED

On the discovery, content, and origin of the *Gospel of Peter* see above, pp. 56–57. An important motive of the passage is the women's intention to bewail Jesus' death. Indirectly or directly, it is mentioned four times (verses 50, 52, 53, 54).

12:50: Only Luke (24:1) also uses "dawn" in the Easter account. In the *Gospel of Peter*[208] as in Rev. 1:10 "the Lord's day" is a conventional designation, though it is absent from the New Testament gospels. Mary Magdalene's role in finding the tomb empty is as prominent here as in John. "Female disciple" appears elsewhere in the New Testament only in Acts 9:36. By calling Mary Magdalene a disciple he aligns her with the other male disciples. For the phrase "fear of the Jews" see John 7:13; 9:22; 19:38a; 20:19. The content of the custom "to do for loved ones who had died" is specified in verses 52–53.

12:51: Since the names of her female friends are not given, Mary Magdalene remains the focus of attention. "The reduction of the number of the women at the tomb to Mary Magdalene and friends . . . rather than being a sign of primitive tradition, merely shows the author's concerted efforts to sort out the competing traditions in the Synoptic records and John."[209]

12:52: The fear of the Jews continues the topic of verse 50. The Greek word *mnema* (tomb) is used for Jesus' burial place also in Mark 15:46; 16:2; Luke 23:53; 24:1. The dialogue of the women presupposes the scene of Mark 15:40–41.

12:53: The question asked by the women precisely matches that of Mark 16:3. The phrase "do the expected things" amplifies "do these things" from the previous verse and specifies what has been hinted at in verse 50: It is their duty to bewail the death of a loved one.[210] Note that unlike the corresponding passages in Mark and in Luke the women did not plan to anoint Jesus' dead body.

12:54: The reference to the large stone is reminiscent of Mark 16:4; the women's fear has already been mentioned in verse 52. The second part of the verse underscores the women's duty to weep and to express sorrow.

13:55: Cf. Mark 16:5. For the verb "to bend down" in this verse and in the next verse see Luke 24:12 (Peter), John 20:5 (the other disciple), and John 20:11 (Mary Magdalene).

13:56: From 10:40 the reader knows that Jesus has ascended to heaven.[211] For the other details of the verse cf. Mark 16:6 and Matt. 28:5–6. It is surprising that the women receive no command "to go and tell the disciples about their encounter and that nothing invites the reader to think that they would have done so."[212] The end of the verse is reminiscent of John 16:5a: "But now I am going to him who sent me."[213]

13:57: This verse corresponds to Mark 16:8 except for the latter's information that the women did not pass on the news—something impossible since they had not received an order to do so.

Gospel of Peter 14:58–60: Jesus' appearance to his disciples in Galilee (Fragment)

(14:58) Now it was the final day of the Unleavened Bread; and many were returning to their <u>home</u> since the feast was over. (59) But we twelve disciples of the **Lord** continued to weep and *grieve*; and each one, *grieving* because of what had come to pass, departed to his <u>home</u>. (60) But I, Simon Peter, and my brother Andrew took our nets and went off to the sea. And with us went Levi of Alphaeus whom the **Lord**. . . .

PURPOSE AND TRADITION REWORKED

14:58: The content of this verse, which prepares the reader for the disciples' return to Galilee, has no parallel in the canonical gospels.

14:59: The sorrow of the disciples[214] corresponds to that of the women.[215] "Twelve apostles" is a standard term that simply ignores the traitor Judas. As in Matthew's gospel (chapter 28:16–20) and in the appendix to John's gospel (chapter 21) the appearance will take place in Galilee, the homeland of Jesus and the disciples.

14:60: Apparently this is leading up to something similar to the appearance story in John 21. If that is the case, this gospel reported no appearance to women. The phrase "I, Simon Peter" justifies the name *Gospel of Peter*, of which only a fragment has been preserved.

RESULT

In contrast to the section describing Jesus' actual departure from the tomb (see above, pp. 93–94), these two pieces contain nothing but reminiscences of the canonical gospels, and hence do not reflect a presynoptic tradition.[216] Rather they seem to minimize the role of the women regarding the resurrection of Jesus and may reflect a common viewpoint in the second century.

THE EASTER NARRATIVE IN THE EPISTLE OF THE APOSTLES (EPISTULA APOSTOLORUM)

The Epistula Apostolorum (EpAp) consists of a letter, a Gospel, and a revelatory discourse from the middle of the second century. It purports to convey revelations from the "Risen One" to all Christians everywhere in order to protect them against the false apostles Simon and Kerinth. Originally written in Greek, the document is preserved in a Coptic fragment from the fourth or fifth century on which an Ethiopic translation is based.[217] While the narrative about the empty tomb and the appearances to the disciples resembles the accounts from the New Testament, a dependency should not be too readily assumed. In what follows, then, I want to investigate whether the reports contain older material and what phase of the early Christian Easter story they may reflect.

EpAp 9:4–10:2: The women in the tomb and the appearance of Jesus

(9:4) There went to that place three women: Mary, the daughter of Martha and Mary Magdalene. (5) They took ointment to pour upon his <u>body</u>, *weeping* and mourning over what had happened. (6) But when they had approached the tomb they looked inside and did not find the <u>body</u>.

(10:1) But as they were mourning and *weeping*, the LORD appeared to them and said to them, "For whom are you *weeping*? Now do not *weep*; I am he whom you seek. (2) But let one of you go to your brothers and say, 'Come, the Master has risen from the dead.'"

PURPOSE AND TRADITION REWORKED

9:4–5: The women go to the tomb to take care of the dead body and to mourn, only to discover that the body is not there. The question of who might open the tomb for them is not a concern. The author must have an interest in the women's expression of grief because in 10:1 he reverses and repeats the phrase "weeping and mourning." For the motif of mourning which is generally absent from the New Testament narratives (except for John 20:11a and the later verse Mark 16:10) see the Gospel of Peter (12:52–53).

9:6: The absence of the body corresponds to that in Luke 24:3.

10:1–2: The risen Jesus encounters the women in the tomb, and apart from identifying himself tells them essentially what the angelic figure tells the disciples in the synoptic version. On "brothers" cf. Matt. 28:10; John 20:17.

EpAp 10:3–11:1: The disciples' disbelief of the witness of the women

(10:3) **Martha** came and told it to us. (4) We said to her, 'What do you want with us, O woman? He who has died is buried; could it be possible for him to live? (5) We did not believe her that the Savior had risen from the dead.

(6) Then she went back to the LORD and said to him, "None of them believed me that you are alive." (7) He said, "Let another one of you go to them saying this again to them."

(8) **Mary** came and told it to us again, and we did not believe her.

(9) She returned to the LORD and told him the same thing. (11:1) Then the LORD said to Mary and her sisters, "Let us go to them."

PURPOSE AND TRADITION REWORKED

10:3: Cf. Luke 24:10.

10:4–5: Cf. Luke 24:11. The detailed description of the disciples' unbelief has no counterpart in the New Testament narratives.

10:6: This verse picks up the thread of thought in 10:5; "to be alive" is identical with "to have risen from the dead."

10:7: Jesus' command that another woman tell the unbelieving disciples the good news of his resurrection moves the narrative forward.

10:8: Note the underlines and dotted underlines in the text. They show the parallels between 10:3, 10:5, and 10:8 and reflect narrative schemes.

10:9–11:1: This section corresponds to 10:6–7.

EpAp 11:2–12:4: Jesus' appearance to the disciples

(11:2) And he came and found us inside, and he called us out. (3) But we thought it was a **ghost**, and we did not believe it was the LORD. (4) Then he said to us, "Come, do not be fearful. I am your teacher whom you, Peter, denied three times; and will you now deny me again?"

(5) Still, we went to him, <u>doubting</u> in our hearts whether it was possibly he. (6) Then he said to us, 'Why do you still <u>doubt</u> and remain <u>unbelieving</u>? I am he who spoke to you concerning my flesh, my death, and my resurrection. (7) So you may know that it is I, Peter, <u>put your finger</u> in the nail prints of my hand; and you, Thomas, <u>put your finger</u> in the spear-wounds of my side; you, Andrew, look at my feet and see if they do not touch the ground. (8) For it is written in the prophet, 'The foot of a **ghost** or a demon does not join to the ground'."

(12:1) Then we touched him so that we might know whether he had truly risen in the flesh, (2) and we fell on our faces confessing our sin, that we had been <u>unbelieving</u>. Then the LORD, our redeemer said, (3) "Rise up and I will reveal to you what is above <u>heaven</u>, and what is in <u>heaven</u>, and your rest that is in the kingdom of <u>heaven</u>. (4) For my Father has given me the power to raise you and all those who believe in me."

PURPOSE AND TRADITION REWORKED

Jesus encounters the disciples. The women have disappeared, though according to 11:1 they had planned to go to Jesus. The present text contains three dialogues between Jesus and his disciples, and comes to a climax when the faith of the disciples overcomes their disbelief.

Thus 11:2–4 reports the disciples' disbelief and Jesus' characterization of disbelief as yet another denial; 11:5–8 adduces a proof of the resurrection by a demonstration of Jesus' fleshliness; 12:1–4 tells of the disciples' faith and Jesus' promise to reveal to them what is in and even above heaven. Jesus the lord and redeemer was given the power to raise the disciples and all those who will believe in him.

11:2: Jesus finds the disciples inside because for fear of the Jews they had locked the doors. This seems to reflect John 20:19a.

11:3: Cf. Luke 24:34, 37. The reference to "ghost" looks forward to verse 8.

11:4: On the call to be unafraid, cf. Matt. 28:10. The mention of Peter's denial is based on the well-known story in the New Testament, but the author's designation of disbelief as a further denial is adroitly original.

11:5–6: This is an introduction to the demonstration that follows.

11:7: The three-step proof is based on the story of doubting Thomas,[218] who here is one of the three examples. The reference to hands and feet stems from Luke 24:39, while the mention of hands and the side derive from John 20:27. Thus the author is using both gospels.[219] The episode with Andrew introduces the following proof text from a prophet. Notably, "the command to Andrew does not continue the pattern established with Peter and Thomas. Less surprising would have been a command to examine the *nail-prints* in the Lord's feet; but Andrew is requested to inspect the Lord's feet as they touch the ground and make footprints."[220]

11:8: An unknown text from a nameless prophet refutes the thesis that Jesus is present only in spirit, for the feet of ghosts and demons do not touch the ground as Jesus' feet do. The footprint motif is used in contemporary writings such as the *Acts of John* 93: "And I ('John') often wished, as I walked with him, to see his footprint in the earth, whether it appeared . . . and I never saw it."[221]

12:1: The disciples accept the offer that Thomas refuses in John 20: 24–29; they assure themselves that Jesus has indeed risen in the flesh.

12:2: As in John 20:28 a confession follows.

12:3–4: These verses sketch the program for the revelation in chapters 13–51. On verse 4 cf. John 12:32.

RESULT

The above texts are mostly dependent on the New Testament gospels; and where they are independent, the traditions they reflect do not derive from the earliest strata of the Easter legend.

IN RETROSPECT

In this chapter we have analyzed all early Christian texts directly or indirectly bearing on the resurrection of Jesus, commencing from the oldest tradition preserved in 1 Cor. 15:3–8. We started with the texts about his death, continued on with those concerning his burial, and examined the stories about the empty tomb. We also turned our attention to the one specific resurrection text as well as reports of post-resurrection appearances.

One clear result of the analytical part of our investigation is that the appearance traditions and those of the tomb did not originally have anything in common. The earliest recorded appearance did not take place in or near the tomb, and the narrative of the empty tomb had the ironically twofold purpose of answering questions from adherents *and* opponents. To appeal to objections from within the Christian circles, the empty tomb tradition stresses the corporeal character of Jesus' resurrection. Similarly, accounts addressed to hostile Jews aimed to correct ugly rumors about the theft of Jesus' body by the disciples. As time went on, the traditions of tomb and appearance were brought increasingly closer together, so that the nature of the original appearance stories becomes almost unrecognizable. But through Paul we can gain some idea of the original event. At the beginning of early Christian faith stood visions of the "Risen One," visionary experiences that led to perceiving a formerly dead person as being alive. From these experiences Paul and other early Christian witnesses very early derived such "empirical" statements as the empty tomb accounts.

But if a tomb in Jerusalem must be ruled out as the historical setting of the first resurrection appearance of Jesus, the same must be said about Jerusalem in general. Taken together, the evidence overwhelmingly suggests Galilee as the locus of the original vision. That the disciples immediately fled to their Galilean homes is improbable for a number of reasons. Yet no one has been able to give a plausible explanation of how the Jerusalem appearances could have been followed by visions in Galilee unless the disciples had returned there. Indeed it is most likely that their experiences with Jesus in Galilee retrospectively shaped the appearance stories.

NOTES

1. Morton Smith, "Historical Method in the Study of Religion," Smith, *Studies in the Cult of Yahweh*, vol. 1, *Studies in Historical Method, Ancient Israel, Ancient Judaism*, ed. Shaye J. D. Cohen (Leiden: Brill, 1996), p. 7.

2. Gerhard Ebeling, *Word and Faith* (London: SCM Press and Philadelphia: Fortress Press, 1963), p. 47.

3. In verse 4b I have translated the verb "has been raised" instead of "was raised" because the Greek has a perfect form whereas the other three verbs (died, was buried, appeared) are in the aorist. Perhaps this reflects a deliberate emphasis on the present and continuing significance of the resurrection in Paul. Cf. Paul's frequent use of the perfect participle in "Christ crucified," which seems to indicate the existential presence of Christ for the apostle: 1 Cor. 1:23, 2:2; Gal. 3:1.

4. The Greek word *ektroma* alludes to Paul's sudden and unexpected "birth" into the apostolic family.

5. N. T. Wright, *The Resurrection of the Son of God* (Minneapolis: Fortress Press, 2003), somewhat desperately sees a reference to the empty tomb in this phrase. "The best hypothesis for why 'that he was buried' came to be part of this brief tradition is simply that the phrase summarized very succinctly that entire moment in the Easter narratives" (p. 321). Since the result of his study very much depends on the pillar of the empty tomb, I am puzzled by the laxity of his analysis at this point.

6. Wright, *The Resurrection of the Son of God*, sees it differently. "Precisely because this is such an early formulation there is no chance that this word could have been a proper name without connotation, and every reason to suppose that the early Christians intended it to have its royal des-

ignation" (pp. 319–20). This reasoning cannot reverse the linguistic fact. Further, it is doubtful that Gentile Christians in Antioch—the possible origin of the formula in 1 Cor. 15:3–5—were aware of any Messianic connotation of the name "Christos."

7. Cf. Acts 6–11. See further my *Paul: The Founder of Christianity* (Amherst, NY: Prometheus Books, 2002), pp. 259–82.

8. What follows is in implicit dialogue with a verdict of C. F. Evans, *Resurrection and the New Testament* (London: SCM Press, 1970), which is to my mind too skeptical, namely in his claim that "Paul nowhere in his letters elaborates on what he means by 'seeing the Lord' (it is not clear that Gal. 1.16 refers to this at all; the meaning may be 'to reveal his Son through me to the Gentiles'), and the argument of I Cor. 15 is not sufficiently precise, nor the two parts of it sufficiently closely linked, to be able to deduce from the exposition of the spiritual body of Christians how Paul thought of the risen body of Christ or of the nature of his appearance" (p. 56).

9. James M. Robinson, "Jesus from Easter to Valentinus," *Journal of Biblical Literature* 101 (1982): 7.

10. Ibid.

11. Cf. ibid.

12. On the historical reliability of the book of Acts concerning the "conversion" of Paul, see my *Paul: The Founder of Christianity*, pp. 184–86.

13. Rev. 1:10.

14. See Job 4:12–16; Isa. 6; Dan. 10:4–21; Ezek. 1:1–3:15; Amos 7:1–9.

15. See only 1 En. 14; 4 Ezra 3:1–9:25.

16. See the examples in Adolf Deissmann, *Light from the Ancient East: The New Testament Illustrated by Recently Discovered Texts from the Graeco-Roman World* (New York: George H. Doran, 1927; repr. Peabody, MA: Hendrickson Publishers, 1995).

17. See 2 Cor. 12:2–4; Acts 7:55–56; Rev. 1:13–16. The most recent and thorough work on "Paul the visionary" is the one in German by Bernhard Heininger, *Paulus als Visionär: Eine religionsgeschichtliche Studie* (Freiburg: Herder, 1996). See further my *Paul: The Founder of Christianity*, pp. 176–92.

18. For the recent (in)famous example of Susan Atkins—she was involved with Charles Manson in a series of murders in California in the 1970s—who saw Jesus in a vision and thus gained a new orientation in her life, see Michael Goulder, "The Baseless Fabric of Visions," in *Resurrection Reconsidered*, ed. Gavin D'Costa (Oxford: Oneworld Publications, 1996), pp. 48–61.

19. See R. C. Finucane, *Appearances of the Dead: A Cultural History of Ghosts* (Buffalo, NY: Prometheus Books, 1984). Consider his observation, "Even though ghosts and apparitions may exist only in the minds of their percipients, the fact of that existence is a social and historical reality: the phenomena represent man's inner universe just as his art and poetry do" (p. 1). Also note his concluding sentences, "This study has tried to show how changes in social assumptions, particularly those associated with theological opinions and scientific accomplishments, affected the ways that the living envisaged their dead in England and Europe. Each epoch has perceived its spectres according to specific sets of expectations; as these things change so too do the spectres. From this point of view it is clear that the suffering soul of purgatories in the days of Aquinas, the shade of the murdered mistress in Charles II's era, and the silent grey ladies of Victoria's reign represent not beings of that other world, but of this" (p. 223).

20. Eric Robertson Dodds, *The Greeks and the Irrational* (Berkeley and Los Angeles: University of California Press, 1951), p. 102. The whole of chapter 4 ("Dream Pattern and Culture-Pattern"[pp. 102–34]) is important for our discussion at this point.

21. For the following paragraphs, see my *Virgin Birth? The Real Story of Mary and Her Son Jesus* (London: SCM Press and Harrisburg: Trinity Press International, 1998), and in addition the helpful survey by Rosemary Ellen Guiley, *The Encyclopedia of Ghosts and Spirits* (New York/Oxford: Facts on File, 1992), pp. 214–17 ("Marian apparitions").

22. A. J. M. Wedderburn, *Beyond Resurrection* (London: SCM Press, 1999), in all seriousness regards it as possible "that he (Jesus) was not really dead" (p. 97). He thus wants to avoid "a dogmatism that is not in keeping with the agnosticism which the nature of the evidence demands" (ibid.).

23. The *Epistle of the Apostles* (on this document see below, pp. 134–35) 9:3 places the burial "in a place called the place of a skull." The "place of the skull" according to the four gospels is the place where Jesus was crucified (Mark 15:22; Matt. 27:33; Luke 23:33; John 19:17) and John 19:41 relates that Jesus' tomb was close to the place where he was crucified. Therefore the author of the *Epistle of the Apostle* likely derived his information about the place of Jesus' burial from a harmonization of the New Testament gospels.

24. Mark 14:55, 15:1.

25. Mark 4:11.

26. Mark 12:34.

27. See Mark 1:15.

28. Note the change of terminology: verse 45 says that Pilate had the corpse (*ptoma*) of Jesus given to Joseph. In verse 43 Joseph had asked for the body (*soma*) of Jesus.

29. See Num. 5:2, 9:6–7.

30. Cf. Luke 2:41–52; Acts 3–4; 16:3, 21:26.

31. See John 7:13, 9:22, 20:19 (cf. 12:42); Gospel of Peter 12:50.

32. For "he came" cf. Matt. 27:57 (Mark 15:43; Luke 23:52).

33. Cf. John 18:1. For the subsequent history of the traditions of the garden, see Robert M. Price, "Jesus' Burial in a Garden: The Strange Growth of the Tradition," *Religious Traditions* 12 (1989): 17–30.

34. Cf. Raymond E. Brown, *The Death of the Messiah: A Commentary on the Passion Narratives in the Four Gospels*, 2 vols. (New York: Doubleday, 1994), 2:1317–49.

35. Eusebius *Ecclesiastical History* 6.12.1–6.

36. Eusebius *Ecclesiastical History* 6.12.6.

37. Eusebius *Ecclesiastical History* 6.12.3.

38. Brown, *The Death of the Messiah*, p. 1232.

39. Cf. Deut. 21:23; Josh. 8:29, 10:27

40. See Acts 2:23, 3:13–15, 4:27, 5:30, 7:52, 10:39, 13:28.

41. On the other hand, John 19:31—the request of the Jews that the legs of the crucified ones be broken and that they might be taken away—does not reflect an independent tradition but was formulated on the basis of John 19:38 as the introduction to John 19:31–37 (see Frank Schleritt, in my *Jesus After Two Thousand Years: What He Really Said and Did* [London: SCM Press, 2000 and Amherst, NY: Prometheus Books, 2001], pp. 571–73).

42. In NHC I.2 (5:10–19) the Savior Jesus says to the twelve apostles: "Do you not know that you have yet to be abused and to be accused unjustly; and have yet to be shut up in prison, and condemned unlawfully, and crucified <without> reason, and buried <shamefully>, as (was) I?" (James M. Robinson, gen. ed., *The Nag Hammadi Library in English*, 3d [completely revised] ed. [Leiden: E. J. Brill, 1988], p. 32 [Francis E. Williams]). Note that the literal translation of the last part is "quickly buried in the sand like me" which would enhance the dishonorable burial. Cf. Uwe-Karsten Plisch, in *Nag Hammadi Deutsch* 1. Band NHC I,1-V,1. Herausgegeben von Hans-Martin Schenke, Hans-Gebhard Bethke und Ursula Ulrike Kaiser (Berlin: Walter de Gruyter, 2001), p. 20n39.

43. See John 3:2.

44. Matt. 27:60; Gospel of Peter 6:24.

45. See 2 Kings 21:18, 26.

46. Martin Hengel, *Crucifixion in the Ancient World and the Folly of the Message of the Cross* (London: SCM Press and Philadelphia: Fortress Press, 1977), p. 87.

47. Translation based on *Philonis Alexandrini in Flaccum*, edited with an introduction and commentary by Herbert Box (London and New York: Oxford University Press, 1939), p. 31.

48. Cf., for example, Isa. 7:14 (Matt. 1:23), 8:23–9:1 (Matt. 4:15–16), 11:2 (1 Pet. 4:14), 40:3 (Matt. 3:3), 53:3–4 (Matt. 8:17). New Testament passages that use the various texts are put in parentheses.

49. Deut. 21:23.

50. See Tobit 1:18–20, 2:3–10. Cf. Kathleen E. Corley, *Women and the Historical Jesus: Feminist Myths of Christian Origins* (Santa Rosa: Polebridge Press, 2002), p. 117.

51. Cf. my *Jesus After Two Thousand Years*, pp. 100–102.

52. A. J. M. Wedderburn (*Beyond Resurrection* [London: SCM Press, 1999]) considers such a statement to be dogmatic although he grants that the decomposition of Jesus' corpse is more likely than the hypothesis that Jesus did not really die (p. 97). For me that ultimately amounts to splitting hairs.

53. Homer *Od.* 11.96. See the comments by Gregory J. Riley, *Resurrection Reconsidered: Thomas and John in Controversy* (Minneapolis: Fortress Press, 1995), p. 47.

54. Homer *Od.* 10.535–37, 11.48–50, 11.80.

55. Wright, *The Resurrection of the Son of God*, pp. 32–84, in a rich survey presents the mainstream opinion over against recent attempts by, for example, Stanley E. Porter, "Resurrection, the Greeks and the New Testament," in *Resurrection*, ed. Stanley E. Porter, Michael A. Hayes, and Davis Tombs (Sheffield: Sheffield Academic Press, 1999), pp. 52–81, who tries to demonstrate "that, in fact, the Greeks did have a significant tradition of bodily resurrection that has been neglected in discussion of the resurrection in the New Testament" (p. 53).

56. Aeschylus *Eumenides* 647–48.

57. Greek mythological hero who after his premature death in the Trojan War was allowed by the gods to return to his bride, Laodameia, for three hours from the underworld.

58. Minucius Felix *Octavius* 11.7–9.

59. See Plato *Phaedo* 80–82; *Phaedrus* 245c–247c; *Meno* 81a–e.

60. See Wright, *The Resurrection of the Son of God*, p. 34.

61. On Philo's notion of the immortality of the soul, see ibid., pp. 144–46.

62. See 4 Macc. 9:8, 13:16, 15:2, 17:5, 18, 18:23, and see further, Emil Schürer, *The History of the Jewish People in the Age of Jesus Christ (175 B.C.–A.D. 135)*, rev. and ed. Geza Vermes, Fergus Millar, and Matthew Black (Edinburgh: T & T Clark, 1979), 2:540 n. 93.

63. For the origin of Israelite belief in the resurrection, see Wright, *The Resurrection of the Son of God*, pp. 124–27. The old thesis that Jews borrowed it from Zoroastrianism—the official religion of the Persian Empire— has been recently defended by Colleen McDannell and Bernhard Lang, *Heaven: A History* (New Haven, CT, and London: Yale University Press, 1988), pp. 12–14.

64. I pass over miracles of resurrection performed by Elishah (2 Kings 4:8–37) and by his dead bones (2 Kings 13:21), which meant a resuscitation to life with a subsequent death and not resurrection to immortal life.

65. Ps. 137 seems to reflect the captivity in Babylon. See verse 1: "By the waters of Babylon, there we sat down and wept. . . ."

66. Cf. Adela Yarbro Collins, *The Beginning of the Gospel: Probings of Mark in Context* (Minneapolis: Fortress Press, 1992), p. 126. See further, John J. Collins, *Daniel: A Commentary on the Book of Daniel, Hermeneia* (Minneapolis: Fortress Press, 1993), p. 398: "The stereotypical assumption that resurrection in a Jewish context was always bodily is in need of considerable qualification."

67. Cf. 1 Thess. 4:13.

68. See Collins, *The Beginning of the Gospel*, p. 126.

69. Translation following James H. Charlesworth, ed., *The Old Testament Pseudepigrapha*, vol. 2, *Expansions of the "Old Testament" and Legends, Wisdom and Philosophical Literature, Prayers, Psalms, and Odes, Fragments of Lost Judeo-Hellenistic Works* (New York: Doubleday, 1985), p. 102 (O. S. Wintermute).

70. Ibid. Another—in my view less probable—way of understanding the verse is to see it as "an example of poetic hyperbole, describing those who die with assurance that justice has been done. They are portrayed as joyous dead who lie in the earth contented with God's certain vindication of the righteous" (ibid.).

71. See the *Second Book of Maccabees* (esp. 2 Macc. 7:11: the martyr expresses his hope to get his hands again) and the comments by Wright, *The Resurrection of the Son of God*, pp. 150–62, and Martin Hengel, "Das Begräbnis Jesu bei Paulus und die leibliche Auferstehung aus dem Grabe," in *Auferstehung—Resurrection*, ed. Friedrich Avemarie and Hermann Lichtenberger (Tübingen: J. C. B. Mohr [Paul Siebeck], 2001), pp. 158–64.

72. See note 64.

73. Hengel, "Das Begräbnis Jesu bei Paulus," would even argue that Matt. 27:52–53 presupposes the *descensus ad inferos*: the region where the bodies of the deceased saints have been waiting for the general resurrection (pp. 172–73).

74. John Dominic Crossan, "Empty Tomb and Absent Lord (Mark 16:1–8)," in *The Passion in Mark: Studies in Mark 14–16*, ed. Werner H. Kelber (Philadelphia: Fortress Press, 1976), p. 136.

75. Ibid.

76. Harvey K. McArthur; "On the Third Day (1 Cor 15,4b and Rabbinic Interpretation of Hosea 6,2)," *New Testament Studies* 18 (1971/72): 81–86.

77. Martin Hengel, "Das Begräbnis Jesu bei Paulus," pp. 132–33.

78. This argument counters the fanciful presumption that "something did indeed happen on that first day of the week, something that initially involved some of Jesus' female followers, and something that loomed so large and ranked as so important in the memory of the early Christians that they held this day of the week to be their Lord's special day and theirs too. The evidence points to something having happened on that day, but it does not tell us what exactly that something was: it may simply have been a fruitless search for a body" (Wedderburn, *Resurrection Reconsidered*, p. 65). These remarks stand in stark contrast to the historical agnosticism that the author displays in other passages (see pp. 141n22, 143n52).

79. See *New Testament Apocrypha*, rev. ed., ed. Wilhelm Schneemelcher, *II Writings Related to the Apostles, Apocalypses and Related Subjects* (Louisville: Westminster John Knox Press, 1992), pp. 34–41 (W. Schneemelcher).

80. Clement of Alexandria *Stromateis* 6.6.48 (translation following *New Testament Apocrypha II*, p. 39).

81. See Martina Janssen, "Mystagogus Gnosticus? Zur Gattung der 'gnostischen Gespräche des Auferstandenen'," in *Studien zur Gnosis*, ed. Gerd Lüdemann (Frankfurt: Peter Lang, 1999), pp. 21–260.

82. For the analysis of Acts 2:1–13, see my *Early Christianity according to the Traditions in Acts: A Commentary* (London: SCM Press and Minneapolis: Fortress Press, 1989), pp. 37–43.

83. See Exod. 19:16–19; Num. 11:25; Deut. 4:11.

84. Hans Conzelmann, *Acts of the Apostles: A Commentary on the Acts of the Apostles. Hermeneia* (Philadelphia: Fortress Press, 1987), p. 16.

85. Cf. verses 6, 8.

86. Cf. Acts 17:32; 28:24.

87. See Luke 24:29.

88. Cf. Acts 8:14–24,19:1–7.

89. The Levite Barnabas is *Kyprios to genei* (Acts 4:36; cf. 11:20); cf. also *apo pantos ethnous* (Acts 2:5) and *te idia dialekto* (2:8).

90. Conzelmann, *Acts of the Apostles,* p. 15.

91. Hans-Josef Klauck, *Magic and Paganism in Early Christianity: The World of the Acts of the Apostles* (Edinburgh: T & T Clark, 2000), p. 8.

92. Thus apparently Conzelmann, *Acts of the Apostles,* p. 16.

93. Ibid.

94. See Gustave Le Bon, *The Crowd: A Study of the Popular Mind* (New York: Viking Press, 1960), p. 29.

95. Ibid., p. 67.

96. Ibid., p. 41.

97. Ibid., pp. 41–42.

98. Paul Wilhelm Schmiedel, "Resurrection- and Ascension-Narratives," *Encyclopaedia biblica* (London: A. and C. Black, 1903), 4:188–89.

99. Translation following *New Testament Apocrypha,* vol. 1, *Gospels and Related Writings,* rev. ed. Wilhelm Schneemelcher, English translation ed. R. McL. Wilson (Louisville: Westminster John Knox Press, 1991), p. 178. For parallel texts, cf. A. F. J. Klijn, *Jewish-Christian Gospel Tradition* (Leiden: E. J. Brill, 1992), pp. 80–83.

100. Wilhelm Pratscher, *Der Herrenbruder Jakobus und die Jakobustradition* (Göttingen: Vandenhoeck & Ruprecht, 1987), p. 47.

101. See Mark 3:21 and my *Jesus After Two Thousand Years,* pp. 23–25.

102. Cf. Carsten Colpe, *Das Siegel der Propheten. Historische Beziehungen zwischen Judentum, Judenchristentum und Islam* (Berlin: Verlag Kirche und Judentum, 1990), p. 85, and my *Opposition to Paul in Jewish Christianity* (Minneapolis: Fortress Press, 1989), pp. 40–63, 119–28.

103. See the careful discussion by Robert H. Gundry, *Mark: A Commentary on His Apology for the Cross* (Grand Rapids, MI: William B. Eerdmans, 1993), pp. 1009–21.

104. See Acts 20:7; Rev. 1:10; 1 Cor. 16:2 (?).

105. Cf. John 20:11a; Gospel of Peter 12:52–53.

106. Cf. Mark 1:31.

107. Other examples of such Markan frameworks are: 1:21–28 to 6:1–6 (miracle), 6:30–44 to 8:1–9 (feeding story), 8:22–26 to 10:46–52 (healing of a blind man), 15:40–41 to 15:47 (list of women).

108. Cf. other passages with double indications of time in Mark: 1:32, 35; 4:35; 10:30; 13:24; 14:21, 30, 45; 15:42.

109. Similarly the beloved disciple remains longer with Jesus than the other disciples (John 19:26) and is the author of the Fourth Gospel (John 21:24).

110. 2 Macc. 3:26, 33: Two young men in radiant garments take action against Heliodorus, the plunderer of the temple.

111. See Tob. 5:5, 7, 10.

112. Cf. John 21:6, etc.

113. Cf. Dan.7:9; Rev. 21:5.

114. One must always be aware of the fact that the Gospel of Mark was circulating in different versions with Matthew and Luke using a different copy from the one available to us. Further, the "Secret Gospel of Mark" might derive from still another version. See Marvin Meyer, *Secret Gospels: Essays on the Gospel of Thomas and the Secret Gospel of Mark* (Harrisburg: Trinity Press International, 2003), pp. 107–78. For example, Mark 14:51–52 may be related to a later edition of Mark's gospel.

115. Mark 8:31, 9:31, 10:34.

116. Cf. Mark 1:24, 10:47, 14:67.

117. Cf. Acts 9:2; 19:23; 22:4; 24:14, 22.

118. Cf. the similar duplication in Mark 14:50.

119. Cf. 1 Cor. 15:5: "(Christ) appeared to Cephas, then to the Twelve."

120. I concur with Michael Goulder, "The Baseless Fabric of a Vision," pp. 57–58. See also my *Primitive Christianity: A Survey of Recent Studies and Some New Proposals* (London/New York: T & T Clark, 2003), pp. 52–54, for comments on a book by Michael Goulder (*A Tale of Two Missions* [London: SCM Press, 1994] US edition, *St. Paul versus St. Peter: A Tale of Two Missions* [Louisville: Westminster John Knox Press, 1995]), where the author develops the thesis more broadly.

121. Here the parallel passages follow in parentheses the corresponding verses of the conclusion or "long ending" of Mark: verses 9–10 (Luke 8:2; John 20:1, 11–18); verse 11 (Luke 24:11); verses 12–13 (Luke 24:13–35); verse 14 (Luke 24:36–43; Acts 1:4); verses 15–16 (Luke 24:47); verses 17–18 (Acts 16:16–18, 2:1–11, 28:3–6, 3:1–10, 9:31–35, 14:8–10, 28:8–9); verse 19 (Acts 1:9, Luke 24:51); verse 20 (Acts generally; Heb. 2:3–4). On Mark 16:9–20, see the impressive study by James A. Kelhoffer, *Miracle and Mission: The Authentication of Missionaries and Their Message in the Longer Ending of Mark* (J. C. B. Mohr/Paul Siebeck: Tübingen, 2000).

122. Cf. only "gathered" (26:3, 57; 27:17, 27; 28:12).

123. For the increased tension between "Christians" and the official

representatives of Judaism, see Matt. 23:1–13, 15–38 and Mark 12:38–40. See below on Matt. 28:13.

124. They are identical with those of Matt. 27:61.

125. After the women's presence at the tomb reported in Matt. 27:61 ("they sat opposite the tomb"), the phrase "going to see the tomb" is quite puzzling.

126. Cf. 2 Kings 4:21.

127. Though the guards did not observe the process of resurrection, which Matthew did not narrate, what they actually saw did not allow any other conclusion.

128. Matt. 27:63.

129. Matt. 27:65.

130. Cf. Eusebius *Ecclesiastical History* 4.18.7.

131. Joseph McCabe, *The Myth of the Resurrection and Other Essays* (Amherst, NY: Prometheus Books, 1993), p. 27. Note the author's sarcastic comment: "But, of course, this is only '*if* it comes to the governor's ears' (v. 14); and a trifle such as a resurrection from the dead, in a quiet city like Jerusalem, was not likely to reach his ears."

132. Cf. Matt. 5:1, 15:29, 17:21.

133. Jesus says to the sinking Peter, "O man of little faith, why did you doubt?"

134. Cf. Luke 24:11, 25, 37–38, 41; John 20:29.

135. See Matt. 4:3, 8:19, 9:28, etc.

136. Cf. Matt. 11:27a; John 3:35; Phil 2:9–11.

137. See Matt. 6:10, 16:19, 18:18.

138. Cf. Matt. 13:52, 27:57.

139. Gal. 3:27.

140. 1 Cor. 1:13; Acts 8:16, 19:5.

141. To be sure, the combination of God, Jesus, and Spirit has already been prepared for by Paul (2 Cor. 1:21–22, 13:13; 1 Cor. 12:4–6).

142. "Fulfill," "all," "command," "remember" (cf. 28:9); "end of the world" (13:39–40, 49; 24:3).

143. Hans Dieter Betz, "Zum Problem der Auferstehung im Lichte der griechischen magischen Papyri," Betz, *Hellenismus und Urchristentum. Gesammelte Aufsätze I* (Tübingen: J. C. B. Mohr [Paul Siebeck], 1990), p. 251.

144. Cf. Luke 2:49; Acts 1:11. In both cases, as in Luke 24:5b, the question expresses blame.

145. This last sentence is not contained in important manuscripts. For the question of the originality of this reading, see the commentary on verse 12.

146. Accordingly Luke has not picked up Mark 14:28–29.

147. For the parallel John 20:3–10, see above, p. 120.

148. Cf. Luke 22:23; Acts 6:9.

149. Only he uses the Greek word for "before" which appears here: see Luke 1:6, 20:26; Acts 7:10, 8:32 (Isa. 53:7).

150. Cf. Acts 7:51–53 and the exoneration of Pilate in Luke's passion narrative.

151. See Luke 1:68, 2:38; Acts 1:6.

152. See the end of Acts.

153. See Acts 8:35.

154. Cf. Rev. 3:20.

155. The explicit statement that the one who appears vanishes is typical of the third evangelist: Luke 1:38, 2:15, 9:33; Acts 10:7, 12:10.

156. "Christ appeared to Cephas, then to the Twelve."

157. See Peter's speeches in Acts 2:14–40, 3:12–26.

158. Hermann Gunkel, *Zum religionsgeschichtlichen Verständnis des Neuen Testaments* (Göttingen: Vandenhoeck & Ruprecht, 1903), p. 71.

159. Apart from Gen. 18:1–15 to which Gunkel alludes, see Judg. 6:11–24. See further, Tobit 5.

160. Ovid *Metamorphoses* 8.616–724 (Philemon and Baucis).

161. Eusebius *Ecclesiastical History* 3.11, 4.22.4

162. That the disciples did look at them is assumed, but not made explicit.

163. Translation based on William R. Schoedel, *Ignatius of Antioch: A Commentary on the Letters of Ignatius of Antioch. Hermeneia* (Philadelphia: Fortress Press, 1985), p. 225.

164. Cf. To the Magnesians 7:1: "The Lord did nothing without the Father, since he was united with him." On Ignatius's place in the history of earliest Christianity's credal tradition, see my *Heretics: The Other Side of Early Christianity* (London: SCM Press and Louisville: Westminster John Knox Press, 1996), pp. 187–89.

165. Cf. Tob. 12:19.

166. See Hans Dieter Betz, "Zum Problem der Auferstehung Jesu," Betz, *Hellenismus und Urchristentum. Gesammelte Aufsätze* I (Tübingen: J. C. B. Mohr/Paul Siebeck, 1991), pp. 249–50.

167. See John 20:24–29; 1 John 1:1, 4:1–2; 2 John 7.

168. See 1 Cor. 15:35: "But some one will ask: 'How are the dead raised? With what kind of body do they come?'" See my *Primitive Christianity: A Survey of Recent Studies and Some New Proposals* (London/New York: T & T Clark, 2003), pp. 160–61.

169. David Friedrich Strauss, *The Old Faith and the New,* 2 vols., introduction and notes by G. A. Wells (Amherst, NY: Prometheus Books, 1997), 1:80–81.

170. See Luke 24:27.

171. Cf. Acts 2:32–33, 38; 3:15–16, 19; 5:28–32; 10:39, 43.

172. Cf. Acts 1:22

173. See the time-references in Luke 24:1 ("at dawn on the first day of the week"), 13 ("that same day"), 33 ("immediately"), 36 ("as they were discussing these events"), 44 ("then").

174. See Exod. 24:18, 34:28; 1 Kings 14:8.

175. See Acts 13:31.

176. Luke 2:46.

177. Acts 2:46, 3:1, 5:42.

178. Luke 1:65–66, 80; 2:20, 40, 52; Acts 1:14.

179. Here and later in the present section on the Gospel of John, an asterisk designates text without later revisions.

180. Mark 16:6; Matt. 28:6; Luke 24:6.

181. Mark 16:7; Matt. 28:7.

182. Matt. 28:9–10.

183. Cf. John 7:9; 9:6; 11:11, 28, 43; 18:1, 38; 20:22.

184. Cf. Matt. 27:62–66; 28:11–15, where the same suspicion is dismissed by other means.

185. Cf. Gen. 2:7; Ezek. 37:5–10, 14; Ws. 15:1.

186. Cf., e.g., John 14:16, 26; 16:7, 13; 7:39.

187. Cf. Luke 24:49; Acts 2.

188. Cf. John 1:42.

189. Cf. John 11:27.

190. Cf. John 5:18, 10:30.

191. Cf. John 6:30, 36, etc.

192. Cf. Luke 24:11, 21ff., 37–38, 41; Matt. 28:17.

193. Anton Dauer, *Johannes und Lukas* (Würzburg: Echter Verlag, 1984), p. 253.

194. Gregory J. Riley, *Resurrection Reconsidered: Thomas and John in Controversy* (Minneapolis: Fortress Press, 1995), pp. 100–26.

195. On this question, see below, p. 180.

196. Cf. John 20:24.

197. Cf. John 1:45–49.

198. Cf. the seven communities in Rev. 2–3.

199. Cf. Luke 5:5.

200. Cf. John 20:20:4; Luke 24:16.

201. Cf. Luke 5:4–6.

202. Cf. John 13:23–26a.

203. Cf. John 1:42.

204. Cf. John 10:1–18.

205. John 18:17, 25–27.

206. Cf. Matt. 16:17–19; Luke 22:32.

207. For practical reasons the description of how Jesus left the tomb was already examined in an earlier section (see above, pp. 93–94). The most recent and thorough analysis of The Gospel of Peter 12:50–14:60 is by Jozef Verheyden, "Silent Witnesses: Mary Magdalene and the Women at the Tomb in the Gospel of Peter," in R. Bieringer, V. Koperski, and B. Lataire, eds., *Resurrection in the New Testament. Festschrift J. Lambrecht* (Leuven: University Press, 2002), pp. 457–82 (lit.).

208. Cf. Gospel of Peter 9:35.

209. Corley, *Women & the Historical Jesus*, p. 135.

210. Cf. John 20:11a: "Mary Magdalene stood weeping outside the tomb."

211. For Gospel of Peter 10:39–41 see above, pp. 93–94.

212. Verheyden, "Silent Witnesses," p. 477.

213. See further John 13:1, 3; 16:28.

214. Cf. Gospel of Peter 7:26–27.

215. Cf. Gospel of Peter 12:52 and 12:54.

216. See Verheyden, "Silent Witnesses," for details.

217. Cf. Julian Hills, *Tradition and Composition in the Epistula Apostolorum* (Minneapolis: Fortress Press, 1990), pp. 1–9. My translation is in general based on the Coptic text reprinted by Judith Hartenstein, *Die zweite Lehre. Erscheinungen des Auferstandenen als Rahmenerzählungen frühchristlicher Dialoge* (Berlin: Akademie Verlag, 2000), pp. 108–110 and the English translation in *New Testament Apocrypha*, vol. I, pp. 254–56.

218. John 20:24–29.

219. Cf. also the affirmation of the apostles at the beginning of their "letter" which is preserved only in the Ethiopic translation, chapter 2: "We have heard and felt him after he had risen from the dead."

220. Hills, *Tradition and Composition in the Epistula Apostolorum*, p. 88.

221. Ibid., p. 91, where Hills discusses further examples of the footprint motif.

4

The Faith of the Early Christians in Jesus' Resurrection

Origin and History of a Self-deception

The only real tyrants that humanity has known have always been the memories of its dead or the illusions it has forged itself.[1]

Of all the forces at the disposal of humanity, faith has always been one of the most tremendous, and the Gospel rightly attributes to it the power of moving mountains. To endow a man with faith is to multiply his strength tenfold. The great events of history have been brought about by obscure believers, who have little beyond their faith in their favour. It is not by the aid of the learned or of philosophers, and still less of sceptics, that have been built up the great religions which have swayed the world, or the vast empires which have spread from one hemisphere to the other.[2]

I n this chapter, I want to focus on the origin of the belief in Jesus' resurrection and narrate its history in the first century. The analyses in the previous chapters have produced two important results: First, the confession that God has raised Jesus from the dead is rooted in Peter's ecstatic vision of Jesus in his heavenly glory, which he received sometime after Good Friday. Second, the only other person in earliest Christianity who had a similar primary experience of the "Risen One" is Paul. Thus the discovery of the origin of the faith in Jesus' resurrection is really the quest for the origin and nature of these two transformational experiences. I commence with that of Peter, continue with that of Paul, and afterward reconstruct the early history of the faith in Jesus' resurrection. Thereby I take fully into account that though initiated by individuals, the earliest Christian faith involved the witness of a group and therefore cannot be understood as the sum of unique personal experiences.

THE ORIGIN OF THE SELF-DECEPTION

The primary witness Peter and his vision

Peter's vision

1 Cor. 15:5a contains a formula describing the first appearance to Peter, a statement that is also reflected in the "cry of Easter jubilation" in Luke 24:34. This corresponds to Peter's status as the uncontested leader of the earliest Jerusalem community. We read in Gal. 1:18 that Paul, three years after his conversion near Damascus, visited Peter in Jerusalem. The probable explanation for such a visit is that Paul wanted to become acquainted with the leader of the new messianic group, and undoubtedly the conferral of this leadership had been legitimized by a direct experience of the "Risen One." Thus 1 Cor. 15:5 should be tied to that event.

Apart from 1 Cor. 15:5, we do not have any clear texts that derive from Peter's vision of the heavenly Jesus. Yet there are some stories about the earthly Jesus that may well be Easter narratives reassigned to Jesus' lifetime. Two examples are Luke 5:1–11 and Matt. 16:17–19, which we shall now proceed to investigate.

Luke 5:1–11: Fragments of Peter's "Easter" vision

(1) *Once when he [Jesus] was standing by Lake Gennesaret with the crowd pressing around him to hear the word of God, (2) he saw two boats lying on the shore, but the fishermen had got out of them and were washing their nets. (3) He got into one of the boats, the one that*

belonged to Simon, and asked him to go out a little way from the shore. And he sat down and taught the multitude from the boat.

(4) When he had finished speaking, he said to Simon, "Go out into the deep water, and cast your nets for a catch." (5) And Simon answered and said, "*Master*, we have worked all night and caught nothing; but if you say the word, I will let down the nets." (6) And when they did, they caught *such a great mass of fish* that their nets began to tear. (7) And they beckoned to their partners in the other boat to come and pull with them. And they came and filled both boats so full that they were [almost] sinking. (8) When Simon Peter *saw* that, he fell at Jesus' feet and said, "Lord, keep away from me, for I am a sinful man!" (9) For *he was amazed and fearful*, as were his crew, at the catch they had made, (10a) and so were his partners James and John, the sons of Zebedee. (10b) And Jesus said to Simon, "Don't be afraid, from now on you will be catching people."

(11) And they brought the boats to land *and left everything and followed him.*

LUKE'S PURPOSE

This call story follows less from the events in Capernaum (Luke 4:31–44) than from the Nazareth story (Luke 4:16–30), to which it provides the positive complement. The rejection of Jesus by his neighbors forms the background for the description of the appropriate relationship to Jesus: one that comes about through a calling.

Verses 1–3: The exposition is based on Mark 1:16–20 and 4:1–2. A crowd appears—in good redactional style—and presses in on Jesus. "Word of God" in verse 1 echoes the two references to Jesus' "words" (speech) in the previous passage (4:32, 36). Luke takes the expression "the word of God" from the Christian tradition[3] and from Paul's writings.[4] The mention of the two boats in verse 2 prepares for verse 7.

Verse 4: First the main character, Simon, is addressed, and then the whole group (cf. verse 9).

Verse 5: The description of the fruitless effort prepares for the great miracle. For "word" see above on verse 1. Peter's obedience was prepared for by 4:38–39.

Verses 6–7: The miracle is effected by the power of Jesus' word.

Verse 8: This verse conflicts with what has gone before. Peter can hardly fall at Jesus' feet nor expect him to keep away in a boat that is about to founder. Nor does his confession of sinfulness bear any relation to the miracle (see further on verse 10b).

Verses 9–10a: Here we see reactions to the miracle. Verse 10a is an appendix in which, on the basis of Mark 1:19, Luke has inserted the sons of Zebedee among those who are amazed at the miracle.

Verse 10b: This is also in tension with the context, since it refers to Peter's missionary activity after Easter. We must assume that verses 8 and 10b were connected in the tradition (see below).

Verse 11: Verse 11a concludes the story; verse 11b is an insertion that does not square with verse 10b, which records no general invitation to discipleship. Verse 11 turns the whole story into a call that is set within Jesus' lifetime.

THE TRADITION REWORKED BY LUKE

On the basis of the tensions within Luke's story, we can probably reconstruct the narrative thus:

a) The oldest discernable element is a miracle story reflected in verses 4b–7, 9, 11a. It ran roughly as follows:

> (4b) (Jesus said to Simon,) "Put out into the deep, and cast your nets for a catch." (5) And Simon answered and said, "We have worked all night and caught nothing; but at your word I will let down the nets." (6) And when they did that, they caught such a great mass of fish that their nets began to fail. (7) So they beckoned to their partners in the other boat to come and to pull with them. And they came and filled both boats almost to the point of sinking. (9) (And all were delighted) about this catch which they had made together. (11) And they brought the boats to land.

b) At a later stage, but before Luke learned the story, verses 8 and 10a were added, turning the miracle story into an Easter narrative.

c) On the basis of Mark 1:16–20, Luke added verses 1–4a, 10 and 11b.

THE RELATIONSHIP OF LUKE 5 TO JOHN 21

The miracle story at the heart of Luke 5:1–11 seems to be a variant of the miraculous catch narrative (John 21:2–4a, 6, 11) that forms the basis of John 21:1–14 (see above, pp. 124–28). Yet if Luke 5 and John 21 are based on the same miracle story, one is faced with a strange paradox: The authors of John 21 have transformed the miracle story into an Easter narrative—by placing it after the Easter stories of John 20 and combining it with a recognition legend—while Luke has found the miraculous catch of fish as an Easter story but has relocated it within Jesus' lifetime.

Matt. 16:17b–19: The "Easter" commission to Peter

[Peter's confession that Jesus is Christ, the son of the living God receives the following response by Jesus:] (17b) *"Blessed are you, Simon bar Jonah; for flesh and blood have not revealed [that] to you, but my Father in heaven.* (18) And I will also tell you that you are Peter [the Rock], and on this rock I will build my community, and the gates of hell shall not prevail against it. (19) *I will give you the keys of the kingdom of heaven:* and what you bind on earth shall also be bound in heaven, and what you loose on earth shall also be loosed in heaven."

MATTHEW'S PURPOSE

Verse 17b: The similarity of this verse to 11:25–27 and its transitional function (see 16:16 and 16:20) indicate a creation by the first evangelist.

Verses 18–19: In the context of the first gospel, this piece of tradition provides a basis for the authority of the community and its leader (cf. 18:15–18).

THE TRADITION REWORKED BY MATTHEW
AND ITS HISTORICAL VALUE

In his classic work, *The History of the Synoptic Tradition*, Rudolf Bultmann rightly defends the considerable antiquity of this passage. He writes,

> the Church preserved a tradition of a saying by Jesus in which Peter is promised authority in matters of doctrine, or authority.[5]

That follows, he argues, from the verbs "loose" and "bind" in verse 19. The whole idea of verse 18 points to earliest times:

> in the end, when the powers of the underworld overcome mankind, the church will be saved. Here the Palestinian Church expresses its eschatological consciousness of being the eschatological community of the Just.[6]

Later Bultmann expands his thoughts on Matt. 16:18-19:

> The words can hardly have been formulated in any other place than in the earliest Palestinian Church, where Peter was looked up to as the founder and leader of the Church and the blessing of Peter was put into the mouth of the risen Lord. . . . Peter's experience of Easter was the time when the early Church's messianic faith was born. . . . Just as Jn. 20:22f. is a parallel to Matt. 16:19 so the whole story of the confession has a clear parallel in the Easter story in Jn. 21:15-19.[7]

This view of Bultmann's has dominated the debate since. However, Ulrich Luz has raised important objections to it. Concerning Peter he writes,

> the more one emphasizes his position of primacy in the early church the more difficult it is to understand why he left Jerusalem and at the time of the apostolic council already was one (and not the first one mentioned!) of several pillars in the structure of the church (Gal. 2:9).[8]

In Luz's view the saying in Matt. 16:17–19 is at most a retrospective summation of Peter's activity.[9] In defending this thesis he adduces Eph. 2:10; Rev. 21:14; and the substantive parallel in John 21:15–17. Luz goes on to say:

> It was not through his leading role in the primitive church that Peter became the church's most important apostolic founding figure. Naturally it was important that the first appearance after Easter was to Peter and that he played a central role in the earliest Jerusalem church. However, it is indeed amazing that there is in the New Testament no detailed report about the first appearance to Peter and that his emerging leading role in the primitive Jerusalem church actually becomes important only in the late Book of Acts.[10]

Rebuttal: First, Luz does not pay enough attention to the *fundamental* changes within the Jerusalem church in the earliest period. Second, the traditions behind Eph. 2:20 and Rev. 2:20 that Luz adduces are more formulaic and colorless than the texts referred to by Bultmann in connection with a first appearance. In short, we must stick with Bultmann's reconstruction.

Furthermore, narratives about Peter's Easter experience were circulating in the communities. Differently from Paul's case, they were told as accounts of a first appearance and largely for this reason were evidently "chopped up" (as a result of changing situations and rivalries in the earliest Jerusalem community), and their elements set in other narrative contexts. Notwithstanding these changes, subsequent to the crucifixion Peter (like Paul later) had an auditory and visual experience of Jesus alive in his heavenly glory, and this experience was causally connected to the leadership of the church, the task of mission, and the authority to forgive sins.

We cannot be certain to what degree these last three points represented direct historical results of the appearance or arose subsequently from Peter's interpretation. Nor can we completely rule out that—consciously or not—a desire to forgive sins and to succeed Jesus as leader was the underlying stimulus behind this vision of Jesus.

Of course, in light of these statements one could dismiss the historical investigation as futile due to the paucity and unreliability of available sources. Yet as concerns Peter's "Easter" vision, the New Testament traditions may not have been exhausted. This is especially true of Peter's denial of Jesus, which is said to have occurred just after the latter's arrest. Luke 5:8 most likely reflects that tradition which, if historical, would suggest that the denial of Jesus *prior* to his death and the vision of Jesus subsequent to his death should be related in the interest of yielding deeper insight into the origin and nature of Peter's vision.[11]

Mark 14:54, 66–72: The prehistory of the "Easter" vision: Peter's denial of Jesus[12]

(54) And Peter had followed him at a distance right into the court-yard of the high priest, and sat there among the servants, keeping warm by the fire.

(66) Meanwhile, Peter was still below in the courtyard, when one of the maids of the high priest came by, (67) and seeing him there warming himself, she looked at him and said, "You also were with the Nazarene, Jesus." (68) But he <u>denied</u> it and said, "I don't know what you are talking about." Then he went out into the fore-court. (69) And the maid noticed him again and began to say to the bystanders, "This man is one of them." (70) And again he <u>denied</u> it. A little while later the bystanders said to Peter, "You must be one of them, for you are also a Galilean." (71) Then he began to curse, and with an oath he said, "I do not know this man you are talking about!" (72) *And immediately the cock crowed the second time. Then Peter remembered what Jesus had said to him: 'Before the rooster crows twice, you will <u>deny</u> me three times.' And he broke down and wept.*

MARK'S PURPOSE AND THE TRADITION REWORKED BY HIM

This episode harks back to the announcement of the denial (verses 26–31) and realizes the latter of Jesus' predictions there. Verse 54, which sets the scene, was intentionally placed by Mark to connect with the depiction of the events before the Supreme Council (verses 53, 55–65). Verse 66a ("when Peter was below in the courtyard") continues the interrupted story line. Mark's purpose in relating the denial to the events before the Supreme Council is to build contrast between Jesus' confession (14:62) and Peter's threefold denial, thereby entreating Christians to openly acknowledge their faith in Jesus' example.

Verses 66–68a: The *first* denial is portrayed in these verses. Strictly speaking, Peter denies only his discipleship; he does not yet repudiate Jesus. But since he disavows any knowledge of Jesus, the total denial of verse 71 is anticipated.

Verses 68b–70a: The *second* denial occurs in the forecourt. Once more the maid spots Peter and announces that Peter is one of Jesus' companions. Unlike the prior denial, the second is tersely declared, which suggests that the maid is not speaking to Peter and only telling the bystanders.

Verses 70b–71: Now the onlookers initiate an accusation endorsing the maid's report and based on the fact that like Jesus, Peter is a Galilean. This third denial is intensified by curses and an oath. At this moment the abjuration of Jesus is complete, and the prediction in 14:30 fulfilled.

Verse 72: This verse reconnects the denial to its prediction; and just as Mark's Jesus can foresee Peter's disavowal, so he already anticipates the "betrayal" of Judas[13] and his own death and resurrection.[14]

Whether the tradition available to Mark had one, two, or three denials remains unclear. What is certain is that he relied on a tradition that originally circulated independently of the passion story, for the link between the two derives from Mark's pen.

In all probability it was Peter himself who first reported his denial; "though not in connection with a description of the Passion so much as in connection with his Easter experience."[15] As an analogy, I would like to point to Paul's citation of a report on his hostile past and his present preaching of the gospel: "The one who once persecuted us now proclaims the faith which he sought to destroy."[16] Clearly this represents an oral tradition that circulated in the Syrian communities persecuted by Paul, and must have been known in the churches he had founded. Indeed, Paul explicitly notes that the Galatians know of his former zealotry.[17] In a similar way the present report of Peter's denial and his subsequent Easter experience amount to a "once it was, but now it is" formula. Both instances derive from personal traditions that correspond to historical facts.

HISTORICAL ELEMENTS

Scholars have challenged the historicity of Peter's denial.[18] Yet the criterion of offensiveness from historical Jesus research[19] applies here, for no Christian would have sullied the reputation of the leader of the Jerusalem church. Furthermore, we do not know of any opponent of Peter who might have created such a story. Therefore, the tradition of Peter denying Jesus during the latter's arrest has a solid historical foundation. Thus the following historical sequence unfolds itself: Jesus' arrest forced the disciples to flee Jerusalem. To preserve his life, Peter publicly disavowed association with his imprisoned leader.[20]

Possibly the denial had a prehistory. Let me try to put the puzzle together. In Mark 8:33b Jesus denounces his foremost disciple by shouting, "Get behind me, Satan! For you are not on the side of God, but of man!" Obviously the later Christian community cannot have created this denunciation of Peter, because it casts aspersions on the character of the first leader of the Jerusalem church. Then in what context does it belong? I propose that Jesus was reacting to Peter's suggestion that he adopt the role of a political messiah. This led to the sharp rebuke that identified Peter with Satan, whom Jesus—as he had said elsewhere—had seen fall like lightning from heaven.[21]

Likely enough strong tensions existed within the group on the decisive journey to Jerusalem, and among these were ambivalences between Jesus and his "first" disciple. The growth of this divergence of opinion is most reasonably dated to the Jerusalem journey. Soon enough another disciple—Judas—would even collaborate in Jesus' arrest although he did not "betray" him.[22]

Peter's "Easter" encounter: the result of unsuccessful mourning

So that we may visualize how, after denying Jesus, Peter saw him alive in heavenly glory, I shall now depict what might in all likelihood have happened within him between Good Friday and Easter. I am concerned with tracing this process, analyzing it with the help of modern psychological studies, in order to understand the rise of Easter faith.

With the dramatic events of Good Friday following close upon his denial of Jesus, Peter's world had collapsed. Then in the Easter event, despite everything that had happened, Jesus speaks again to a shattered and mourning Peter. As a consequence, Peter suddenly "saw" Jesus anew.

To recognize Peter's situation as one of mourning one need only peruse reports by other mourners, not a few of which attest to the image of a beloved person who has died. Yorick Spiegel[23] cites several cases:

> The grief sufferer hears the steps of the deceased on the stairway, hears the sand crunch in front of the house, and believes that the door opens. "I saw Kay standing just inside the front door, looking as he always had coming home from work. He smiled and I ran into his outstretched arms as I always had and leaned against his chest. I opened my eyes, the image was gone." A mother who has lost a baby may hear it cry while she is half asleep and rush to his bed before realizing that all of this was only a desire.[24]
>
> Children who have lost their father or mother very often tell in illustrative ways how their parents sit at the edge of the bed and talk to them. Almost half the patients [Colin Murray] Parkes[25] examined told about similar visual disturbances. Often shadows are perceived as visions of the deceased.[26]
>
> Not infrequent are auditory hallucinations; a creak at night or a sound at the door is interpreted as the husband moving about the house or coming home. One patient of Parkes's reported that she, while sitting in a chair, has the feeling the deceased caresses her ear and whispers that she should rest. In another study, widows reported that they hear their husband cough or call out at night.[27]
>
> Besides visual and auditory hallucinations, the feeling that the

dead person is present is an even more common phenomenon. Some of the widows told Parkes: "I still have the feeling he is near and there is something I ought to be doing for him or telling him . . . He is with me all the time, I hear him and see him, although I know it's only imagination"; "When I am washing my hair I have the feeling he is there to protect me in case someone comes in through the door." For some, the presence of the dead is particularly strong at his grave.[28]

To the category of breakdown of reality testing to prevent the loss belong the dreams about the deceased. . . . Widows are by far the most regular dreamers about the lost persons compared to the rest in the interviewed group of bereaved. . . . In the dream of the mourner a remarkable compromise is made between the desire that the deceased be alive again and the acceptance of the reality that he is lost. For the psychoanalytically trained, the bereaved's dreams are important information about the process of grief.[29]

Let me also cite two reports that were sent to the journal *Swiss Observer* (*Schweizerischer Beobachter*) in response to the question of whether readers had experienced appearances of spirits, intimations, etc. One woman's account is particularly germane:

When I was nine I lost my father. I was inconsolable and mourned him for many years. . . . Then one Christmas Eve I had gone to bed but had planned to go to Midnight Mass. It was just time for me to get up when I was overcome by terrible stomach colic and had to stay in bed. The pain soon passed off, but then it was too late for Mass. So I stayed in bed. Suddenly I heard the door open and there were soft footsteps with a strange noise of knocking—I was alone at home and was rather frightened. Then the miracle happened—my beloved father came towards me, shining and lovely as gold, and transparent as mist. He looked just as he did in life. I could recognise his features quite distinctly, then he stopped beside my bed and looked at my lovingly and smiled. A great peace entered into me and I felt happier than I had felt before. . . . Then he went away.[30]

Another woman's report is equally instructive:

In a neighboring village there was a very dear, religious woman whom I knew. I heard she had died and made up my mind to go to her funeral. It was on the day of the funeral, about eleven in the morning. I was just preparing the fire in the stove when suddenly I felt I was not alone—I turned round, and there this woman stood behind me. She was transparent but perfect in her glory and beauty. Her hair, gray in her lifetime, was wonderfully fair and curled halfway down her arms. Her face was clear and white, her eyes were shining, and her teeth in her smiling mouth were beautiful. Her dress, which reached up to her chin, and the sleeves which fell down over her wrists, were of an unearthly splendour.[31]

To use psychoanalytic terminology, one might say that the mind sometimes calls up unconscious memories under the dramatic stress of loss. The disintegration of the mourner's world often unleashes libidos and aggressive drives.[32] Frequently, questions of guilt gain intense magnitude during this regressive stage.[33] Here normal reality controls can break down when the unconscious is unable to bear the loss of a beloved person and creates artificial fulfillments for itself. Judged in this way, however, Peter's vision would be delusion or wishful thinking. Indeed, his vision is an example of unsuccessful mourning, because it abruptly cuts off the very process of mourning, substituting fantasy for unromantic reality.

Also instructive along these lines are investigations undertaken at Harvard into cases of mourning and the painful loss associated with them.[34] The researchers followed forty-three widows and nineteen widowers through the bereavement process, interviewing them at three weeks, eight weeks, and thirteen months after the spouse's death. The aim was to investigate what enabled people to work their way through the mourning process. Three primary factors were identified as inhibiting or preventing a successful passage through the mourning period: *first*, a sudden death; *second*, an ambivalent attitude toward the deceased, involving feelings of guilt; and *third*, a dependent relationship.

In the case of all the disciples, but especially that of Peter,[35] we should note that all three factors that inhibit grieving apply. *First*, Jesus' death was violent, unexpected, and sudden. *Second*, even the gospel accounts offer evidence that the relationship between the disciples and Jesus was colored by a sense of guilt and profound ambivalence: only recall that Judas was involved in Jesus' arrest and then committed suicide; that Peter denied him and wept bitterly. *Third*, the dependent relationship of the disciples to Jesus is evident in that most of them had given up their work and homes and families to be with him. This merging was clearly further magnified by their status as a tiny group that had effectively cast off its religious and social moorings, withdrawing from much of the larger culture.[36]

By a bold if unconscious leap Peter entered the world of his wishes. As a result he "saw" Jesus and thus made it possible for the other disciples to "see" Jesus as well. And if that was not enough, a few years later another Jew, Paul—later missionary to the Gentiles— "saw" Jesus, too, although he had never met him personally. The consequences of this vision have in large measure directed the course of Western civilization for almost two thousand years.

The primary witness Paul and his vision

Paul's vision again

Let me at the outset remind the reader of two crucial points. First, in Paul's mind his vision of Jesus put him on an equal footing with the other Easter witnesses. Second, the earlier characterization (see pp. 44–48) of his vision as esoteric and ecstatic, yet proceeding from within the mind of a visionary, must be central to any attempt to understand the nature and circumstances of the very first appearances.

Paul's vision—a Christ complex

In what follows I shall analyze—and thus, I hope, come to better understand—some of the conscious and unconscious motivations that resulted in Paul's dramatic adoption of the Christian faith. The question is, "What was the real reason for Paul's conversion?"[37]

Paul's pre-Christian period, which lasted until he was around thirty, had been characterized by a great zeal for the law (Phil. 3:6) and a sense of religious obligation that expressed itself in the persecution of Christians (Gal. 1:23). It is evident that this course of action was prompted by his condemnation of their proclamation of a crucified Messiah and, even more, his outrage at their *de facto* disregard of the Torah that was an all but inevitable concomitant of their social mingling with Gentile Christians from the time of Stephen and the Hellenists onward. It should be noted that Paul's active persecution of Christians came at a time when such leading Jews as his putative teacher Gamaliel seem to have been counseling a wait-and-see approach (Acts 5:38–39). In other words, it was not the case that early Christian preaching automatically generated anti-Christian oppression, but rather that the persecution of the new sect came from a particular Jewish group of which Paul was a particularly zealous member.

The sources tell us little about Paul's radical about-face from persecuting Christians to proclaiming Christ except to support the apparent fact that it was a both unexpected and sudden upheaval. Especially valuable in establishing this latter point, however, is Gal. 1:23 ("He who once persecuted us is now preaching the faith he once tried to destroy"), which as part of a thanksgiving to God attests to Christian surprise and satisfaction at an abrupt change of heart on the part of this erstwhile persecutor of Christians.

A passage from Paul's letter to the Romans (Rom. 7:7–25a) was for a long time taken to reflect the inner turmoil that led to his transformation, but that understanding is now generally repudiated. Three objections have been made to a biographical understanding of this ostensible "ego-analysis" by which Paul purports to describe his mental agitation before he turned to Christ: (a) The ego is a rhetorical or stylistic form, one commonly and effectively employed in the Psalms of the Hebrew Bible; (b) Rom. 7 is to be understood in the context of the letter: its retrospective form indicates a theological, not historical, description of the pre-Christian self; (c) In Phil. 3:6 ("as to righteousness under the law, blameless") and in Gal. 1:14, where Paul claims to have surpassed most of his contemporaries in observing the Jewish law, he never gives any indication that an inward moral struggle afflicted his pre-Christian life.

Against the first two points must be said that a biographical understanding is certainly not ruled out here. Indeed, a clear acknowledgment of the theological nature of this retrospective does not necessarily exclude the historical question of how far Paul's theological interpretation of his own life has a biographical nucleus. In defending the third point, quite a few scholars affirm that the solid self-confidence that is reflected in Phil. 3:6 excludes any split in the personality of the pre-Christian Paul. "Paul believed that he could live up to the high demands of perfect observance of the torah of a pharisaic kind, without qualifications."[38] However, such a reference to Phil. 3:6 takes too little account of the argumentative character of that text, in which the apostle was manifestly eager to accentuate his perfection in the fulfillment of the law in order to contrast his zealous commitment to "rubbish" with the "surpassing value of knowing Christ" (Phil. 3:8). Moreover, one may need to dedicate a great deal of pride in one's nomistic achievements to placate the insatiable psychic demands of unconsciously coping with a conflict.

This question brings me to assay an analysis of Paul's situation in terms of depth psychology, an approach that, broadly speaking, orients itself on the psychodynamics of the unconscious.[39] It will seek on the one hand to increase our understanding of Paul's conversion, and on the other to grasp its significance as one element of a process of conflict resolution. The great discovery of researchers in this field is that much of our mental life goes on below the level of consciousness. When a particular pattern of thought or behavior ceases, for example, the energy that prompted it does not disappear, but is redirected or repressed; and even though unconscious, it will continue to demonstrate its presence. Indeed, modifications of experience and behavior often reflect shifts in the boundary between our consciousness and unconscious modes of mental activity. The very essence of therapeutic practice is to effect such shifts of boundary in a positive direction by empathic interpretations that reveal unconscious modalities in a manner that enables the subject to come to terms with them.

The validity of psychological questions and the need to ask them must be stressed. If, for example, one studied Primitive Christianity as a whole, or one of the communities of which it was comprised, or for that matter a modern religious group like the Mormons in an exclusively historical and source-critical way, one would be skirting the problem of personal dynamics and thus failing to deal with the enigmas often posed by both the founders of these groups and the adherents who find meaning and personal direction in them. It is not enough to study the reports from and about these groups and persons. The faith of the first Christians, for example, derives from emotions, assumptions, and goals we can at least begin to identify and understand. And surely a historical study of the resurrection of Jesus or the belief of individual Christians that they "saw" Jesus after his death has to be supplemented by the enhanced understanding of the human mind and personality that modern psychology has afforded us. This is nothing but an application of new knowledge, an entirely consistent attempt to extend and deepen the process of historical investigation by pursuing it into the subconscious sources of perception and motivation within the life of the individual.[40]

As I have already indicated above, the source texts indicate that the pre-Christian Paul was a committed, zealous persecutor of Christians. That his response to the new sect was so vehement as to be noteworthy indicates that the basic elements of the preaching of Christians had a powerfully disturbing effect on him. In other words, his encounter with Christians and their preaching and practice took place not only at a cognitive level but also at an emotional and unconscious one. Indeed, this is probably true of all social and religious experiences. Behind Paul's intense antagonism to Christians and Christianity there must have been a steady intensification of the sort of inner conflict that depth psychology has ascertained in other cases to be the basic motivation for aggressive behavior. This is not an entirely new concept; the phenomenon of ambivalence leading to psychic turmoil—along with its sometimes tragic consequences—has been amply dramatized in art and literature. It is not difficult to imagine that the basic elements of Christian preaching and practice unconsciously attracted Paul, nor that, recoiling against his subconscious but all-consuming needs for acceptance and self-importance, he projected them onto the Christians so as to justify attacking them all the more savagely.

Sometimes another explanation of Paul's excessive zeal for the law is introduced: namely, that his fanaticism sprang from an authoritative belief that the teachings of the Christians whom he persecuted sullied God's honor and destroyed the divinely ordained purity of the Jewish community, and therefore had to be exterminated. A model for such violent action was Phinehas, whose zeal "has been reckoned to him as righteousness."[41] His fervent advocacy of God's law, on which the story about Phinehas in the Old Testament book of Numbers[42] possibly serves as a commentary, may indeed have given *one* stimulus to Paul's persecuting the Christians, the more so since as a Christian Paul later formulates a doctrine of justification through faith that employs much the same language.[43] One suspects that he must have pondered deeply about Phinehas before becoming a Christian. Yet the view that derives Paul's action as a persecutor solely from an authoritative belief makes it difficult to understand the sudden change from persecutor to preacher, unless one writes it off as a miracle. In that case, however, all efforts to arrive at a historical understanding must be subordinated to arbitrary invocations of divine thaumaturgy.

Of course, fanatics often suppress the very doubts that define and commission their views of life and the ends they strive for. Paul shows clear evidence of conflicting emotions: a radical sense of guilt and unworthiness combined with an exalted self-image that results in the need to be an authority figure. Likely enough, the latter was an overcompensation for the former. At any rate, caught up in an intellectual and emotional maelstrom that can only have been intensified by his growing familiarity with the sect he was harassing, he seems at last to have discovered the resolution of his problems for himself. (I emphasize "for himself" for Paul's conflict—if I describe it correctly—is based on a misrepresentation of Judaism.) The humble and self-sacrificing Jesus represents for Paul a new vision of the Almighty: no longer a stern and demanding tyrant intent on punishing even those who could not help themselves, but a loving and forgiving leader who offered rest and peace to imperfect humans who accepted his grace. Again, the Rabbinic corpus, Josephus, Philo, and the other sources of the period represent a loving and not a wrathful deity. The latter is Paul's personal problem. Further, by transforming this Jesus into a mythic Christ-Redeemer, Paul could become the Apostle-in-Chief of a new program of salvation with a culture-wide appeal. Something of that nature was in all likelihood the dynamic that impelled the persecutor turned proclaimer (dare one say promoter?) whose religious zeal stands as a measure of the inner tension that was powerfully released and transformed in a vision of Christ.

Ironically, it was no doubt the proclamation of forgiveness by Christians whom he persecuted that brought Paul's simmering yet unconscious yearning toward a Christ-figure to a boil: his compulsion to find release by fighting an external enemy collided with a message of reconciliation that became his "destiny."

What may we suppose the source of this inner revolt to have been? *First*, it must have had to do with the law. The argument presented in Romans 7 is too authentic, too "loaded with experience," and too alive for Paul to have developed it as a purely theoretical construct. In other words, it reflects real life. Although a theological exposition, it is clearly a retrospective formulation that describes the unconscious conflict that Paul endured before his conversion. *Second*, it is eminently reasonable that this conflict could have been sparked by the proclamation of a crucified Messiah (a crucified Messiah could not be the real Messiah). When Paul approached Damascus, there was a catastrophic breakthrough. Paul fled from his painful situation into the world of hallucination from which he soon returned to make himself the apostle of Jesus Christ, and finally the apostle to the Gentiles, commissioned by Christ himself.

But why was it not enough for Paul simply to be a member of the Christian movement? Why did he have to be an apostle, even *the* apostle to the greater world? The answer to this is no doubt rooted in his character. Put it simply, as a Jew he claimed to have surpassed his Jewish contemporaries in ardor, piety, and practice; the same was true for him afterward. As a Christian he claimed to have worked more than all the other apostles[44] and to have a greater gift for speaking in tongues than any of the Corinthians.[45] A person like Paul must always be "number one." Since at the time of his conversion no one had emerged to assume the obviously vital role of foremost apostle to the Gentiles, Paul was eager—of course subconsciously—to assume that exalted position.

THE HISTORY OF THE SELF-DECEPTION CONCERNING THE RESURRECTION OF JESUS

The Roman prefect Pontius Pilate sentenced Jesus to be crucified on a Friday in the spring of about 30 CE. At or just after his arrest, the male disciples who had traveled with him from Galilee to Jerusalem—apparently to share a never-to-be-forgotten Passover—abandoned him and fled in fear back to their native Galilee. Several women who were part of that same entourage stayed with the master longer. They remained as near as possible, even though of course they could not prevent his fate. Among them, we may be sure, was a woman named Mary from the Galilean fishing village of Magdala.

Pilate's reason for executing Jesus is clear. Here was a troublemaker who had to be permanently put out of action. Evidently, members of the Jerusalem priesthood had lodged false political charges against him as a result of perceived eschatological and messianic pretensions, which may have included a claim to be the long-awaited Son of Man.

The condemnation and death of Jesus occurred on a single day. The next day was the Sabbath, which that year fell on the first day of the Passover feast.[46] This raised the problem of what to do with the body of Jesus, for Jewish law and custom forbade leaving a corpse on the cross overnight.[47] Even more offensive to Jewish sensibilities, of course, would be its remaining there on a Sabbath which was also the first day of Passover. For whatever reason, Pilate apparently gave permission for Jesus' body to be taken down from the cross. Perhaps the Jewish authorities entrusted Joseph of Arimathea to place the body in a tomb; perhaps persons unknown to us buried the corpse elsewhere. At any rate, as far as the Jewish authorities and Pilate were concerned, that ended the matter.

Completely unknown are Jesus' thoughts and feelings in his last hours. The words attributed to him during the trial and on the cross are certainly creations of the Christian community, since none of his followers were present to hear and pass them on. Moreover, they are variously reported and clearly complement the agendas of the various evangelists.[48]

For Jesus' disciples his death was so severe a shock that it required an explanation proportionate to their devastation. John Dominic Crossan, however, seems to underestimate the shock of Good Friday. He writes:

> Easter faith . . . did not start on Easter Sunday. It started among those first followers of Jesus in Lower Galilee long before his death, and precisely because it was faith as empowerment rather than faith as domination, it could survive and, in fact, negate the execution of Jesus itself. It is absolutely insulting to those first Christians to imagine either that faith started on Easter Sunday through apparition or that, having been temporarily lost, it was restored by trance and ecstasy that same Sunday. . . . But Christian faith itself . . . was the continued presence of absolutely the same Jesus in an absolutely different mode of existence.[49]

Rebuttal: a) A little bit more concreteness is called for concerning "absolutely the same Jesus in an absolutely different mode of existence." b) Where and how does Paul fit in, who claimed to have seen Jesus and was able to convince at least some of the disciples? c) Faith included domination if the idea of the Twelve goes back to Jesus, for it included "judging the twelve tribes of Israel" (Matt. 19:28b).[50] d) The disciples claim exactly what Crossan negates, namely that "Easter" was decisive and not the historical Jesus. e) Why is Crossan using such inflammatory language ("insulting") here?

The process of reconceptualization began in Galilee and was marked by visions that involved admonitions and interpretations. Not long after Good Friday, Peter experienced a vision of Jesus that included auditory features, and this event led to an extraordinary chain reaction. Peter reconstituted the circle of the Twelve in Galilee, apparently modeling the fellowship on that founded by Jesus. This regathering reflected the hope—which may also have been Jesus'—

that at the imminent arrival of the kingdom of God the twelve tribes of Israel would be fully represented.

The disciples had, after all, followed Jesus to Jerusalem yearning for and perhaps half expecting the advent of the kingdom of God, the arrival of which was somehow intertwined in their minds with the message and example of their Master. At first his crucifixion and death had destroyed their hope, but these appearances rekindled, fulfilled, and at last even surpassed it. "The kingdom of God had begun, though differently from the way they had expected it."[51] Peter experienced Jesus' appearance to him as reacceptance by the one whom he had repudiated; the other disciples experienced it as forgiveness for their desertion.

The traditions of Israel provided the disciples with several choices for interpreting the appearances of Jesus: exaltation from the midst of life to the throne of God,[52] ascension after death,[53] resurrection of a martyr,[54] and outpouring of the Spirit of God.[55] We should also be aware of various notions of resurrection in first century Palestine, ranging from fleshly to bodily and even to spiritual forms thereof.[56] At the same time it is true that Jewish beliefs about the afterlife did not normally lead to "anyone's rising from the dead before the general resurrection at the end of the world."[57] But also true is the observation that Peter's faith started as a vision. It was not until reflection began that Peter's faith developed into faith in the "Risen One." Paul, a trained Pharisaic theologian, therefore designed Christ as the "first fruits of the risen dead, who will join him at his return (1 Cor. 15:23)."[58]

Peter had seen and heard Jesus. Naturally the content of the vision and the audition was passed on to others, and the news swiftly spread that God had not abandoned Jesus in death, but indeed had exalted Jesus to himself. To this may well have been added—at first, perhaps as a merely speculative notion—the report that Jesus would soon be appearing as the Son of Man on the clouds of heaven. That created a new situation, and the Jesus movement embarked on a tremendous new venture. Now the women and men who had attached themselves to Jesus could return to Jerusalem and there take up the work their master had left unfinished: to call on both the people and the authorities to undergo a change of heart and mind. (Perhaps this was seen and proclaimed as the very last reprieve that God would offer.) The first vision of Peter proved formally infectious, and was reportedly followed by others—one to the Twelve, and another to more than five hundred at one time.[59] At this point, at least, any nonecstatic interpretation comes to grief. It is surprising that Crossan writes, "The risen apparitions are not historical events in the sense of trances and ecstasies, except in the case of Paul."[60] The clear witness of 1 Cor. 15:6 to the appearance to "more than five hundred at one time" speaks against this, especially if the event behind Acts 2 can be combined with it, and the identity of Christ and the (ecstatic) Spirit thus adduced.[61]

Ernest Renan has aptly described the phenomenon thus:

> It is the characteristic of those states of mind in which ecstasy and apparitions are commonly generated, to be contagious. The history of all the great religious crises proves that these kinds of visions are catching; in an assembly of persons entertaining the same beliefs, it is enough for one member of the society to affirm that he sees or hears something supernatural, and the others will also see and hear it. Amongst the persecuted Protestants, a report was spread that angels had been heard chanting psalms in the ruins of a recently destroyed temple; the whole company went to the place and heard the same psalms. In cases of this kind the most excited are those who make the law and who regulate the common atmospheric heat. The exaltation of individuals is transmitted to all the members. . . . When, then, an apparition is brought forward in such meetings as these, the usual result is, that all either see it or reject it.[62]

It is worth recalling Renan's subsequent applications of his insights to Jesus' disciples. At the outset one should remember their low degree of intellectual culture. They "believed in phantoms; they imagined that they were surrounded by miracles; they took no part whatsoever in the positive science of the time."[63]

We must not underestimate the dynamic power of such a beginning. It was so compelling that the natural brothers of Jesus[64] were caught up in the excitement, and went to Jerusalem. James even received an individual vision[65]—the same James who had little to do with his brother during Jesus' lifetime, and seems to have participated in the attempt to have his "crazy" brother put away.[66]

A number of concurrent and mutually supporting elements can be identified in the earliest Christian experience. In addition to the personal visionary encounters with the "Risen One," we find the recurrence of three powerful historical themes galvanizing the community's faith: a) the act of breaking bread together enabled the members to recapture the presence of the Master who had been so cruelly killed but was now so wonderfully restored; b) recalling his words and works at table and in worship set him again in their midst; c) the messianic promise of scripture, and especially the familiar Psalter hymns, now took on new meaning as expressions of the present reality of the exalted Son of Man. Even at this early stage, the movement took on new dimensions when Greek-speaking Jews in Jerusalem joined it and began to spread the message about Jesus throughout Palestine. This attracted the attention of the Pharisee Saul, who set out to suppress the new preaching until his own Christ complex reversed his plans by interrupting his trip to Damascus with a vision of the heavenly Jesus. This event marked a turning point in the development of the earliest Easter faith, though hardly its culmination, and it would ultimately prove to be of worldwide historical importance.

The original Easter faith sprang from a visionary perception of Jesus being with God in heaven. This phenomenon is properly denominated a vision, for though seen as being alive, Jesus was and remained in fact dead. Ontologically speaking, this "risen Jesus" existed only in the memory of the disciples. According to them, however, Jesus continued to intervene in world history, and had not only sent his disciples forth into the world to preach and teach, but also endowed them with the power to forgive sins. Thus the "Risen One," though in objective terms no more than a fancy of the mind, not only had tremendous power himself, but even granted his disciples a share in this might. In order to describe such a phenomenon and its implications, the ordinary notion of "vision" is insufficient; the original Easter vision of the disciples had so developed as to display the features of a shared hallucinatory fantasy.

More than two hundred years ago Thomas Paine offered the following description of the earliest Easter faith that is worth quoting at this point. He wrote,

> The story of Jesus Christ appearing after he was dead is the story of an apparition, such as timid imaginations can always create in vision, and credulity believe. Stories of this kind had been told of the assassination of Julius Caesar, not many years before; and they generally have their origin in violent deaths, or in the execution of innocent persons. In cases of this kind, compassion lends its aid and benevolently stretches the story. It goes on a little and a little further till it becomes *a most certain truth*. Once start a ghost and credulity fills up the history of its life, and assigns the cause of its appearance! one tells it one way, another another way, till there are many stories about the ghost and about the proprietor of the ghost, as there are about Jesus Christ in these four books.[67]

Paine continued,

> The story of the appearance of Jesus Christ is told with that strange mixture of the natural and the impossible that distinguishes legendary tale from fact. He is represented as suddenly coming in and going out when the doors were shut, and of vanishing out of sight and appearing again, as one would conceive of an unsubstantial vision; then again he is hungry, sits down to meat, and eats his supper. But as those who tell stories of this kind never provide for all the cases, so it is here; they have told us that when he arose he left his grave clothes behind him; but they have forgotten to provide other clothes for him to appear in afterward, or to tell us what he did with them when he ascended.[68]

As time went on the early Christians must have become aware of the ambiguous character of visions, the more so since in their environment these were readily related to apparitions of demons and ghosts. For this reason and because their religious sensibilities were rooted in Judaism, the disciples' visionary faith took on physical manifestations in different communities at almost the same time. Hence at this point it is appropriate to introduce the notion of convergence.

Having laid claim to the mission to the Gentiles, who neither knew nor understood the concept of "bodily resurrection,"[69] the apostle Paul emphasized during his missionary preaching that Christians would receive new transformed ("spiritual") bodies just as Christ had at his resurrection. Interestingly, the communities of Mark, Matthew, Luke, and John also adopted the doctrine of bodily resurrection as a shibboleth of orthodoxy, and it must be stressed that to the degree that Jewish tradition persisted, the idea of Jesus' resurrection from the dead tended to include the corpse in the resurrection event. Even Paul, whose deeply religious nature cannot be denied, was unwilling to tolerate any doubt concerning a future bodily resurrection and that it is the dead who are to be raised. He went so far as to insist that without it Christ would have died in vain, the apostles would be mere deceivers, and Christians the most pitiable of human beings (1 Cor. 15:19).[70]

On the other hand, it is clear that almost from the beginning members of many Christian communities did not understand the resurrection literally, that is, as the resuscitation and/or the transformation of a dead body. Rather, they understood the proclamation as a symbolic statement. Certainly this is true of Paul's converted Gentiles and, I am tempted to say, all Christians from the first generation whose inner promptings were sufficiently sophisticated to remind them that religious truths can never be understood literally.

The next generation of those who denied the bodily resurrection can be found among the Christian Gnostics of the late first and early second centuries who ironically referred to Paul. Two examples may suffice: First, from the *Letter to Rheginos* (NHC I. 4):

45:14–46:2: The Savior swallowed up death—you are not reckoned among the ignorant—for he put aside the world which is perishing. He transformed it into an imperishable Aeon and raised it up, having swallowed the visible by the invisible, and he gave us the way of our immortality. Then, indeed, as the Apostle [Paul] said, "We suffered with him, and we arose with him, and we went to heaven with him." Now if we are manifest in this world wearing him, we are that one's beams, and we are embraced by him until our setting, that is to say, our death in this life. We are drawn to heaven by him, like beams by the sun, not being restrained by anything. This is the spiritual resurrection which swallows up the psychic in the same way as the fleshly.[71]

According to the author of this text "spiritual resurrection" replaces future bodily resurrection that has now become superfluous. Similarly, the unknown author of the *Gospel of Philip* (NHC II. 3) writes (*Logion 90a*):

> 73:1–5: Those who say they will die first and then rise are in error. If they do not first receive the resurrection while they live, when they die they will receive nothing.[72]

One wonders why these Gnostics could refer to Paul, "when in such letters as First Corinthians and Philippians Paul had opposed precisely that view."[73] At this point we must note that one wing of Paul's school asserted that the resurrection had already taken place and for that reason had become the target of criticism by the author of the Pastoral letters in 2 Tim. 2:16–18: "Avoid such godless chatter, for it will lead people into more and more ungodliness, and their talk will eat its way like gangrene. Among them are Hymenaeus and Philetus, who have swerved from the truth by holding that resurrection is past already."

Understandably the Gnostics' symbolic and *explicitly* nonphysical interpretation of the resurrection (and of all basic theological concepts) faced stiff opposition from the church fathers and was at last eradicated, the more readily since already "orthodox" followers of Paul attacked any nonbodily resurrection.[74]

For some time now, North American scholars have taken the lead in advocating the thesis that Christians from the communities behind the *Gospel of Thomas* never believed in the bodily resurrection of Jesus. Thus John Dominic Crossan regards Paul's Corinthian opponents ("the strong") as a group analogous to the people behind the *Gospel of Thomas*;[75] and Helmut Koester writes,

> The Gospel of Thomas and Q challenge the assumption that the early church was unanimous in making Jesus' death and resurrection the fulcrum of Christian faith. Both documents presuppose that Jesus' significance lay in his words, and his words alone.[76]

These authors along with others derive this from their finding that the oldest nonapocalyptic stratum of the Q-Gospel presents Jesus' teaching in a symbolic or sapiental way.[77] But this is doubtful, for a considerable portion of the Gospel of Thomas reflects an earlier apocalyptic tradition.[78] And unfortunately, we know very little about Thomas communities before 70 CE.[79]

Therefore we have no sound way to place the symbolic interpretation of Jesus' resurrection within the context of earliest Christian resurrection belief. Since the chief obstacle to that belief was the Palestinian setting of primitive Christianity, the resurrection was from the very beginning understood in bodily terms. Still, we can recognize the somewhat ironic nature of the process thus far described, since the real origin of early Christianity's resurrection belief was a vision—which, as a subjective representation of a reportedly objective "event," comes very close to a symbolic or a nonliteral understanding of the resurrection.

It is doubtless that one point or another of this historical outline of the earliest Christian belief in the resurrection needs to be corrected. The reason for this is not only the relatively meager amount of source material, but also the nature of the event itself. Martin Hengel rightly observes:

> During these momentous months of beginning, which are so obscure to us but which shone out so splendidly for the disciples, many movements and discoveries alongside and with each other and sometimes confusingly "through each other" were possible. The encounters with the Risen Christ formed a complex knot along with the formation of the earliest exaltation christology; but we can no longer neatly disentangle the individual strands and put them in chronological order, especially as the world of ideas of the first disciples, shaped by eschatological enthusiasm, does not correspond to the rules of our analytical method.[80]

However, this does not represent a gap or anything of the kind, as some have maintained,[81] but rather the beginning of a religious enthusiasm with its own dynamic.[82]

At the end of this summary history of the earliest resurrection faith, I would like to dispose of the often-repeated argument that the belief in Jesus' resurrection from the dead would not have survived in Jerusalem if his tomb had not been empty. In that case, many have argued, the Jewish leadership would have easily refuted the earliest faith in Jesus' resurrection by exhibiting the "full" tomb.[83] This argument is unpersuasive for the following three reasons:

> a) We know neither how long the disciples stayed in Galilee nor when their public appearance in Jerusalem began. If as Luke reports in Acts, for example, their preaching started fifty days after Jesus' crucifixion, then nobody—if only because of the rapid decay of flesh in that climate—would have been able to identify Jesus' body. (Such modern methods of identification as DNA analysis or dental examination were of course unknown in the first century.)
>
> b) The place of burial was unknown.
>
> c) The Jerusalem community, for whatever reason, did not ascribe any significance to the location of Jesus' burial place; had it done so, a tradition about it would in all likelihood have arisen early and been preserved.

Bishop Melito of Sardis, who visited Jerusalem in the latter half of the second century,[84] has sometimes been claimed as a witness to the veneration of Jesus' tomb. But his remarks are rhetorical and do not attest to his personal knowledge of its existence or veneration. In his *Homily on the Passion 93–94* he writes the following:

> You [Jews] killed your Lord **in the middle** of Jerusalem
> Listen all you families of nations, and see!
> An unprecedented murder has occurred **in the middle** of
>   Jerusalem;
>   in the city of the law,
>   in the city of the Hebrews,
>   in the city of the prophets,
>   in the city accounted just.
> And who has been murdered? Who is the murderer?
> I am ashamed to say and I am obliged to tell.
> For if the murder had occurred at night,
>   or if he had been slain in a desert place,
>   one might have had recourse to silence.

But now, **in the middle** of the street, and **in the middle** of the
city,

>   **in the middle** of the day for all to see,
>   has occurred a just man's unjust murder.[85]

Some scholars connect the repeated assertion "that Christ died in
the middle of Jerusalem . . . with the fact that the traditional site of
the crucifixion was enclosed within Herod Agrippa's wall of A.D.
41–44, and with Melito's claim to have visited Jerusalem."[86] Yet in
Melito's homily "in the middle" clearly has a rhetorical polemical
function of accusing the Jews of a shameless murder during the day-
light in the middle of Jerusalem in order to enhance their guilt. This
attack reveals nothing of what Melito had actually seen in Jerusalem.
Therefore his Passover homily cannot be seen to provide evidence
for the ongoing memory of the location of Jesus' tomb.

Indeed, nobody seems at first to have missed the tomb. Not until
326 CE, according to the report of the church father Eusebius, was it
"rediscovered" under a temple of the goddess Venus as the "cave of
salvation."[87]

NOTES

1. Gustave Le Bon, *The Crowd: A Study of the Popular Mind* (New York:
Viking Press, 1960), p. 146.

2. Ibid., pp. 119–20.

3. Cf. esp. Mark 4:13–20.

4. Cf. 1 Thess. 1:6–8.

5. Rudolf Bultmann, *The History of the Synoptic Tradition*, rev. ed.
(Oxford: Basil Blackwell, 1968), p. 138.

6. Ibid., pp. 139–40.

7. Ibid., pp. 258–59.

8. Ulrich Luz, *Matthew 8–20: A Commentary.* Hermeneia (Minneapolis: Fortress Press, 2001), p. 359.

9. Ibid., p. 359.

10. Ibid., p. 368.

11. Martin Rese ("Exegetische Anmerkungen zu G. Lüdemanns Deutung der Auferstehung Jesu," in *Resurrection in the New Testament*, ed. R.

Bieringer, V. Koperski, and B. Lataire. Festschrift J. Lambrecht [Leuven: University Press, 2002], pp. 55–71) too easily dismisses Luke 5:8 as a source for Peter's guilt (p. 65), and obviously refuses to equate sin with guilt (p. 67). Yet I think that equation can stand.

12. There is no need to include the account of the Gospel of John (18:15–18, 25–27) here nor that of Matthew (26:57–75) or Luke (22:54–71) for all of them are dependent on Mark at this point. It is worth noting, however, that Luke 22:31–32a is likely a reaction to the story of the denial. See my *Jesus After Two Thousand Years: What He Really Said and Did* (Amherst, NY: Prometheus Books, 2001), pp. 394–96.

13. Mark 14:18–21.

14. See Mark 8:31, 9:31, 10:32–34.

15. Martin Dibelius, *From Tradition to Gospel* (New York: Charles Scribner's Sons, 1965), p. 215.

16. Gal 1:23.

17. Gal. 1:13: "For you have heard of my former life in Judaism, how I persecuted the church of God violently and tried to destroy it."

18. See the survey by Raymond E. Brown, *The Death of the Messiah: A Commentary on the Passion Narratives in the Four Gospels*, 2 vols. (New York: Doubleday, 1994), 1:614–20.

19. See my *Jesus After Two Thousand Years*, p. 4.

20. See Mark 14:50.

21. Luke 10:18. On the authenticity of this verse, see my *Jesus After Two Thousand Years*, pp. 327–30.

22. The Greek verb *paradidomi* designates "the deed for which Judas is almost universally blamed—that of 'betraying Jesus'—. . .[It] does not mean 'betray' in any classical text . . .; never in Josephus and never in the New Testament" (William Klassen, *Judas: Betrayer or Friend of Jesus* [Minneapolis: Fortress Press, 1996]), p. 202, but simply "to hand over." Yet the historical contexts of this action and of Judas's suicide remain unclear. See Klassen's excellent book for details.

23. Yorick Spiegel, *The Grief Process: Analysis and Counseling* (Nashville: Abingdon Press, 1978).

24. Ibid., p. 182.

25. Colin Murray Parkes, *Bereavement: Studies of Grief in Adult Life* (London: Tavistock Publications, 1972).

26. Spiegel, *The Grief Process*, p. 184.

27. Ibid.

28. Ibid.

29. Ibid., p. 185.

30. Aniela Jaffé, *Apparitions: An Archetypal Approach to Death Dreams and Ghosts*, with a foreword by C. G. Jung (Irving, TX: Spring Publications, 1979), p. 57.

31. Ibid.

32. Cf. Spiegel, *The Grief Process*, p. 73.

33. Ibid., p. 76.

34. Colin Murray Parkes and Robert S. Weiss, *Recovery from Bereavement* (New York: Basic Books, 1983).

35. For what follows, see Carol Leet Kerr, *Dreams and Visions of Those Who Grieve* (DMin, Newton Center, MA, 1987).

36. See my *Jesus After Two Thousand Years* for detailed comments on the historical authenticity of Jesus' sayings in Matt. 6:25–33; Luke 9:57–62, 14:26. Cf. also Gerd Theissen, *Social Reality and the Early Christians: Theology, Ethics, and the World of the New Testament* (Minneapolis: Fortress Press, 1992), pp. 33–93.

37. For the following, see my *Paul: The Founder of Christianity* (Amherst, NY: Prometheus Books, 2002), pp. 187–91.

38. Martin Hengel, *The Pre-Christian Paul* (Philadelphia: Trinity Press International, 1991), p. 79.

39. Cf. Gerd Theissen, *Psychological Aspects of Pauline Theology* (Philadelphia: Fortress Press, 1987), pp. 11–28.

40. At the same time, I am fully aware of the difficulty in psychoanalyzing a person who has been dead for two thousand years. Yet a "this-worldly" explanation at least sheds historical light on what may have happened as opposed to a "theological" interpretation that explains an X (the rise of Easter faith) by a Y (God).

41. Ps. 106:3.

42. Num. 25:6–11.

43. See Rom. 4:3b quoting Gen. 15:6: "Abraham believed God, and it was reckoned to him as righteousness."

44. 1 Cor. 15:10.

45. 1 Cor. 14:18.

46. See John 18:28, 19:14, 13:1. According to the Synoptics, Friday is already the first day of Passah. Yet that seems quite improbable.

47. See Deut. 21:23.

48. For details see my *Jesus After Two Thousand Years* on the various last words of Jesus: Mark 15:34; Matt. 27:46; Luke 23:34, 43, 46; John 19:25–27, 30. Yet Jane Schaberg—referring to Mark 15:34—thinks that "the

women's witness to the crucifixion may have included the tradition that Jesus cried out the words of Ps 22:1 or similar words" (*The Resurrection of Mary Magdalene: Legends, Apocrypha, and the Christian Testament* [New York/London: 2002], p. 280). Clearly, one cannot rule out this possibility completely. Yet what counts is whether it is probable.

49. John Dominic Crossan, *Who Killed Jesus? Exposing the Roots of Anti-Semitism in the Gospel Story of the Death of Jesus* (San Francisco: HarperSan-Francisco, 1995), pp. 209–10.

50. See my *The Great Deception: And What Jesus Really Said and Did* (Amherst, NY: Prometheus Books, 1999), pp. 79–80, 102–103.

51. Gerd Theißen, *Die Religion der ersten Christen: Eine Theorie des Urchristentums* (Gütersloh: Chr. Kaiser, 2000), p. 77. This sentence is absent from the English version: Gerd Theissen, *A Theory of Primitive Christian Religion* (London: SCM Press, 1999).

52. Cf. Gen. 5:24: "Enoch walked with God; and he was not, for God took him"; 2 Kings 2:11: "And Elijah went up by a whirlwind into heaven."

53. This is presupposed at least for Moses and Jeremiah. Though according to Deut. 34:7 Moses had died, he had supposedly appeared along with Elijah (Mark 9:4–5), and Jeremiah "showed himself" stimulating the Maccabees to beat their enemies (2 Macc. 15:13–16).

54. See 2 Macc. 7.

55. See Joel 3:1–5. Cf. Acts 2:17–21.

56. See above, pp. 64–66.

57. Michael Goulder, "The Explanatory Power of Conversion-Visions," in *Jesus' Resurrection: Fact or Figment? A Debate between William Lane Craig and Gerd Lüdemann*, ed. Paul Copan and Ronald K. Tacelli (Downers Grove, IL: InterVarsity Press, 2000), p. 95 (quoting a statement made by William Lane Craig).

58. Ibid.

59. See 1 Cor. 15:6 and the analysis above, pp. 73–81.

60. Crossan, *Who Killed Jesus?* p. 209. A few pages earlier Crossan translated 1 Cor. 15:5–7 and pointed out the "profoundly political implications" of these and other similar texts. He continued: "They are not primarily interested in trance, ecstasy, apparition, or revelation but in authority, power, leadership, and priority" (p. 203). Yet this does not *exclude* the ecstatic character of the apparitions.

61. See above, p. 79.

62. Ernest Renan, *The Apostles* (New York: Carleton, 1886), pp. 63–64.

63. Ibid., p. 64. Renan's reference to the disciples' belief in phantoms

is backed by Mark 6:49/Matt. 14:26. He rightly continues: "The science flourished amongst a few hundreds of men who were only to be found in the countries to which the civilization of the Greeks had penetrated" (ibid., pp. 64–65).

64. Cf. 1 Cor. 9:5.

65. See 1 Cor. 15:7 and the analysis above, pp. 81–83.

66. Mark 3:21, 31–35 (cf. John 7:5). The episode in Mark derives from a historical bedrock because it is quite offensive. For that very reason both Matthew and Luke—who used Mark as a source—omit it (cf. Matt. 12:46–50; Luke 8:19–21).

67. Thomas Paine, *The Age of Reason* (Amherst, NY: Prometheus Books, 1984), p. 164. This powerful work was originally published in two volumes 1794/95.

68. Ibid.

69. See above, pp. 63–64 and cf. my *Paul: The Founder of Christianity*, pp. 123–25.

70. In passing I refer the reader to the rebuttal of 1 Cor. 15:14, 17–19 by Christian theologian A. J. M. Wedderburn, *Beyond Resurrection* (London: SCM Press, 1999). He writes: "Here it seems to me that Paul's logic simply cannot hold water today. His rhetoric has led him astray here. For by implication it utterly devalues Jesus' existence and ministry and all that he achieved during his life on earth, and it devalues Christians' lives on earth as well, including Paul's own life" (p. 154). Welcome to the camp of dissenters!

71. Translation based on my *Heretics: The Other Side of Christianity* (London: SCM Press and Louisville: Westminster John Knox Press, 1996), pp. 225–26 and James M. Robinson, gen. ed., *The Nag Hammadi Library in English*, 3d (completely revised) ed. (Leiden: E. J. Brill, 1988), p. 54–55 (M. Peel).

72. Translation based on ibid., p. 153 (Wesley Isenberg).

73. James M. Robinson, "Jesus from Easter to Valentinus," *Journal of Biblical Literature* 101 (1982): 19.

74. See my *Heretics*, pp. 187–89 and passim. Note that the title of Bishop Irenaeus's work against the heresies, *Unmasking and Refutation of the Gnosis Falsely So Called*, borrows from 1 Tim. 6:20b.

75. John Dominic Crossan, *The Historical Jesus: The Life of a Mediterranean Jewish Peasant* (San Francisco: HarperSanFrancisco, 1991), pp. 228–30.

76. Helmut Koester, *Ancient Christian Gospels: Their History and Development* (London: SCM Press and Philadelphia: Trinity Press International, 1990), p. 86.

77. John Dominic Crossan, *The Birth of Christianity: Discovering What Happened in the Years Immediately After the Execution of Jesus* (San Francisco: HarperSanFrancisco, 1998), p. 411, remarks about Kloppenborg and Patterson: "Those two visions of the eschatology of the sayings tradition as Kloppenborg's 'radical wisdom of the Kingdom of God' or as Patterson's 'social radicalism' are necessary correctives to Koester's almost contentless emphasis on the 'words of Jesus' in that tradition."

78. See my *Jesus After Two Thousand Years*, pp. 589–645.

79. See above, pp. 122–24, on John 20:24–29.

80. Martin Hengel, "Psalm 110 und die Erhöhung des Auferstandenen zur Rechten Gottes," in *Anfänge der Christologie*, ed. Cilliers Breitenbach and Henning Paulsen, Festschrift für Ferdinand Hahn (Göttingen: Vandenhoeck & Ruprecht, 1991), p. 72.

81. See, e.g., C. F. D. Moule and Don Cupitt, "The Resurrection: A Disagreement," *Theology* 75 (1972): 507–19. Moule thinks that in connection with the Easter events he must be concerned with "something beyond history," "something transcendent," and continues, "The N[ew] T[estament] calls it the resurrection of Jesus" (p. 509). See also the remarks by Don Cupitt, *Christ and the Hiddenness of God* (Philadelphia: Westminster Press, 1971), pp. 138–53.

82. Cupitt in all seriousness thinks that the Easter faith precedes the Easter experiences: "The arguments that led to the Easter faith are logically prior to the Easter appearances" (ibid., p. 8). Edward Schillebeeckx, in *Jesus: An Experiment in Christology* (New York: Seabury Press, 1979), has tried to put historical flesh on such "logic" and argued that the Easter faith is historically earlier than the appearance (p. 397). See the objections to such a thesis by N. T. Wright, *The Resurrection of the Son of God* (Minneapolis: Fortress Press, 2003), pp. 701–706.

83. See, e.g., Wolfhart Pannenberg, "Die Auferstehung Jesu—Historie und Theologie," *Zeitschrift für Theologie und Kirche* 91 (1994): 327; here the author follows in the footsteps of Hans von Campenhausen, "The Events of Easter and the Empty Tomb," von Campenhausen, *Tradition and Life in the Church: Essays and Lectures in Church History* (Philadelphia: Fortress Press, 1968), pp. 42–89.

84. Eusebius *Ecclesiastical History* 4.26.13f.

85. Melito of Sardis *On Pascha and Fragments*, text and translations ed. Stuart George Hall (Oxford: Clarendon Press, 1979), p. 53 (bold print added by G. L.).

86. Ibid., p. 53n55.

87. See Eusebius *Life of Constantine* 3.26–28.

5

Can We Still Be Christians—Despite the Nonresurrection of Jesus?

I have no intention of disputing that Jesus was an extraordinary man. What I hold is only this: It is not because of what he was, but because of what he was not; not because of the truth he taught, but on the strength of a prediction which was not fulfilled, and which therefore was not true, that he has been made the central point of a church, a cult. So soon as we see that he was not that because of which he was raised to such a position, then we have no further ground, nor even, if we would be truthful, any right to belong to such a church. Mere human excellence even at its highest perfection . . . gives no title to ecclesiastical veneration; least of all can it give such title when, having its root in conditions and in spheres of thought which are remote from ours, and to some extent the reverse of ours, it grows daily less fitted to be the pattern for our lives and our thoughts.[1]

Liberal Protestantism means the end of Christianity:—it is really an atheism covered with a thin layer of belief in God. "With God everything is possible, even that He should exist," said Ernest Renan. We must not deny that Protestantism has done a great service by increasing intellectual independence throughout the world. We only insist that every reform movement of this kind, whether it be Liberal Protestantism, or Reformist Judaism or Brahmanism, must necessarily end in atheism or in a still more rigorous established religion. Logically, if one wishes to be religious, one can only be orthodox, or one is no longer religious.[2]

THE RESULT

Thus we have come full circle. Although early Christian faith confesses the resurrection and the church is built on it, historical research shows with definite clarity that Jesus was not raised from the dead. "So there was no resurrection of Jesus. Psychological explanations are available for the early, appearance tradition; and known intra-ecclesial controversies about the nature of the resurrection explain the Gospel additions."[3] Lest there be any uncertainty or misunderstanding, let me go a step further: the insistence by Paul and early Christian faith generally on the "fact" of Jesus' resurrection by God must now be regarded as a falsification. Therefore, unless we totally redefine the word, people can no longer justify calling themselves Christians.[4]

Deriving such corollaries from the inescapable conclusions of our historical analysis is very difficult for me. For if it is valid, this process of deduction has destroyed the basis of the world's largest religious community, and shows the Christian faith, like the emperor's new clothes in the Andersen fairy tale, to be a great imposture. For two thousand years an abiding faith in Jesus' resurrection has displayed enormous power, but because of its utter groundlessness we must now acknowledge that it has all along been a worldwide historical hoax.

The example of David Friedrich Strauss, an eminent nineteenth-century theologian, has long encouraged me to insist on clarification on this point. In addition to offering some quotations from his work, I shall first outline his career as a historical Jesus scholar who, while rejecting the historicity of the resurrection, remained a Christian theologian and yet became an implacable critic of the church. Second, I shall delineate the reaction to the challenge of Strauss, and third, I will sketch the upshot of my argument in this book.

A HISTORICAL SURVEY

Between his first major book, *The Life of Jesus* (1835–36), and his last work, *The Old and the New Faith* (1872), the subtitle of which designates it *A Confession*, David Friedrich Strauss underwent a deep theological change. This is particularly significant since his historical-critical conclusions remained essentially unaffected. In *The Life of Jesus* Strauss was already aware of the possibly ruinous effect of his work on Christian faith. In its conclusion he writes,

> The results of the inquiry which we have now brought to a close, have apparently annihilated the greatest and most valuable part of which the Christian has been wont to believe concerning the Saviour Jesus, have uprooted all the animating motives which he has gathered from his faith, and withered all consolations. The boundless store of truth and life which for eighteen centuries has been the aliment of humanity, seems irretrievably dissipated; the most sublime levelled with the dust, God divested of his grace, man of his dignity, and the tie between heaven and earth broken.[5]

Yet at the same time Strauss considers the inner kernel of Christian faith to be completely independent of the historical results of his investigation. In the preface to volume I of *The Life of Jesus* (1835) he assures the reader as follows:

> The author is aware that the essence of Christian faith is perfectly independent of his criticism. The supernatural birth of Christ, his miracles, his resurrection and ascension, remain eternal truths, whatever doubts may be cast on their reality as historical facts. The certainty of this can alone give calmness and dignity to our criticism, and distinguish it from the naturalistic criticism of the last century, the design of which was, with the historical fact, to subvert also the religious truth, and which thus necessarily became frivolous. . . . In the meantime let the calmness and the sang-froid with which in the course of it, criticism undertakes apparently dangerous operations, be explained solely by the security of the author's conviction that no injury is threatened to the Christian faith.[6]

In *The Old and the New Faith* (1872) the consequences have changed.[7] Now Strauss writes that in Christianity

> the founder is at the same time the most prominent object of worship; the system based upon him loses its support as soon as he is shown to be lacking in the qualities appropriate to an object of religious worship. This, indeed, has long been apparent; for an object of religious adoration must be a Divinity, and thinking men have long since ceased to regard the founder of Christianity as such.[8]

At the same time Strauss does not think that one can avoid the dilemma by orienting Christian faith solely on the message of Jesus. He writes,

> But it is said now that he himself never aspired to this, that his deification has only been a later importation into the Church, and that if we seriously look upon him as man, we shall occupy the standpoint which was also his own. But even admitting this to be the case, nevertheless the whole regulation of our churches, Protestant as well as Catholic, is accommodated to the former hypothesis; the Christian *cultus*, this garment cut out to fit an incarnate God, looks slovenly and shapeless when but a mere man is invested with its ample folds.[9]

A little later Strauss continues in a similar vein:

> It may be humiliating to human pride, but nevertheless the fact remains: Jesus might still have taught and embodied in his life all that is true and good, as well as what is one-sided and harsh—the latter after all always producing the strongest impression on the masses; nevertheless, his teachings would have been blown away and scattered like solitary leaves by the wind, had these leaves not been held together and thus preserved, as if with a stout tangible binding, by an illusory belief in his resurrection.[10]

Thus in the course of his development as a theologian, historical facts became increasingly important to Strauss. At the same time he identified the cultic veneration of Jesus as a divine being and the belief in Jesus' resurrection from the dead as the hard kernel of traditional Christianity. Yet the onslaught of historical criticism nullified these two traditional objects of faith along with other eternal truths that Strauss had clung to earlier in his life. For Jesus' divinity and his resurrection were available only together with the old faith that historical criticism had refuted once and for all.

ALTERNATIVES TO DAVID FRIEDRICH STRAUSS

Objections to Strauss's conclusions take one of two forms. The first defends the historicity of Jesus' resurrection; the second, though agreeing with Strauss's denial of the historicity of Jesus' resurrection, affirms the possibility of rejecting that belief and remaining a Christian. I shall first turn to the latter approach.

The vain resort of the kerygma theology

Together with several colleagues Rudolf Bultmann argued from the viewpoint of dialectical theology that the proper object of Christian faith is the Christ of the proclamation, not the Jesus extracted from the text and reconstructed by historical scholars.[11] For Bultmann and his fellow theologians, the Good News to be proclaimed does not concern the miracles or the divine self-understanding of Jesus, but consists in the message that in this humble, rejected, and humanly conflicted Galilean, the Divine One had made known his own supreme goodness as well as the relative and thus flawed nature of human pretensions to righteousness. They saw in the failure of older attempts to establish the Jesus of history an opportunity to recapture a scriptural ethos and an honest historicism. The scriptural validity would rest on the fact that neither Paul nor the Fourth Gospel reflects either the personal faith or the teachings of Jesus. The attributed miracles, after all, are not matters of belief, but contextualized representations of early Christianity's faith in the reality of God's self-revelation. The essential New Testament message, they proposed, was that the divine had become fully involved in humanity within the context of everyday historical events. For despite all biographical uncertainties and ambiguities, in Jesus God's word had been made manifest, and only through faith can this interpenetration of the human and divine natures be apprehended.[12]

Thus basing his argument in large part on the apostle Paul for whom faith is the result of preaching,[13] Rudolf Bultmann understands the death and the resurrection as a "salvation occurrence." Yet this is a one-sided use of Paul, since—contrary to Paul—Bultmann presupposes the nonhistoricity of the resurrection of Jesus, and, while criticizing Paul's argument in 1 Cor. 15:3–8, stresses that one cannot come to faith on the basis of the "fact" of the resurrection. Bultmann writes,

> The resurrection cannot . . . be demonstrated or made plausible as an objectively ascertainable fact on the basis of which one could believe. But insofar as it or the risen Christ is present in the proclaiming word, it can be believed—and only so can it be believed. . . . The word which makes this proclamation is itself part of the event; and this word, in contrast to all other historical tradition, accosts the hearer as personal challenge. If he heeds it as the word spoken to him, adjudicating to him death and thereby life, then he believes in the risen Christ.
>
> Any counter-questioning as to the proclamation's right to its claim means that it is already rejected. Such questioning must be transformed into the question which the questioner has to ask himself—whether he is willing to acknowledge the Lord-ship of Christ which is putting this decision-question to his self-understanding.[14]

Bultmann's reflections deserve support in several regards. First, full agreement must be accorded to his plain statement that, historically speaking, Jesus did not rise from the dead. Second, he correctly emphasizes that the statement "Christ rose" does not belong to the same category as any statement about the influence or impact of any other historical person, as for example, "George Washington rose." For in the latter case, it would be a historical judgment, whereas in Jesus' case, we assert an eschatological event, something that transcends history. Third, it follows clearly that for Bultmann any questioning of this "event" is already a rejection of it.

The last two points invite intensive criticism, for they reflect the dogmatic basis of Bultmann's statement. For one thing, we may legitimately ask why he takes such pains to demythologize the message of the New Testament if at last he is going to employ a strategy of immunization against criticism. The other question that arises is why Bultmann invites—or even promotes—misunderstanding by using the parallel construction "death and resurrection of Jesus" as if the two were parallel occurrences. The two expressions suggest an ontological similarity that simply does not exist, and indeed in Bultmann's analysis the resurrection did not take place, but is only a faith-inspired interpretation of the cross. Having abandoned the traditional basis of Christian faith, can he claim to be a Christian theologian? According to Bultmann modern Christians ought to participate in the faith that motivated the early Christians, the kerygma that embodied their interpretation—in spite of the fact that they themselves claimed a faith rooted in the risen Christ, one that includes both fact and interpretation.

Bultmann's suggestions remind me of Andersen's fairy tale of the *Emperor's New Suit.* He wants to avoid the consequence that without mythology the loom of traditional Christian faith is emptied, but he refuses to accept the natural result of his project for Christian claims to objectivity. Like the emperor, he chooses—for fear of appearing a fool—to affirm at a different level what candid people know to be obedient credulity. In the last analysis, Bultmann simply substitutes new mythology for the old—something that he wanted passionately to avoid. His approach is therefore not a valid alternative to David Friedrich Strauss's criticism.

The vain resort of the objective vision hypothesis

The German systematic theologian Hans Grass, while also presupposing the nonhistoricity of Jesus' resurrection, tries to avoid Strauss's dilemma by introducing the objective vision hypothesis. He writes:

> When historical criticism is carried to such extremes that even the most radical conclusions are considered—for example, that in dealing with the resurrection one cannot place the empty tomb

and appearances of the risen Christ in the "space-time world," but only the disciples' visions; and when conversely one declines to surrender the belief that Christ lives as the exalted Lord on the grounds that in the absence of its living Lord the church would have forfeited its reason for existence, then one must seek to merge the two modalities. The objective vision hypothesis embodies this attempt: it both posits the trans-subjective origin of the Easter vision and Easter faith, and accepts the reality of the transcendent content and result of these visions.[15]

Yet Grass's thesis of an objective vision has understandably found almost no support in recent scholarship; after all, it can be nothing more than an apologetic move, since by their very nature visions cannot be examined. Indeed, it does not make much sense for a scholar to distinguish between subjective and objective vision unless he has already decided what conclusion he wishes to draw. Notwithstanding this weakness, Grass deserves respect for his attempt to take historical research fully into account.

Recently the Heidelberg New Testament scholar Gerd Theissen has proposed a variant of the objective vision hypothesis. He writes:

It completely depends on our construction of reality whether we think it possible that an objective message can also be communicated to people through internal psychological processes. To take an analogy: in my view there can be no doubt about the "objectivity," i.e. the factual correctness, of some transfer of information after the death of people (of which stories are told above all in time of war), even if we cannot fit them into our scientific constructions of reality. We cannot exclude them.[16]

Clearly, this statement faces the same objections as Grass's reasoning. Even worse, perhaps, it attempts to use modern parapsychology to pave a way to the early Christian confession that God has raised Jesus from the dead. The ghosts and demons that occasionally appear in accounts of contemporary spiritualism bear only indirect relation, if any at all, to Jesus' resurrection, and in any case such a strategy is specifically rejected by early witnesses.[17] Furthermore, I cannot escape the suspicion that introducing various constructions of reality too often serves the purpose of avoiding embarrassing questions. Why must we hypothesize multiple constructions for a single reality? For example, I would ask Theissen and his followers whether they think that a different construction of reality enabled the early Christians to establish real communication with the risen Jesus. If so, would we not have to take most of the "visions" from the ancient world seriously? What would follow from this for our own construction of reality? Last but not least, would this not repopulate the heavens with all the divinities that modern scholarship has at long last managed to evict? In short, I consider utterly invalid any recourse to objective visions or parapsychology as a defense of the resurrection of Jesus.

Today apologetic theologians like to emphasize that the scientific understanding of the world is a rather recent perspective and therefore should not be uncritically applied to the analysis of early Christian Easter texts. Yet on this point we would do well to pay attention to what the German theologian Alexander Bommarius said on the occasion of a debate on the resurrection of Jesus:

> Even if we are aware of the relativity of our own world-view—it is, indeed, only "our" image—nevertheless we must rely on it since we are restricted by our finitude. A different question is how long we shall rely on this world-view—an unanswerable question, for how long this will last has yet to be seen.[18]

That may be, but acknowledging that the scientific worldview entails certain assumptions hardly requires one to conclude that Jesus left the tomb with a newly created and transformed body or that God sent Peter a video message from heaven to confirm the objective nature of the event.[19]

The vain resort of understanding the resurrection of Jesus as a metaphor

The Catholic theologian Hans Kessler from the University of Frankfurt regards the resurrection of Jesus as

> a metaphor of an event that has really taken place which, however, withdraws itself from the senses and an empirical approach.[20]

A little later Kessler remarks:

> The process of resurrection and the Risen One . . . is a real event, yet not a "historical" occurrence to be examined by us.[21]

By way of criticism, I question the basic cogency of such sentences. If we are dealing with a real event, its factuality can be evaluated.

This rebuttal of Kessler is also directed against every method of interpretation that simultaneously admits the nonhistoricity of Jesus' resurrection and still seeks to interpret it metaphorically in order to preserve the kernel of Early Christian resurrection faith.[22] While I do not for a moment question the honest intent of such an undertaking, it stands in stark contrast, if not contradiction, to the Christian creed from the earliest times on. Those who made this confession assumed an act of God upon the dead body of Jesus if only because they were unable to think in nonbodily terms. Thus a merely metaphorical interpretation of Jesus' resurrection is but a pale counterfeit of the earliest belief in God's raising Jesus from the dead.

The vain resort of replacing the risen Christ by the historical Jesus

Quite a few theologians compensate for the loss of the risen Christ by going back to the preaching of the historical Jesus in an effort to renew the content of the gospel. A few years ago I myself participated in this error and wrote,

> Jesus formally lived out for his disciples the message of the boundless grace of God—in word and in action. Human beings have nothing to boast about to God. . . . At the centre of his message stands the kingdom of God, which begins to come about with him—completely of its own accord. The kingdom of God literally breaks into the present, so that from now on all life is lived in the presence of God. . . . His announcement of the kingly rule of God was accompanied by a praxis which opened up participation in the kingdom of God to sinners—or better, the godless—unconditionally.[23]

Such a view of Jesus may certainly provide a stimulus toward humanistic ideals and for that reason should be respected. Yet a theology based on the doctrine of the risen Christ cannot be saved by a detour to the teachings of Jesus; replacing Christology with a sort of "Jesuology" that denies the resurrection has no valid basis. One who wishes to abjure the confession that God raised Jesus from the dead must repudiate the faith of most early Christians.

This same judgment must be asserted against attempts to ground Christian faith on Jesus' moral code or on that of the early Christians. Apart from the fact that the ethics of Jesus and of the first Christians have many parallels in the Jewish and Hellenistic environment, such attempts overlook Christian specifics, namely the cultic veneration of Jesus and/or his proclamation as the Lord of the universe. It was not until these specifics had developed that it makes sense to speak of Christian ethics. Christian ethics without the aforementioned presuppositions is vacuous, an imperative without an indicative.

Furthermore, attempts to build Christianity on Jesus' teachings quite often present a Jesus who is tacitly based on the image of a post-Easter Jesus. This can be observed wherever Jesus is reported to have initiated the mission to the Gentiles or to have attacked Judaism after the style of Paul. Proponents of such theories too easily tend to forget that Paul, who never knew Jesus personally,[24] was the one who forced the personal disciples of Jesus in Jerusalem to deal with the divisive cultic and ethical issues raised by Gentiles who were not bound by the Jewish law.[25]

The vain resort of "theological explanation"

Proponents of such a view restrict the historical question and seriously reintroduce God as a historical agent whose actions such as raising Jesus bodily from the dead could be known by people. Indeed, one theologian asserts, "It is simply not possible to investigate whether Jesus rose from the dead without taking a view about how probable it is that there is a God likely to intervene in human history in this kind of way,"[26] while another claims, "To believe in the resurrection is no more difficult than to believe in God's reality."[27] Moreover, authors who share such a view regularly refer to biblical sayings that with God everything is possible[28] and regard a strictly historical approach *etsi deus non daretur* as "Enlightenment bias."[29]

A couple of fine examples of scholarship led astray by theology can be found in N. T. Wright's recent book, *The Resurrection*.[30] He begins chapter 18, "Easter and History," by asserting "that Jesus of Nazareth was bodily raised from the dead,"[31] and disingenuously attests this to be a "historical datum" on the grounds that "(t)his belief was held by virtually all the early Christians for whom we have evidence."[32] But even if one were to restrict the category "early Christians" sufficiently to make that problematic statement true, no proof of its factuality results. As Thomas Paine made clear a little over two hundred years ago in *The Age of Reason*, evidence provided by scripture and by those who create it is at least as likely to be spurious as accurate.[33]

Further, in attempting to demonstrate the validity of the resurrection story, Wright relies on "two things, which must be regarded as historically secure . . . the emptiness of the tomb and the meetings with the risen Jesus."[34] One of his seven "points" of this contention is that for Jews of the second-Temple period to believe in a bodily resurrection, it would have to be known that a body had disappeared and that the person had been discovered to be thoroughly alive again. Once more Wright betrays what is no doubt an unconscious naiveté, for to a would-be believer the *report* that the deceased master had been seen alive would no doubt have sufficed. It is not everyone—not even in first century Palestine—who insists on putting his finger into nail-holes.

Last, he seems to have gotten himself into a bit of a quagmire in the footnote in which he assails my lack of critical acumen in asserting that modern science assures us that dead people do not rise, and therefore Jesus did not either. He explains his reason in a parenthesis, "as though the ancient world had been ignorant of the fact that dead people stayed dead."[35] So, Mr. Wright, you agree that the ancients were—as we moderns are—aware of the fact that death is an irreversible occurrence: it seems a serious inconsistency that you elsewhere dismiss *the fact* known to ancients and moderns alike, and claim that in one special case the facts don't apply.

Yet, twenty pages later, Wright adds what seems to me to be an inescapable "theological" conclusion,

The fact that dead people do not ordinarily rise is itself part of early Christian belief, not an objection to it. The early Christians insisted that what happened to Jesus was precisely something new; was, indeed, the start of a whole new mode of existence, a new creation. The fact that Jesus' resurrection was, and remains, without analogy is not an objection to the Early Christian claim. It is part of the claim itself.[36]

A little later, we understand why Wright is able to raise such claims for his own work—he has introduced "theology" in the proper sense, namely "god" or even "God":

The challenge for any historian, when faced with the question of the rise of Christianity . . . comes down to . . . the direct question of death and life, of the world of space, time and matter and its relation to whatever being there may be for whom the word "god," or even "God," might be appropriate. Here there is, of course, no neutrality. Any who pretend to it are merely showing that they have not understood the question.[37]

Yet, who decides at what point of historical study a "theological explanation" ought to begin? If the gods of the individual religions should determine the results of the various studies about their "reality" and "actions," goodbye scholarship!

Much better is an affirmation of the substance of historical study. In the words of Van Harvey,

what we call historical inquiry is really the formalization by professional historians of our modern, Promethean desire to know, a desire that is actually rooted in everyday life. Historical reasoning is merely the formalization of one method that has, over time, proved to be our best guarantor of achieving this desire and of holding in check the special pleading, obscurantism, and tendentiousness that are omnipresent in human existence.[38]

In other words, for reasons of self-protection against ideologies cloaked as "theological explanations," straightforward historical study of any religion and its beliefs, including the resurrection of

Jesus, is mandatory and should not be transformed into a metaphysical or speculative sphere.

The vain resort of accepting the resurrection of Jesus as a historical fact

Recently we have witnessed a resurgence of fundamentalism; dogmatic thinking seems to be gaining adherents not only in the world at large but also within the church. Credulous acceptance of the historicity of Jesus' resurrection goes hand in hand with attacks on rationalism's alleged narrowing of the notion of reality—a scurrilous subterfuge, according to doctrinaire believers, that excludes the very investigation of the possibility of the resurrection.

Yet occasionally the conflict still arises in both Protestant and Catholic academic theology. Speaking from the Protestant side, Christian Hartlich has remarked that in spite of the incomplete and often dubious treatment of the other miracle accounts, research still concentrates on examining the validity of the historical-critical method as a means of evaluating the central miracle of Christianity—the resurrection of Jesus. He continues:

> Positions have recently been taken on this subject in numerous theological publications—with the prevailing tendency, in spite of the diversity of arguments, to protect the ontic primacy of Jesus affirmed by his resurrection, which elevates him above all other creatures, against historical criticism. The resurrection of Jesus is supposedly a singular fact; and regarding its determination the historical-critical method founders, and, according to its own presuppositions, must founder. The fundamental theological axiom at work here can be summarized in one sentence: *Without an objective, ontic grounding for Christology in the resurrection event Christian faith has no basis.* At the same time, however, there is also the desire—so far as possible—to proceed in a historical-critical way, in order to make the event of the resurrection of Jesus historically plausible.[39]

Similarly, Catholic theologian Ingo Broer observes,

> In dealing with Jesus' miracles, and perhaps the virgin birth, one may yield some leeway to historical criticism, but no latitude can

be allowed in the case of the resurrection. . . . Only in that instance is that methodology—despite its wide acceptance—claimed to be inapplicable. Many theologians, at least, argue that the resurrection should, must, and can offer what was once derived from the virgin birth, miracle, and resurrection accounts conflated from the Gospels: a sound basis for faith. The more problematic any objective understanding of the miracles and the virgin birth became, the more people focused on the resurrection—and in particular on the appearances—hoping to discover an unassailable position.[40]

However, despite such conservative efforts at "damage control," Christian resurrection faith is in a deep crisis that reflects not so much the results of natural science as conclusions based on historical criticism and sober insight. The latter may at last lead to the following assessment:

> That a resuscitated Jesus exited his tomb, that he physically ascended to the reputed location of God's throne, and that he will in the same body return to pronounce divine judgment on the world—these claims constitute so interdependent a sequence of events that modifying any element must invalidate the whole. Today, however, imagining a body rising to enter a heavenly throne room and subsequently returning in the company of an angelic escort is impossible, for our knowledge of the cosmos admits of no such heaven.[41]

It is interesting to note that retired Episcopalian Bishop John Shelby Spong, an eloquent spokesman for the liberal wing of modern Protestantism says much the same thing:

> There appears to be no place in our universe for heaven. It has been radically dislocated from its ancient spot just beyond the clouds. If heaven is no longer a locatable concept, then we have to recognize that neither is God, since heaven was God's abode. We can and do rationalize this by saying that that heaven is not a place and God cannot be thought of spatially. That is of course true, but a God who cannot be located or envisioned begins to fade into an oblong blur. Once God had been removed from the position beyond the sky from where divine judgment, to say nothing of personal intervention, was believed to occur, then the major pillars

upholding the concept of heaven were removed and the believ-
ability of heaven collapsed.[42]

Clearly, both Academy and Church are forced to wrestle with the
problem of what to put in place of a doctrine that no longer makes
sense, but the abrupt dismissal of which would rend the curtain of
what until recently seemed an impregnable Temple. One could even
suggest a sterner metaphor: when the keystone of Christ's resurrection is removed, as it must be at last, the arch of faith must fail, and
Christianity must collapse.

Summary: we can no longer be Christians even if we wanted to be, for Jesus did not rise from the dead

The overall picture does not change when some—notably Protes-
tants—de-emphasize or dismiss the virgin birth so as to make the
resurrection a more defensible plank in the church's shaky platform.
This is the final desperate volley of a faith that has become a pale
shadow of its former self, but imagines that the "resurrection" will
serve as its enduring anchor of salvation. This arbitrary and self-con-
tradictory latter-day Christianity both believes and disbelieves at the
same time. The problem with this Christianity becomes evident if
one asks such questions as whether Jesus really answers prayers,
whether he will return in judgment on the clouds of heaven, and
whether God is a real being or only a symbol. Here again the
responses will vary widely, from attacking any who presume to question the deity's reality to assuring the petitioner that God's existence
inheres in the process of becoming. Such opaque answers necessarily raise more and murkier questions.

    This "modern" circle, which always wants to be in tune with the
times, has recently criticized me for being an Enlightenment fundamentalist, for slashing and burning religion, and sowing only doubt.
But one should recall that the "capacity to doubt, and in particular
the ability to endure doubt for a long time, is one of the rarest things
on this planet. As a matter of fact, man is a mammal who cannot
well endure uncertainty. He cherishes a profound longing for firm
convictions."[43] Precisely because our nature is such that we cannot

face life without illusions, I happily accept the taunting label of historical or Enlightenment fundamentalist. And precisely because the resurrection is so doubtful and can no longer serve as a basis for our lives, I choose to live in a house built on a solid foundation rather than in a priestly domicile suspended in the sky. Those who protest that radical historical criticism is recklessly destroying religion should examine their own foundations without delay, lest they prove vulnerable to the charge that their faith is illusory.

If we take seriously the nature of historical knowledge and our own human dignity, we cannot be Christians any longer. Since Jesus did not rise from the dead, those who nonetheless continue to claim that obsolete title are deceiving themselves.[44]

NOTES

1. David Friedrich Strauss, *The Old Faith and the New*, introduction and notes by G. A. Wells, 2 vols. (Amherst, NY: Prometheus Books, 1997), 1:xliv–xlv.

2. Theodor Reik, *Dogma and Compulsion: Psychoanalytic Studies of Religion and Myths* (New York: International Universities Press, 1951), p. 153.

3. Michael Goulder, "The Baseless Fabric of Visions," in *Resurrection Reconsidered*, ed. Gavin D'Costa (Oxford: Oneworld Publications and Rockport, MA, 1996), p. 58.

4. In passing, let me hasten to question the following statement by Pheme Perkins, *Resurrection: New Testament Witness and Contemporary Reflection* (Garden City, NY: Doubleday, 1984), when she writes, "Nor . . . can one insist that if a tomb containing the body of Jesus were to be found by archaeologists, the Christian proclamation of Jesus as the one who has been raised and exalted by God would be destroyed and with it the Christian claims about Jesus' place in salvation" (p. 84).

5. David Friedrich Strauss, *The Life of Jesus Critically Examined*, edited and with an introduction by Peter C. Hodgson, translated from the fourth German edition by George Eliot (Philadelphia: Fortress Press, 1972), p. 757.

6. Strauss, *The Life of Jesus*, p. lii.

7. To be sure, these altered consequences had been in the making since as early as 1840, when Strauss published *The Christian Faith: Its Doctrinal Development and Conflict with Modern Science* (*Die christliche*

Glaubenslehre in ihrer geschichtlichen Entwicklung und im Kampfe mit der modernen Weltanschauung dargestellt, 2 vols. [Tübingen: C. F. Osiander, 1840–41]). For a comparison of *The Life of Jesus* of 1835 with these and other works of Strauss, see Peter C. Hodgson, "Editor's Introduction: Strauss' Theological Development from 1825–1840," *The Life of Jesus*, pp. xv–xivii. Regrettably, Hodgson does not include *The Old and the New Faith* in his comparison—a book that according to Joseph McCabe, *A Biographical Dictionary of Modern Rationalists* (London: Watts & Co., 1920), was Strauss's "greatest work" (p. 768).

8. Strauss, *The Old Faith and the New*, 1:54.

9. Ibid., pp. 54–55.

10. Ibid., p. 83.

11. See the most recent renewal of Bultmann's position by Georg Strecker, *Theology of the New Testament* (New York/Berlin: Walter de Gruyter and Louisville: Westminster John Knox Press, 2000), pp. 270–75. See Strecker's comment, "Rudolf Bultmann coined the statement, 'Jesus rose into the kerygma.' This means that we can learn who Jesus really is not by historical investigation but from the Easter kerygma alone" (p. 275).

12. For an excellent introduction into this aspect of Bultmann's theology, see Van A. Harvey, *The Historian and the Believer: The Morality of Historical Knowledge and Christian Belief. With a New Introduction by the Author* (Urbana and Chicago: University of Illinois Press, 1996), passim.

13. See Rom. 10:17a.

14. Rudolf Bultmann, *Theology of the New Testament* (New York: Charles Scribner's Sons, 1951), 1:305–306.

15. Hans Grass, *Ostergeschehen und Osterberichte*, 4th ed. (Göttingen: Vandenhoeck & Ruprecht, 1970), p. 248.

16. Gerd Theissen, *A Theory of Primitive Christian Religion* (London: SCM Press, 1999), p. 334n5. For a critique of Theissen's thoroughly apologetic book, see my *Primitive Christianity: A Survey of Recent Studies and Some New Proposals* (London/New York: T & T Clark, 2003), pp. 163–77.

17. See Luke 24:37–43; Acts 12:9.

18. Alexander Bommarius, in Bommarius, ed. *Fand die Auferstehung statt? Eine Diskussion mit Gerd Lüdemann* (Düsseldorf and Bonn: Pargerga Verlag GmbH, 1995), p. 122. A little earlier Bommarius had said, "Even if it is clear that our technical rationalism is not the last resort of wisdom, we should prefer to drive on a bridge that was built on the basis of the scientific rather than the mythological worldview" (pp. 121–22).

19. Researchers of the last two centuries had spoken of a "telegram

from heaven" with the same consequences as those of Grass and Theissen. See the instructive survey by A. Michael Ramsey, *The Resurrection of Christ* (Philadelphia: Westminster Press, 1946), pp. 50–52 (Theodor Keim and Burnett Hilman Streeter).

20. Hans Kessler, *Sucht den Lebenden nicht bei den Toten. Die Auferstehung Jesu Christi in biblischer, fundamentaltheologischer und systematischer Sicht.* Erweiterte Neuausgabe (Würzburg: Echter Verlag, 1995), p. 475.

21. Ibid., p. 476.

22. Cf. recently James D. G. Dunn, "Beyond the Historical Impasse? In Dialogue with A. J. M. Wedderburn," in *Paul, Luke and the Graeco-Roman World: Essays in Honour of Alexander J. M. Wedderburn,* ed. Alf Christophersen, Carsten Claussen, Jörg Frey, and Bruce Longenecker (London/New York: Sheffield Academic Press, 2002), pp. 250–64, esp. pp. 261–64. According to Dunn, "metaphor takes us into a more extended linguistic reality than history as such, and thus provides the possibility of transcending the blind alley of the 'historical impasse'" (p. 263). Later he writes the astounding sentences, "Christians have continued to affirm the resurrection of Jesus, as I do, not because they know what it means. Rather, they do so because, like the affirmation of Jesus as God's Son, 'the resurrection of Jesus' has proved the most satisfactory and enduring of a variety of options, all of them inadequate in one degree or other as human speech, to sum up the impact made by Jesus, the Christian perception of his significance. They do so because as a metaphor, 'resurrection' is perceived as referring to something otherwise inexpressible, as expressing the otherwise inchoate insight that this life, including Jesus' life, is not a complete story in itself but can only be grasped as part of a larger story in which God is the principal actor and in which Jesus is somehow still involved" (p. 264). With due respect, this is inflated, irrational talk with many parallels in contemporary theological literature.

23. See my *Heretics: The Other Side of Early Christianity* (London: SCM Press and Louisville: Westminster John Knox Press, 1996), p. 210.

24. See my *Paul: The Founder of Christianity*, pp. 193–212.

25. Ibid., pp. 213–26, and passim.

26. Richard Swinburne, *Resurrection of God Incarnate* (Oxford: Clarendon Press, 2003), pp. 202–203.

27. Joachim Ringleben, *Wahrhaft auferstanden. Zur Begründung der Theologie des lebendigen Gottes* (Tübingen, J. C. B. Mohr/Paul Siebeck, 1998), p. 49n102.

28. See Matt. 19:26; Luke 1:37.

29. Alan G. Padgett, "Advice for Religious Historians: On the Myth of a Purely Historical Jesus," *The Resurrection: An Interdisciplinary Symposium on the Resurrection of Jesus*, ed. Stephen T. Davis, Daniel Kendall, and Gerald O'Collins (Oxford/New York: Oxford University Press, 1997), p. 304. Understandably, this verdict receives support from Gerald O'Collins, "The Risen Jesus: Analogies and Presence," in *Resurrection*, ed. Gerald O'Collins, Michael A Hayes, and Davis Tombs (Sheffield: Sheffield Academic Press, 1999), p. 207n17. I should remind the author that resurrection of a corpse to life is not a small thing and should be considered as a possibility only if the available sources are unanimous.

30. N. T. Wright, *The Resurrection of the Son of God* (Minneapolis: Fortress Press, 2003).

31. Ibid., p. 685.

32. Ibid.

33. Thomas Paine, *The Age of Reason* (Amherst, NY: Prometheus Books, 1984), pp. 77–190.

34. Wright, *The Resurrection of the Son of God*, p. 686.

35. Ibid., p. 685n2.

36. Ibid., p. 712.

37. Ibid.

38. Van A. Harvey, *The Historian and the Believer: The Morality of Historical Knowledge and Christian Belief* (Urbana and Chicago: University of Illinois Press, 1996), pp. xx–xxi.

39. Christian Hartlich, "Historical-Critical Method in Its Application to Statements Concerning Events in the Holy Scriptures," *Journal of Higher Criticism* 2, no. 2 (Fall 1995): 122.

40. Ingo Broer, "'Seid stets bereit, jedem Rede und Antwort zu stehen, der nach der Hoffnung fragt, die euch erfüllt" (1Petr 3,15). Das leere Grab und die Erscheinungen Jesu im Lichte der historischen Kritik'," Broer and Jürgen Werbick, eds., *Biblische und systematische Beiträge zur Entstehung des Osterglaubens*, SBS 134 (Freiburg: Herder, 1988), pp. 29–61: 48.

41. Emanuel Hirsch, *Hauptfragen christlicher Religionsphilosophie* (Berlin: Walter de Gruyter, 1963), pp. 326–27.

42. John Shelby Spong, *Why Christianity Must Change or Die: A Bishop Speaks to Believers in Exile* (San Francisco: Harper, 1998), p. 205.

43. Reik, *Dogma and Compulsion*, p. 161.

44. Note Michael Goulder's remark, "Perhaps the sapient sutlers of the Lord may manage without Jesus' resurrection, or reinterpret it; but it will not, I think, be the same religion" ("The Baseless Fabric of Visions," p. 59).

Epilogue

Does my thesis—that since Jesus did not rise from the dead, Christians cannot reasonably hope for immortality—lead to spiritual despair and moral misconduct? That is the opinion of many Christians today—as it was of the apostle Paul, according to whom a person with such a view as mine should follow the precept, "Let us eat and drink, for tomorrow we die."[1] Moreover, based on the findings of natural science, one could feel compelled to ask, "What meaning to life remains if all we face is death, not only as individuals but collectively as a species destined to extinction in the inevitable heat death of the universe?"[2] Christians whose faith is founded on life after death must ask such questions, and I do not deny that "a philosophy which maintains that the world is morally meaningful, that death is not the end, and that human beings—or at least some of them—will have another chance is emotionally more satisfying than naturalism."[3] Nevertheless, I neither adopt such a simplistic stance nor share such a pessimistic outlook. True, I can no longer relate "Easter" directly to the Bible and the creed. The resurrection of Jesus is not a historical event, and therefore he will not come again. But being solidly based on historical scholarship, that conclusion is quite liberating. It enables me to see that "resurrection" must be understood metaphorically by applying it to this present life—in which we find ourselves, as it were, on a small raft adrift on a vast, dark ocean. An icy wind blows, and we on the raft are ultimately united only by the bond of the death that will come to all of us. Nor can we expect any compassion from the impersonal universe. Yet we may come to terms with the reality of such terrors by seeking a deeper foundation for life. We strive to create meaning in our lives by living in humility, wisdom, and love. Faith, understood as that which empowers life, is effective in every act of courage on the face of this earth. Once this happens I cross the threshold of a new existence. Henceforth, I am no longer cowed by the notion that death is a punishment for my sin. Nor do I hope for a resurrection.[4] Like Bertrand Russell, I believe that when I die my body will rot, and my selfhood will vanish.[5] And yet I know that genuine happiness is no less precious because it must come to an end—nor do humility, love, wisdom, and courage lose their value because they must forever be renewed. Indeed, accepting my perishability gives rise to a truer Easter vision. Now freed from the undertow of fear and in defiance of the absurd, I can join myself to all humanity by striving in all things to give the best that is in me, and to dedicate my efforts to the welfare of my fellow-voyagers.[6]

NOTES

1. 1 Cor. 15:32b—quoting Isa. 22:13b. See the critique of Paul at this point by A. J. M. Wedderburn, *Beyond Resurrection* (London: SCM Press, 1999), p. 154, quoted above, pp. 186–87n70. Later, Wedderburn expresses his concern "to move 'beyond resurrection' and a faith bewitched by that concept to a faith that is thoroughly this-worldly, both for the sake of this world and also in the conviction that the traditions concerning the resurrection of Jesus justify nothing else than a thoroughgoing agnosticism concerning what may or may not have happened on that 'third day' and that the concept of individual survival after death is anyway riddled with incoherence" (p. 167).

2. William Lane Craig, "Closing Response," in *Jesus' Resurrection: Fact or Figment? A Debate Between William Lane Craig and Gerd Lüdemann*, ed.

Paul Copan and Ronald K. Tacelli (Downers Grove, IL: InterVarsity Press, 2000), p. 205.

3. Paul Edwards, introduction to *Immortality*, ed. Paul Edwards (Amherst, NY: Prometheus Books, 1997), p. 1. Edwards rightly adds, "However, the question can hardly be avoided whether this emotionally more satisfying outlook is supported by adequate evidence" (ibid.).

4. As much as I am impressed with John Shelby Spong's straightforward book *Resurrection: Myth or Reality?* (San Francisco: HarperSanFrancisco, 1994), in view of the author's deconstruction of the resurrection myth I am unable to comprehend his "Yes to life after death—because one who has entered a relationship with God has entered the timelessness of God" (p. 292). To me this is cloudy talk and, alas, leaves unresolved the relationship between God and the victims of humankind's bloody history. One could almost hope for the reinstatement of a final judgment. In view of so much injustice on the face of this earth I would wish that the victims gain a better life in heaven to compensate for mortal suffering. Yet for the reasons given in this book, there is no evidence for a future resurrection or judgment.

5. Cf. Bertrand Russell, "What I Believe," in *Why I Am Not a Christian and Other Essays on Religion and Related Subjects*, edited, with an appendix on the "Bertrand Russell Case," by Paul Edwards (London: Allen & Unwin and New York: Simon and Schuster, 1957), p. 54.

6. Thus I agree in essence with Spong, who characterizes the religious life as "living fully, loving wastefully, and daring to be all that each of us has the capacity to be" (*Why Christianity Must Change or Die: A Bishop Speaks to Believers in Exile* [San Francisco: HarperSanFrancisco, 1998], p. 218). Yet, I do not agree with him that we can with honesty relate this humanistic attitude to Jesus. Spong writes, "When the community of faith wrote their accounts of the life of this Jesus, these were the human qualities that they discovered residing underneath the theistic interpretation of the meaning of Jesus of Nazareth. Here was a whole human being who lived fully, who loved wastefully, and who had the courage to be himself under every set of circumstances. He was thus a human portrait of the meaning of God, understood as the source of life, the source of love, and the ground of being" (pp. 128–29).

Appendix 1

Mary Magdalene—
A Confidante of Jesus
and a Rival of Peter

I n the later tradition (since Gregory the Great, c. 600), Mary Magdalene was identified with Mary of Bethany (Luke 10:38–42; John 11:2f, 12:3) and with the "sinful woman" in Luke 7:36–50 (cf. Luke 8:2b), where a former life of vice is ascribed to demonic possession. Much earlier, however, Gnostic Christian literature had portrayed Mary Magdalene as the preferred recipient of special revelations of the "Risen One" as well as the object of criticism by the male disciples.[1] The key factors in assessing the importance of these texts are their age and their relationship to the canonical writings. In the following I shall deal with the most important documents.[2]

MARY MAGDALENE—A CONFIDANTE OF JESUS

In the *Wisdom of Jesus Christ* (NHC III. 4) Maria Magdalene is among the seven female followers of Jesus[3]—along with the twelve disciples—to whom the savior appears on a mountain in Galilee (90:10). She is the only woman whose name is mentioned and who twice asks a question. From that one may conclude that the author intends to accord her a special status.

A similar conclusion can be drawn in the case of the *Dialogue of the Savior* (NHC III. 5), where again Mary is the only woman who speaks, fourteen times asking questions or raising issues. Because of her intelligent contributions she is recognized as an enlightened interpreter of scripture who "had understood completely" (139:13). Unfortunately, the texts in question have sustained so much damage that more precise analyses are impossible.

Two passages from the *Gospel of Philip* (NHC II.3) are also important for determining Mary Magdalene's role in Gnostic Christianity. *Gospel of Philip*, Logion 32:[4]

> *59:6–11*: There were three (women) who kept company with the Lord at all times: Mary his mother and her (read: his) sister and Magdalene, who was called his companion. His sister and his mother and his companion were each a Mary.[5]

The Gospel of John evidently underlies this, for in John 19:25—and only there in the canonical texts—is it said that Mary the mother of Jesus was present under the cross. The notion of Mary Magdalene as the companion of Jesus is unique in Early Christian literature. "Apart from the *Gospel of Philip*, Mary Magdalene is nowhere introduced as the companion of the Lord. Neither is this epithet attributed to any other disciple in extant early Christian writings."[6] It likely portrays Mary Magdalene as Jesus' "spiritual consort."[7] At the same time, the close connection between Simon and Helena[8] comes to mind, as well as the Gnostic notion of syzygies (couples), in which Wisdom is the consort of Jesus.

Gospel of Philip, Logion 55b:

> *63:33–35*: [The Savior loved Maria Magdalene] more than [all] the disciples [and used to] kiss her[. . . .] The rest of [the disciples. . . .] They said to him, "Why do you love her more than all of us?" The Savior answered and said to them, "Why do I not love you like her?"[9]

The lacuna after "kiss her" is tantalizing and can be filled by quite a few words: "feet," "cheek," forehead," or even "genitals." Yet internal evidence suggests "mouth" as the correct substitution. Logion 31 (59:4–5) "juxtaposes talk of nourishment from the mouth and the kiss by which the perfect conceive and give birth . . . from the grace which is in one another."[10] This resembles John 20:22 where Jesus breathed on the disciples and thereby imparted to them the Holy Spirit.

Logion 55b likewise seems to display a Johannine coloring, in that here Mary Magdalene occupies the "beloved disciple" role that we know only from the Gospel of John.[11] The kiss on the mouth is to be understood entirely within the framework of the Valentinian Gnostic ceremony of the bridal chamber, "a formalized 'redemption' ritual."[12] It is regarded as "the 'Holy of Holies' and ranks above the other sacraments."[13] In this regard we should also note the *Second Apocalypse of James* (NHC V.4):

> *56:14–57:19*: (James on Jesus): And he kissed my mouth. He took hold of me, saying: "My beloved! Behold, I will reveal to you those (things) that (neither) [the] heavens nor their archons have known. . . . But now, stretch out your [hand]! Now, take hold of me!" [And] then I stretched out my [hands] and I did not find him as I thought (he would be). But afterward I heard him saying, "Understand, and take hold of me." Then I understood, and I was afraid. And I was exceedingly joyful.[14]

The kiss on the mouth and the embrace could well indicate for the author a kind of " beloved disciple" conception.

MARY MAGDALENE—A RIVAL OF PETER

The other noteworthy feature of the Gnostic picture of Mary Magdalene is the rivalry with Peter.[15] One finds this motif in the Gospel of Mary, the Gospel of Thomas, and the Pistis Sophia.

Gospel of Mary

A Coptic translation of this brief work, eight pages (about one half) of which are relatively intact, was discovered at the end of the nineteenth century.[16] It consists of two parts which an editor has brought together. The first part is presumably a dialogue of Jesus with his disciples. Upon his departure the disciples are perplexed and fearful:

> *9:7–12:* "How shall we go to the Gentiles and preach the Gospel of the kingdom of the Son of Man? If they did not spare him, how will they spare us?"

But this section ends with the successful comforting of the disciples by Mary Magdalene. She addresses them as follows:

> *9:14–23:* "Do not weep and do not grieve nor be irresolute, for his grace will be entirely with you and will protect you. But rather let us praise his greatness, for he has joined us together and made us into human beings." When Mary said this, she turned their hearts to the good, and they began to discuss the words of the [Savior].[17]

The second part (10:1–19:2, of which 11–14 have not been preserved) is introduced by a request of Peter:

> *10:1–6:* Peter said to Mary, "Sister, we know that the Savior loved you more than the rest of women. Tell us the words of the Savior which you remember—which you know (but) we do not, nor have we heard them."[18]

Thereupon Mary tells the disciples hidden knowledge she has received in a vision:

> *10:7–16:* Mary answered and said: "What is hidden from you I will proclaim to you." And she began to speak these words: "I," she said, "I saw the Lord in a vision and I said to him: 'Lord, I saw you today in a vision.' He answered and said to me: 'Blessed are you that you did not waver at the sight of me. For where the mind is, there is the treasure.'"

Yet Andrew is skeptical (17:10–15), and Peter exclaims,

> *17:18–22:* "Did he really speak with a woman without our knowledge (and) not openly? Are we to turn about and all listen to her? Did he prefer her to us?"[19]

However, Mary Magdalene's answer and Levi's retort to Peter corroborate Mary's authority:

> *18:1–20:* Then Mary wept and said to Peter, "My brother Peter, what do you think—that I thought this up myself in my heart or that I am lying about the Savior?" Levi answered and said to Peter, "Peter, you have always been hot-tempered. Now I see you contending against the woman like the adversaries. But if the Savior made her worthy, who are you indeed to reject her? Surely, the Savior knows her very well. That is why he loved her more than us. Rather let us be ashamed and put on the perfect humanity and acquire it for ourselves as he commanded us, and preach the gospel, not laying down any other rule or other law beyond what the Savior said."[20]

As the final sentences of the work have been preserved in Greek (Rylands Papyrus no. 463, dating to the early third century), it is certain that the original was in that language. The age of the papyrus indicates that the work was probably composed in the second century. In contrast to the demands for women's submission and silence that we see reflected in 1 Tim. 2:8–15,[21] Gnostic Christians asserted Mary Magdalene's significance as a bearer of special revelation.[22] The *Gospel of Mary* may very well be part of the struggle between Gnostic and orthodox Christians in the second century, the more so since "the accusation expressed by Andrew that Mary Magdalene's revelation is not in agreement with the teachings of Jesus, is a claim frequently used by orthodox Christians in their anti-Gnostic polemic."[23]

Gospel of Thomas, Logion 114:

> (1) Simon Peter said to them, "Mariham [Mary] should go from us. For women are not worthy of life." (2) Jesus said, "Look, I myself will lead her in order to make her male, so that she, too, becomes a living spirit resembling you males. (3) For every woman, if she makes herself male, will enter the kingdom of heaven."[24]

This logion—"one of the most studied and debated logia in the entire gospel"[25]—is in tension with Gospel of Thomas 22:5, which speaks of the dissolution of sexuality ("when you make the male and the female into a single one"); for here we have a transformation of the female into the male, a theme that occurs in numerous Gnostic texts. Cf. as an example

Excerpts from Theodot 21:3:

> The males are drawn together with the Logos, but the females, becoming men, are united to the angels and pass into the Pleroma. Therefore the woman is said to be changed into a man, and the church here on earth into angels.[26]

In Logion 114 of the *Gospel of Thomas* Peter serves as a "representative of a developing ascetic perspective in which male celibates view the presence of women as threatening."[27] Cf. *Dialogue of the Savior* (NHC III.5) 144:16: "Pray in the place where there is no woman."

Pistis Sophia[28]

This extensive Gnostic work consists of four parts and goes back to two underlying documents, whose Greek originals date from the third century. In them the disciples and above all Mary Magdalene (together with Mary the mother of Jesus, Martha, and Salome) put questions to the risen Jesus and are given extensive instructions. "Indeed, *Pistis Sophia* is that Gnostic writing which, besides the *Gospel of Mary*, is most often used to delineate a portrait of the Gnostic Mary Magdalene."[29] She has tremendous significance here and carries on the dialogue almost alone, but the content rests exclusively on New Testament and Valentinian (Gnostic) doctrines.

Jesus praises Mary Magdalene because her "heart is more directed to the Kingdom of Heaven than all thy brothers" (26:18–20). This attitude "does not reflect a penitent mind or a new moral consciousness or a correct cultic behavior but an ability to hear and perceive the mysteries Jesus is revealing. In this respect Mary Magdalene is the most capable one among the disciples."[30] And yet Peter's critical remarks about Mary Magdalene are striking:

58:11–14: "My Lord, we are not able to suffer this woman, who takes the opportunity from us and does not allow anyone of us to speak, but she speaks many times."

Mary Magdalene's reaction is also directed to Jesus:

162:14–18: I am afraid of Peter because he threatens me and hates our race (*genos*).

"Race" here hardly refers to the human race or the Gnostic community, but to the female sex.[31] In view of the texts that portray Peter's misogyny[32] this seems to be the correct understanding of the present text. The modern reader may find Mary Magdalene's statement offensive, for it portrays Peter as sexist. But the dispute is imbedded in a controversy over the right of women to speak in the church led by Peter, and thus its context is the controversies of the second century, when the church was becoming increasingly patriarchal. "Peter's problem with Mary Magdalene is that she is spiritually more advanced than his male colleagues and that she is a woman."[33]

RESULT

The above texts from the *Sophia of Jesus Christ,* the *Dialogue of the Savior,* the *Gospel of Philip,* the *Gospel of Thomas,* the *Gospel of Mary,* and the *Pistis Sophia* reflect conflicts within the Christian church of the second century and thus cannot be used as additional sources for the first century. All this supports my earlier finding that not until the latter part of the first century did the tradition of a first appearance of Jesus to Mary Magdalene arise.

Yet according to Susanne Heine, the reason Mary Magdalene is not mentioned in the earliest texts on the resurrection (e.g., 1 Cor. 15:3–7 and Luke 24:34) is that

Christophany and authority roles . . . are reciprocally related. . . . Since she is not a community leader, she fades into the background following the first institutional conflicts over supremacy among the burgeoning Christian communities. Nonetheless, she may have retained a degree of religious prestige as an immediate disciple of Jesus and an arbiter of spirituality.[34]

But for reasons already noted, even this measured verdict may be too optimistic for the early period. As concerns the passion accounts, while the tradition of Mary Magdalene is historical, her role as the first witness to the "resurrection" cannot be confirmed. Still, Heine is quite certainly right in the following comment,

> At any rate, Mary Magdalene is significant for her theological symbolism. The record of the strife between orthodox and Gnostic churches provides ample evidence that women's roles in community life long remained a source of conflict. Far from standing for the emancipation of women—an anachronistic notion—Mary Magdalene represents the understanding that receiving the Holy Spirit and the Redeemer's grace, coming to faith and handing it on by proclaiming and instructing, as well as performing the related community functions, cannot be limited to men.[35]

The work of two other well-known feminist scholars and a massive new contribution by Jane Schaberg should be noted in passing.[36]

The first, Elisabeth Schüssler Fiorenza, was trained in Würzburg under Rudolf Schnackenburg and has taught in the United States at Notre Dame and since 1983 at Harvard. Her book *In Memory of Her: A Feminist Theological Reconstruction of Christian Origins* appeared in 1983 and has become internationally recognized as a pioneer work in the feminist reconstruction of early Christianity. Schüssler Fiorenza flatly states that all the Gospels assume "that Mary Magdalene was the first resurrection witness."[37] Here she has tacitly claimed the Gospel of Mark in favor of her thesis of the androcentric selection of historical traditions. But in Mark, Mary is in fact not a witness to the resurrection, but together with two other women hears an announcement of Jesus' resurrection (Mark 16:6). It does not help to say that in the pre-Markan story of Mark 16:1–6, 8a the early Christian confession, "Jesus of Nazareth, the crucified one, was raised," was revealed first in an appearance to the Galilean women disciples of Jesus.[38] A confession can hardly be revealed in an appearance.

The second is Luise Schottroff, a pupil of Herbert Braun, who produced a feminist social history of early Christianity in 1994 under the title *Lydia's Impatient Sisters*.[39] Schottroff agrees with Schüssler Fiorenza both that there were women followers of Jesus and that women were the first witnesses to the resurrection of Jesus. But their theses are far from unassailable on two crucial points.

(a) The involvement of women in the Jesus movement

The only direct textual reference to women among Jesus' followers is Mark 15:40. Since Matt. 27:55–56 and Luke 23:49 as well as Luke 8:2 derive from Mark, they offer no further attestation or additional information. Therefore, the main thesis of these two scholars has very tenuous textual support. It should also be noted that the role description in Mark 15:41 is limited to the purveyance of domestic services. In view of Mark 1:13, 31, therefore, stretching it to include anything more than feeding, clothing, or other personal services seems problematic.

(b) Women as the first witnesses of the resurrection

Both zealously defend this thesis; indeed they rely on it in assessing women's standing in the Jesus movement. Could it be demonstrated, women must have been important members of Jesus' entourage. But here again the texts provide little support. Paul never refers to women as resurrection witnesses; John 20:1–23 comes so late in the tradition as to be of dubious value; and the fleeting vision in Matt. 28:9–10 has too derivative a ring to pass for historical recollection. The empty tomb and appearance stories were undoubtedly originally separate, but became joined as the tradition developed, and only in this merging of narratives did appearances to women come to be added. Accordingly, such traditions cannot be used to support the thesis that Mary Magdalene and/or a group of women provided the first testimony to the resurrection.

Finally, Jane Schaberg—whose work I have already used in the course of the present book—has made an even more thoroughgoing attempt than any of the other feminist theologians I know of to make a new and convincing case for the bedrock tradition

> that women were at the crucifixion, burial, and tomb. That they found it empty, and that they—or Mary Magdalene alone—claimed to receive a revelation interpreting that emptiness as resurrection. That Mary Magdalene claimed—or it was claimed by others—that she had a visionary experience of Jesus which empowered her with God's spirit.[40]

Yet for reasons given in the analytical part of my work and in response to Schuessler Fiorenza and Schottroff, such claims are not supported by the available sources.

NOTES

1. In the following I shall follow the scholarly consensus that despite different spellings of Mary's name the "Gnostic" Mary is always Mary Magdalene. See F. Stanley Jones, ed. *Which Mary? The Marys of Early Christian Discussion* (Atlanta: Society of Biblical Literature, 2002) for further discussions.

2. A fine book on the subject is Antti Marjanen's *The Woman Jesus Loved: Mary Magdalene in the Nag Hammadi Library and Related Documents* (Leiden: E. J. Brill, 1996). After providing a "Survey of Research" (pp. 1–21) Marjanen makes helpful introductory remarks to the sources and always offers brilliant analyses. Yet his book does not deal with a possible genetic relationship between the "apocryphal" traditions about Mary Magdalene and the New Testament sources. Jane Schaberg has taken up this task in her massive work *The Resurrection of Mary Magdalene: Legends, Apocrypha, and the Christian Testament* (New York/London: Continuum, 2002). (On Marjanen's book, see Schaberg, pp. 233–34.) The above appendix is oriented chiefly on the historical question of the relationship of the Gnostic sources to the earliest witnesses, and therefore does not aim at a full analysis of all the documents.

3. There are also seven female disciples of Jesus in the *First Apocalypse*

of James (NHC V. 3) 38:22–23. Cf. Marjanen, *The Woman Jesus Loved*, pp. 135–37. Unfortunately, the passage in question is badly damaged. Marjanen offers a full analysis of "Mary Magdalene in the First Apocalypse of James" (122–46) although "the name Mary appears only once in the writing and this particular passage (40:22–26) is fragmentary and difficult to interpret" (p. 122). Indeed, in this passage James the Just is advised to turn to Mary Magdalene as a reference person, "as he seeks to preach the gospel" (ibid., p. 218).

4. I have retained the modern division of the *Gospel of Philip* into various Logia and give the page numbers in each case before the translation.

5. Cf. the slightly different translation in James M. Robinson, gen. ed., *The Nag Hammadi Library in English*, 3d (completely revised) ed. (Leiden: E. J. Brill, 1988), p. 145 (Wesley W. Isenberg).

6. Marjanen, *The Woman Jesus Loved*, p. 151.

7. Ibid., p. 154. Marjanen also discusses other possibilities (pp. 151–60).

8. Justin *I Apology* 26:3. See further my *Primitive Christianity: A Survey of Recent Studies and Some New Proposals* (London/New York: T & T Clark, 2003), pp. 97–99.

9. Translation based on Robinson, *The Nag Hammadi Library in English*, p. 148 (Wesley W. Isenberg).

10. Schaberg, *The Resurrection of Mary Magdalene*, p. 154.

11. See John 13:23–25; 18:15–16; 19:26–27, 35; 20:2; 21:7, 20.

12. Kurt Rudolph, *Gnosis: The Nature and History of an Ancient Religion* (Edinburgh: T & T Clark, 1984), p. 245.

13. Ibid.

14. Translation based on Robinson, *The Nag Hammadi Library in English*, p. 274 (Charles W. Hedrick).

15. See esp. Schaberg, *The Resurrection of Mary Magdalene*, pp. 156–66 and passim.

16. I have based my work at this point on the Coptic and Greek text as printed in Judith Hartenstein, *Die zweite Lehre: Erscheinungen des Auferstandenen als Rahmenerzählungen frühchristlicher Dialoge* (Berlin: Akademie Verlag, 2000), pp. 137–42.

17. Translation on the basis of Marjanen, *The Woman Jesus Loved*, pp. 105–106.

18. Ibid., p. 106.

19. Ibid.

20. Ibid., pp. 526–27.

21. On the historical place of the Pastoral letters, see my *Heretics: The Other Side of Early Christianity* (London: SCM Press and Louisville: Westminster John Knox Press, 1996), pp. 135–42.

22. Cf. Marjanen, *The Woman Jesus Loved*, pp. 119–21.

23. Ibid., p. 121.

24. Translation following my *Jesus After Two Thousand Years: What He Really Said and Did* (London: SCM Press, 2000 and Amherst, NY: Prometheus Books, 2001), p. 644.

25. Marjanen, *The Woman Jesus Loved*, p. 44.

26. Translation based on *The Excerpta ex Theodoto of Clement of Alexandria*, edited with translation, introduction, and notes by Robert Pierce Casey (London: Christophers, 1934), p. 57.

27. Marjanen, *The Woman Jesus Loved*, p. 54. Marjanen offers on pp. 32–55 a detailed analysis of Maria Magdalene in the Gospel of Thomas. See further Schaberg, *The Resurrection of Mary Magdalene*, pp. 156–68.

28. Critical text and translation: *Pistis Sophia*, text ed. Carl Schmidt, translation and notes by Violet MacDermot (Leiden: Brill, 1978). I refer to *Pistis Sophia* on the basis of this work. The first number is the page number of the Coptic text, the second number gives the appropriate line. All the English translations of *Pistis Sophia* are taken from MacDermot.

29. Marjanen, *The Woman Jesus Loved*, p. 170.

30. Ibid., p. 177.

31. Ibid., pp. 179–81 with a survey of various opinions.

32. Cf. *Gospel of Thomas* Logion 114; *Gospel of Mary* 18:8–10.

33. Marjanen, *The Woman Jesus Loved*, p. 181.

34. Susanne Heine, "Eine Person von Rang und Namen. Historische Konturen der Magdalenerin," *Jesu Rede von Gott und ihre Vorgeschichte: Beiträge zur Verkündigung Jesu und zum Kerygma der Kirche*. Festschrift für Willi Marxsen zum 70. Geburtstag. Herausgegeben von Dietrich-Alex Koch, Gerhard Sellin und Andreas Lindemann (Gütersloh: Gütersloher Verlagshaus Gerd Mohn, 1989), p. 188.

35. Ibid., p. 194. See also Susanne Heine, *Women and Early Christianity: Are the Feminist Scholars Right?* (London: SCM Press, 1987), pp. 71–81 ("At the foot of the cross").

36. For a detailed critique of Schottroff's and Schüssler Fiorenza's reconstructions of Christian origins, see my *Primitive Christianity*, pp. 83–92.

37. Elisabeth Schüssler Fiorenza, *In Memory of Her: A Feminist Theological Reconstruction of Christian Origins* (New York: Crossroad, 1983), p. 50.

38. Ibid., p. 139.

39. Luise Schottroff, *Lydia's Impatient Sisters: A Feminist Social History of Early Christianity* (Louisville: Westminster John Knox Press, 1995).

40. Schaberg, *The Resurrection of Mary Magdalene*, p. 350. The continuation of the above quote runs as follows: "In some ways it does not matter if this tradition is historical or not, or if it can persuasively be shown to be historical or not. If Mary Magdalene was a fictional, literary character, and these claims for her legendary, she could still empower and be a resource for contemporary wo/men" (ibid.). Susanne Heine has arrived at the same conclusion (see above, p. 220).

Appendix 2

An Analogy from Hellenistic Religions Concerning the Relationship between the Appearances of Jesus and the Empty Tomb

The Greek historian Herodotus (480–c. 420 BCE) reports the following about Aristeas of Proconnesus:
Histories 4.14:

> The story goes that Aristeas, who was as high born as anyone on Proconnesus, died in a fuller's shop he was visiting on the island. The fuller locked up his workshop and went to tell the dead man's relatives what had happened. Word soon spread around the town that Aristeas had died, but then a Cyzican man arrived from the town of Artaca[1] with a contradictory report; he said that he had met Aristeas on the road to Cyzicus, and had had a conversation with him. He was very insistent that he was right and the others were wrong. The dead man's family went to the fuller's workshop with the things they needed to collect the body, but when they opened the door, there was no sign of Aristeas, dead or alive! Seven years later, he reappeared on Proconnesus, composed the poem which is nowadays known in Greece as *On the Arimaspians*, and then vanished a second time.[2]

Clearly adopted from an oral tradition ("the story goes"), this piece is analogous to New Testament reports about the empty tomb and the appearances of Jesus in that despite the death, the body is not found where expected, and that the supposedly dead person appeared to someone. Evidently supporters of Aristeas, who during his lifetime was perhaps a priest of Apollo, told this story after his death.[3] The crucial claim was that he had "appeared" to the Cyzicenian and later in Proconnesus. From this they inferred that his body could not be found. The story is a vivid example of how religious fantasy associates "events" and draws "conclusions."

How opponents possibly reacted to this story may be inferred from Herodotus's *Histories* 4.94f. Of the Thracian tribe of the Getae, Herodotus reports that they think that on death they go to a deity called Salmoxis. "They recognize no god than their own" (4.94). But Herodotus has learned from the Greeks on the shores of the Hellespont and the Pontus that this Salmoxis was a man, and that he deceived his fellow-countrymen. Compare Herodotus's account, *Histories 4.95*:

> I am told by the Greeks who live around the Hellespont and the Euxine Sea that this Salmoxis was a human being—a slave on Samos; in fact, he belonged to Pythagoras the son of Mnesarchos. When he gained his freedom, he amassed a considerable fortune there, and then returned to his native land. Now, Salmoxis had experienced life in Ionia and was familiar with Ionian customs, which are more profound than those of the Thracians, who are an uncivilized and rather naive people; after all, he had associated with the Greeks, and in particular with Pythagoras, who was hardly the weakest intellect in Greece. So they say he furnished a dining-room, where he entertained his most eminent countrymen, and taught them, while he wined and dined them, that he would not die, and neither would they, his guests, and neither would any of their descendants. Indeed, he explained, they would go to the kind of place where they would live forever in possession of every blessing. But all the time, while he was holding these meetings and teaching this doctrine, he was building an underground chamber. When this chamber was finished, he disappeared, as far as the Thracians were concerned; he descended into his underground chamber and lived there for three years. The Thracians missed him and mourned him as if he were dead, but after three years he reap-

peared, and so validated what he had been teaching them. That is what I am told that he did.[4]

The account likely documents a response of those opposed to the assertions of immortality claimed by Salmoxis and his supporters. In a related criticism of Aristeas, the church father Gregory of Nazianzus compares him to Trophonius and others who sequester themselves in order to encourage their own deification.[5] We may surmise that his contemporaries previously said similar things about him, as the above narrative against the followers of Salmoxis signifies. To be sure, this analogy helps to elucidate something of why the justifications for the empty tomb of Jesus were so soon in forthcoming.

NOTES

1. A harbor about five miles from Cyzicus.

2. Translation based on Herodotus *The Histories*, trans. Robin Waterfield, introduction and notes by Carolyn Dewald (Oxford/New York: Oxford University Press, 1998), p. 240.

3. However, Erwin Rohde in his *Psyche: The Cult of Souls and Belief in Immortality Among the Greeks* (London: Kegan Paul, Trench, Trubner & Co. and New York: Harcourt, Brace & Company, 1925) assumes that Herodotus is inaccurate and prefers the account of Maximus of Tyrus (second century CE), according to whom Aristeas was in ecstasy. "When his soul left his body behind, 'being seized by Phoibos' it (as his second self made visible) was seen in distant places" (ibid., p. 300). Eric Robertson Dodds, *The Greeks and the Irrational* (Berkeley/Los Angeles: University of California Press, 1951), could then consistently understand Aristeas as a kind of shaman (p. 141). For a survey of research on Aristeas, see J. D. P. Bolton, *Aristeas of Proconnesus* (Oxford: Clarendon Press, 1962), pp. 119–73, who at pp. 142ff attacks the priority of the version of Maximus of Tyrus preferred by Rohde and others to Herodotus.

4. Translation by Robin Waterfield (note 2), pp. 266–67.

5. Gregory of Nazianzus *Oratio* 4.59 (printed in Bolton, *Aristeas of Proconnesus*, p. 213).

Appendix 3

Some Critical Comments on Mel Gibson's Movie The Passion of the Christ in the Light of Historical Criticism

In memoriam Paul Winter

INTRODUCTION

The Passion of the Christ portrays the last hours of the life of Jesus of Nazareth—from his arrest in the Garden of Gethsemane to the removal of his body from the cross. Its depiction of the extreme brutality of his execution has great visual impact. In his portrayal of the violence inflicted on Jesus, Gibson, who is a practicing Roman Catholic, presents a historically accurate account of the torments to which those condemned to crucifixion by the Romans were commonly subjected. This staged orgy of deliberate maltreatment accorded political rebels and slaves was a bloody reality repeated tens of thousands of times in the Roman Empire. Indeed, Gibson's movie offers a useful corrective to the romanticized and mollycoddling treatments of the crucifixion, old and new, that lead us to forget the cruelty of his execution and the fact that the "Lord" of

---

This essay was first published in *The Bible and Interpretation* (March 2004).

what is perhaps the world's most widely influential religion died a criminal's death on the cross two thousand years ago.

The primary narrative basis for the film is the collective account found in the four New Testament Gospels—the story that Christians call Jesus' passion. Everything that the Gospels say about the circumstances of the trial of Jesus—from the hatred of Jesus by the Jewish leaders and people to the declaration of his innocence by Pilate—is skillfully staged in the film. Mel Gibson simply translates the content of the biblical reports into action. But here the problem begins. It has long been known that the early Christians wrongly put the blame for the death of Jesus on the "unbelieving Jews." By translating this theological interpretation into powerful images on film, Gibson is encouraging anti-Semitism, whether he intended to or not.

Here is what the historical study of the four Gospels reveals about the historical worth of the various narratives.

THE PASSION NARRATIVE IN THE GOSPEL OF MARK

Anti-Judaism permeates the Gospel of Mark and also its passion narrative. This cannot be understood without previously considering Jesus' three prophecies about his suffering (and his resurrection) that punctuate Mark's story. They appear in 8:31; 9:31; and 10:32–34. Either the author received the first from tradition and he himself formulated the last two, or he created all three. Their content is this: *Jesus is going to Jerusalem to be put to death by the Jewish authorities.*

Mark also formulated a parallel passage in 3:6, according to which, after a healing performed on the Sabbath, "the Pharisees went out and immediately conspired with the Herodians to destroy him." This motif runs through the Gospel like a scarlet thread (note Mark 12:12: "They [the Jewish authorities] tried to arrest him, but feared the multitude, for they perceived that he told the parable against them") and finds its fulfillment in the passion narrative.

In view of this, it is hardly surprising that in the Gospel of Mark the high priests, elders, and scribes join in condemning Jesus to death (14:64) and hand him over to Pilate (15:1). Unfortunately for them, Pilate wants to let Jesus go because he "perceived that it was out of envy that the chief priests had delivered him up" (Mark 15:10). But the Jewish authorities thwart his intention by inciting the Jewish people to demand Jesus' crucifixion.

Mark 15:11–14

(11) But the chief priests stirred up the crowd to have him release for them Barabbas instead. (12) And Pilate again said to them, "Then what shall I do with the man whom you call the King of the Jews?" (13) And they cried out again, "Crucify him." (14) And Pilate said to them, "Why, what evil has he done?" But they shouted all the more, "Crucify him."

If Mark's previous differentiation between the Jewish elite and the Jewish people suggests that only the elite were to blame for Jesus' death, this passage contradicts such a conclusion.

THE PASSION NARRATIVE IN THE GOSPEL OF MATTHEW

Matthew's aim can be discovered from a comparison of his account with that of Mark, which served as his model. We find hardly any deviations, but several important additions:

1. Judas repented having handed Jesus over to the authorities for thirty pieces of silver and returned the money to the high priests and elders saying, "'I have sinned in delivering up innocent blood.' They said, 'What is that to us? See to it yourself.' And throwing down the pieces of silver in the temple, he departed, and went and hanged himself" (Matt. 27:4–5). Thus, by way of anticipation, the action against Jesus is represented as being reprehensible, and a devastating verdict is pronounced on the Jews who are hostile to Jesus. The suicide of a disciple who despite his repentance can no longer live with his guilt accentuates the moral degeneracy of the Jewish authorities, who do not repent of their actions.

2. In Matthew, Pilate's wife tells her husband: "Have nothing to do with that righteous man, for I have suffered much over him today in a dream" (27:19). A Roman woman becomes witness to Jesus' innocence, whereas the Jewish people, spurred on by the authorities, call for Jesus' death. Since it is sheer invention on Matthew's part, this scene is an important indication of his intention.

3. According to Matthew, when the Jewish crowd insists on the crucifixion of Jesus, Pilate washes his hands before them (cf. Deut. 21:6; Ps. 26:6) and says, "I am innocent of the man's blood; see it to yourselves" (Matt. 27:24). Accordingly, Pilate endorses his wife's judgment: as a righteous man, Jesus is innocent. This performance by a pagan Roman of the Jewish expiatory rite of washing the hands strikingly demonstrates Matthew's intention to foist blame for the death of Jesus on the Jewish people.

4. This purpose is yet more vividly expressed when the Jewish people next call down a curse on themselves—a feature to be found only in Matthew: "And all the people answered, 'His blood be on us and on our children!'" (Matt. 27:25). Granted, Pilate ordered the crucifixion, but according to Matthew, all Israel assumed the blame for Jesus' death—and in so doing finally forfeited its special status as God's elect. Convinced of Jesus' guilt, they have uttered a limited curse on themselves, but since Jesus is clearly innocent, they will be responsible for the consequences, and Jesus' blood accordingly is charged to them and their children.

THE PASSION NARRATIVE IN THE GOSPEL OF LUKE

In his account of the trial before Pilate (Luke 23:2–5), Luke generally follows Mark, but with significant changes. To Mark's account, he has added verse 2: "And they began to accuse him, saying, 'We found this man perverting our nation, and forbidding us to give tribute to Caesar, and saying that he himself is Christ a king'"—an obvious allusion to the well-known saying about paying taxes to Caesar (Luke 20:25).

By making this connection, Luke shows that the accusation of the Jewish authorities is a falsehood, for Jesus had explicitly endorsed the payment of taxes. The Jewish action against Jesus is therefore grounded in a malicious lie, but Pilate did not fall for it. This is clear from two other statements of his that Luke has added to the Markan scenario:

Luke 23:4

And Pilate said to the chief priests and the multitudes, "I find no crime in this man."

Luke 23:13–16

(13) Pilate then called together the chief priests and the rulers and the people, (14) and said to them, "You brought me this man as one who was perverting the people; and after examining him before you, behold, I did not find this man guilty of any of your charges against him; (15) neither did Herod, for he sent him back to us. Behold, nothing deserving death has been done by him; (16) I will therefore chastise him and release him."

It is further clear from these two added details that, like his predecessors, Luke sees the Jewish elite *and* the people as being of one mind; accordingly, the designation "the Jews" is undeniably hostile in the context of this assignment of guilt.

This reaches a climax in Luke's assertion that it was the Jews, not the Romans, who executed Jesus. He deliberately omits the scourging scene (Mark 15:16–20) so that Jesus is taken away immediately after he has been handed over. Accordingly, the story reads as follows: Pilate handed over Jesus to the will of the Jews (23:25); they led him away (26); they crucified him (33). It follows from this that those who call for Jesus' death also execute him (see Luke 24:20; Acts 3:15).

In short, Luke's account of the passion heightens both the anti-Judaism and the innocence of Pilate that he found in Mark.

THE PASSION NARRATIVE IN THE GOSPEL OF JOHN

The hearing before the Sanhedrin related by all three Synoptic Gospels does not appear in John. The Fourth Evangelist reports only a hearing before Pilate (John 18:28–19:16).

Earlier, the high priest Annas has interrogated Jesus (John 18:19–23) and sent him in fetters to the high priest Caiphas (18:24). From there Jesus goes to Pilate. Although no real hearing is held by the Sanhedrin, the Jews are directly involved in the trial of Jesus. Moreover, they are further incriminated because they have handed Jesus over to Pilate (John 18:35), to whom Jesus explicitly presents this as wickedness: "He who has delivered me to you has the greater sin" (19:11).

Exoneration of Pilate goes hand in hand with the heightened attribution of guilt to the Jews. Pilate expresses his conviction of Jesus' innocence several times (18:38; 19:4, 6) and repeatedly attempts to set the prisoner free.

WHO REALLY CONDEMNED JESUS TO DEATH?

Jesus' death by crucifixion, a Roman form of execution, is an assured fact. From this we can safely draw three conclusions:

a) Jesus' death came at the hands of the Romans; b) his execution followed upon Roman legal proceedings, however summary; c) Jesus was condemned for a political crime.

Further historical details can be extracted only by means of source criticism. Literary-critical analysis leads to the conclusion that both Matthew and Luke—and probably also John—are *dependent* on Mark's report. That means that only the Markan narrative can be used in establishing facts.

In any case, Mark's account of the trial and condemnation by the Jewish authorities is secondary and was composed either by Mark himself or by a predecessor. To see that it corresponds item by item to the hearing before Pilate (Mark 15:1–5, 15b–20), one need only compare the following parallel passages:

Jesus before the Sanhedrin	Jesus before Pilate
14:53a	15:1
14:55	15:3
14:60	15:4
14:61a	15:5
14:61b	15:2
14:62	15:2
14:64	15:15
14:65	15:16–20

It follows from this that the hearing before the Sanhedrin has been based on a tradition of the hearing before Pilate and therefore cannot be considered a historical report.

The apologetic features (note 15:10) and indications of hostility to the Jews (see 15:11–14) contained in the accounts of the hearing before Pilate are certainly to be deleted. The three remaining historical data are a trial before the Roman prefect Pilate, a false political charge by the Jerusalem priesthood that led Pilate to intervene, and the crucifixion of Jesus.

PILATE—A MILD AND PERCEPTIVE RULER?

The New Testament Gospels depict Pilate as a perceptive man who sees through the Jewish authorities and recognizes Jesus' innocence. What is the historical likelihood of such a portrait? The available sources show quite a different picture from that sketched in the New Testament. Here are but two of many:

a) The Jewish philosopher Philo, an older contemporary of the apostle Paul, quotes from a letter of Agrippa I to the emperor Caligula that Pilate's administration was characterized by "corruption, acts of violence, robberies, maltreatments, insults, continual executions without trial, endless and intolerable cruelties" (*On the Embassy to Gaius* 38).

b) Josephus, a younger contemporary of Paul, relates that Pilate misused the temple treasures in Jerusalem to build an aqueduct into the city. He writes:

> At this the multitude were indignant; and when Pilate came to Jerusalem, they gathered at his palace and made a great uproar. Apprised beforehand of this impending disturbance, he ordered armed soldiers disguised as private individuals to mix with the multitude, and not to use their swords, but with their staves to beat those who raised the clamor. When he gave the signal from his palace, the Jews were so savagely beaten that many of them perished from the blows they received, and many others were trodden to death by one another; by which means the multitude was astonished at the calamity of those that were slain, and held their peace. (*Jewish War* II, 175–77)

In keeping with these pictures of a cruel Roman official is Luke's report (13:1) that Pilate had a number of Galileans killed when they were presenting their offerings in the Jerusalem temple.

Clearly, the New Testament portrait of Pilate as a just and perceptive ruler is a great deception. The Gospel report that Pilate was merely a tool by which the Jews carried out their death sentence is sheer wishful thinking.

THE CLAIM THAT THE JEWS WERE GUILTY OF THE DEATH OF JESUS

The learned church father Origen (185/6–254 CE) wrote on Matt. 27:25 and the consequences it had for the Jews:

> Therefore they not only became guilty of the blood of Christ. . . . Therefore the blood of Christ came not only on those who lived formerly but also on all subsequent generations of Jews to consummation.

These words contain the typical Christian view of the Jews that was predominant from earliest Christianity to modern times. Today, scholars have at last shown that the indictment of Jews found in the Gospels is historically untrue and results from their apologetic tendency. One need only read Psalms 22, 38, 69, and 110 to see that the Gospel writers created much of the passion account from ancient scriptures. As Paul Winter aptly observes, their aim was to exonerate the Romans and to present "unbelieving" Jews as enemies.

CONCLUSION

Any discussion of Gibson's movie should pay attention to three important facts: 1. The key statements and representations about Jewish responsibility for Jesus' death that we find in the New Testament passion narratives have no historical foundation, but are rooted in Christian propaganda. 2. Most of the details of the passion narratives derive from later "theological" interpretations and bear no relation to historical truth. 3. Jesus had no idea of dying for the sins of the world. He looked for the kingdom of God, but the church arrived instead.

Select Bibliography

Alsup, John E. *The Post-Resurrection Appearance Stories of the Gospel-Tradition.* Stuttgart: Calwer Verlag, 1975.

Avemarie, Friedrich, and Hermann Lichtenberger, eds. *Auferstehung—Resurrection.* Tübingen: J. C. B. Mohr (Paul Siebeck), 2001.

Bieringer, R., V. Koperski, and B. Lataire, eds. *Resurrection in the New Testament.* Festschrift J. Lambrecht. Leuven: University Press, 2002.

Bommarius, Alexander, ed. *Fand die Auferstehung wirklich statt? Eine Diskussion mit Gerd Lüdemann.* Mit Beiträgen von Gerd Lüdemann, Klaus Berger, Hugo Staudinger, Michael Murrmann-Kahl und Alexander Bommarius. Düsseldorf and Bonn: Parerga Verlag, 1995.

Brown, Raymond E. *The Death of the Messiah: A Commentary on the Passion Narratives in the Four Gospels.* 2 vols. New York: Doubleday, 1994.

Bultmann, Rudolf. *Theology of the New Testament.* 2 vols. New York: Charles Scribner's Sons, 1951, 1955.

Copan, Paul, and Ronald K. Tacelli, eds. *Jesus' Resurrection: Fact or Figment? A Debate between William Lane Craig and Gerd Lüdemann.* Downers Grove, IL: InterVarsity Press, 2000.

Corley, Kathleen E. *Women and the Historical Jesus: Feminist Myths of Christian Origins.* Santa Rosa, CA: Polebridge Press, 2002.

Craig, William Lane. "Closing Response." In *Jesus' Resurrection: Fact or Figment? A Debate Between William Lane Craig and Gerd Lüdemann,* edited by Paul Copan and Ronald K. Tacelli, 162–206. Downers Grove, IL: InterVarsity Press, 2000.

Crossan, John Dominic. *The Historical Jesus: The Life of a Mediterranean Jewish Peasant.* San Francisco: HarperSanFrancisco, 1994.

———. *Who Killed Jesus? Exposing the Roots of Anti-Semitism in the Gospel Story of the Death of Jesus.* San Francisco: HarperSanFrancisco, 1995.

———. *The Birth of Christianity: Discovering What Happened in the Years Immediately after the Execution of Jesus.* San Francisco: HarperSanFrancisco, 1998.

Cullmann, Oscar. *Immortality of the Soul or Resurrection of the Dead? The Witness of the New Testament.* New York: Macmillan, 1958.

Davis, Stephen T., Daniel Kendall, and Gerald O'Collins, eds. *The Resurrection: An Interdisciplinary Symposium on the Resurrection of Jesus.* Oxford and New York: Oxford University Press, 1997.

D'Costa, Gavin, ed. *Resurrection Reconsidered.* Oxford: Oneworld Publications and Rockport, MA, 1996.

Dunn, James D. G. "Beyond the Historical Impasse? In Dialogue with A. J. M. Wedderburn." In *Paul, Luke and the Graeco-Roman World: Essays in Honour of Alexander J. M. Wedderburn,* edited by Alf Christophersen, Carsten Claussen, Jörg Frey, and Bruce Longenecker, 250–64. London/New York: Sheffield Academic Press, 2002.

Ebeling, Gerhard. *Word and Faith.* London: SCM Press and Philadelphia: Fortress Press, 1963.

Evans, C. F. *Resurrection and the New Testament.* London: SCM Press and Naperville: Alec R. Allenson, 1970.

Geering, Lloyd. *Resurrection: A Symbol of Hope.* London/Auckland/Sydney/Toronto: Hodder and Stoughton, 1971.

Goulder, Michael. "The Baseless Fabric of a Vision." In *Resurrection Reconsidered,* edited by Gavin D'Costa, 48–61. Oxford: Oneworld Publications and Rockport, MA, 1996.

———. "The Explanatory Power of Conversion-Visions." In *Jesus' Resurrection: Fact or Figment? A Debate Between William Lane Craig and Gerd Lüdemann,* edited by Paul Copan and Ronald K. Tacelli, 86–103. Downers Grove, IL: InterVarsity Press, 2000.

Grass, Hans. *Ostergeschehen und Osterberichte.* 4th ed. Göttingen: Vandenhoeck & Ruprecht, 1970.

Hartenstein, Judith. *Die zweite Lehre: Erscheinungen des Auferstandenen als Rahmenerzählungen frühchristlicher Dialoge.* Berlin: Akademie Verlag, 2000.

Hartlich, Christian, "Historical-Critical Method in Its Application to Statements Concerning Events in the Holy Scriptures." *Journal of Higher Criticism* 2, no. 2 (Fall 1995): 122–39.

Harvey, Van A. *The Historian and the Believer: The Morality of Historical Knowledge and Christian Belief.* Urbana and Chicago: University of Illinois Press, 1996.

Hengel, Martin. "Das Begräbnis Jesu bei Paulus und die leibliche Auferstehung aus dem Grabe." In *Auferstehung—Resurrection*, edited by Friedrich Avemarie and Hermann Lichtenberger, 119–83. Tübingen: J. C. B. Mohr (Paul Siebeck), 2001.

Hills, Julian. *Tradition and Composition in the Epistula Apostolorum.* Minneapolis: Fortress Press, 1990.

Lake, Kirsopp. *The Historical Evidence for the Resurrection of Jesus.* London: Williams & Norgate and New York: G. P. Putnam's Sons, 1912.

Le Bon, Gustave. *The Crowd: A Study of the Popular Mind.* New York: Viking Press, 1960.

Lüdemann, Gerd. *The Resurrection of Jesus: History, Experience, Theology.* London: SCM Press and Minneapolis: Fortress Press, 1994.

———. *Heretics: the Other Side of Early Christianity.* London: SCM Press and Louisville: Westminster John Knox Press, 1996.

———. *Jesus After Two Thousand Years: What He Really Said and Did.* London: SCM Press, 2000 and Amherst, NY: Prometheus Books, 2001.

———. *Paul: The Founder of Christianity.* Amherst, NY: Prometheus Books, 2002.

———. *Primitive Christianity: A Survey of Recent Studies and Some New Proposals.* London/New York: T & T Clark, 2003.

Marxsen, Willi. *The Resurrection of Jesus of Nazareth.* Philadelphia: Fortress Press, 1970.

Niebuhr, Richard R. *Resurrection and Historical Reason: A Study of Theological Method.* New York: Charles Scribner's Sons, 1957.

Pannenberg, Wolfhart. *Jesus—God and Man.* Philadelphia: Westminster Press, 1968.

Perrin, Norman. *The Resurrection According to Matthew, Mark, and Luke.* Philadelphia: Fortress Press, 1977.

Porter, Stanley E., Michael A. Hayes, and Davis Tombs, eds. *Resurrection.* Sheffield: Sheffield Academic Press, 1999.

Riley, Gregory J. *Resurrection Reconsidered: Thomas and John in Controversy.* Minneapolis: Fortress Press, 1995.

Robinson, James M. "Jesus from Easter to Valentinus." *Journal of Biblical Literature* 101 (1982): 5–37.

————, gen. ed. *The Nag Hammadi Library in English.* 3d ed., completely revised. Leiden: E. J. Brill, 1988.

Schaberg, Jane. *The Resurrection of Mary Magdalene: Legends, Apocrypha, and the Christian Testament.* New York/London: Continuum, 2002.

Schneemelcher, Wilhelm, ed. *New Testament Apocrypha.* Revised edition. English translation edited by R. McL. Wilson. *I: Gospels and Related Writings. II: Writings Related to the postles, Apocalypses and Related Subjects.* Louisville: Westminster John Knox Press, 1991, 1992.

Spiegel, Yorick. *The Grief Process: Analysis and Counseling.* Nashville: Abingdon Press, 1978.

Strauss, David Friedrich. *The Old Faith and the New.* Introduction and notes by G. A. Wells. Amherst, NY: Prometheus Books, 1997.

Swinburne, Richard. *The Resurrection of God Incarnate.* Oxford/New York: Oxford University Press, 2003.

Theissen, Gerd. *A Theory of Primitive Christian Religion.* London: SCM Press, 1999. (US title: *The Religion of the Earliest Christians: Creating a Symbolic Universe.* Minneapolis: Fortress Press, 1999.)

Verweyen, Hansjürgen, ed. *Osterglaube ohne Auferstehung? Diskussion mit Gerd Lüdemann.* Freiburg/Basel/Wien: Herder Verlag, 1995.

Von Campenhausen, Hans. "The Events of Easter and the Empty Tomb." In Hans von Campenhausen, *Tradition and Life in the Church: Essays and Lectures in Church History,* 42–89. Philadelphia: Fortress Press, 1968.

Wedderburn, A. J. M. *Beyond Resurrection.* London: SCM Press, 1999.

Wright, N. T. *The Resurrection of the Son of God.* Minneapolis: Fortress Press, 2003.

Index of Modern Authors